The Goddess and the King in Indian Myth

The Sanskrit narrative text *Devī Māhātmya*, "The Greatness of the Goddess," extols the triumphs of an all-powerful Goddess, Durgā, over universe-imperiling demons. These exploits are embedded in an intriguing frame narrative: a deposed king solicits the counsel of a forest-dwelling ascetic, who narrates the tripartite acts of Durgā which comprise the main body of the text. It is a centrally important early text about the Great Goddess, which has significance to the broader field of Purāṇic Studies.

This book analyzes the *Devī Māhātmya* and argues that its frame narrative cleverly engages a dichotomy at the heart of Hinduism: the opposing ideals of asceticism and kingship. These ideals comprise two strands of what is referred to herein as the *dharmic* double helix. It decodes the symbolism of encounters between forest hermits and exiled kings through the lens of the *dharmic* double helix, demonstrating the extent to which this common narrative trope masterfully encodes the ambivalence of brāhmaṇic ideology. Engaging the tension between the moral necessity for nonviolence and the sociopolitical necessity for violence, the book deconstructs the ideological ambivalence throughout the *Devī Māhātmya* to demonstrate that its frame narrative invariably sheds light on its core content. Its very structure serves to emphasize a theme that prevails throughout the text, one inalienable to the rubric of the episodes themselves: sovereignty on both cosmic and mundane scales.

The book sheds new light on the content of the *Devī Māhātmya* and contextualizes it within the framework of important debates within early Hinduism. It will be of interest to academics in the fields of Asian Religion, Hindu Studies, Goddess Studies, South Asian Studies, Narrative Studies and comparative literature.

Raj Balkaran teaches at the School of Continuing Studies at the University of Toronto, Canada.

Routledge Hindu Studies Series

Series Editor: Gavin Flood
Oxford Centre for Hindu Studies

The *Routledge Hindu Studies Series*, in association with the Oxford Centre for Hindu Studies, intends the publication of constructive Hindu theological, philosophical and ethical projects aimed at bringing Hindu traditions into dialogue with contemporary trends in scholarship and contemporary society. The series invites original, high-quality, research-level work on religion, culture and society of Hindus living in India and abroad. Proposals for annotated translations of important primary sources and studies in the history of the Hindu religious traditions will also be considered.

Hindu Images and their Worship with Special Reference to Vaisnavism
A Philosophical-Theological Inquiry
Julius J. Lipner

River and Goddess Worship in India
Changing Perceptions and Manifestations of Sarasvati
R.U.S. Prasad

The Future of Hindu-Christian Studies
A Theological Inquiry
Francis X. Clooney

Modern Hindu Traditionalism in Contemporary India
The Śrī Maṭh and the Jagadguru Rāmānandācārya in the Evolution of the Rāmānandī Sampradāya
Daniela Bevilacqua

The Goddess and the King in Indian Myth
Ring Composition, Royal Power, and the *Dharmic* Double Helix
Raj Balkaran

For a full list of titles, please see: www.routledge.com/asianstudies/series/RHSS.

The Goddess and the King in Indian Myth

Ring Composition, Royal Power, and the *Dharmic* Double Helix

Raj Balkaran

Routledge
Taylor & Francis Group
LONDON AND NEW YORK

First published 2019
by Routledge
2 Park Square, Milton Park, Abingdon, Oxon OX14 4RN

and by Routledge
52 Vanderbilt Avenue, New York, NY 10017

First issued in paperback 2020

Routledge is an imprint of the Taylor & Francis Group, an informa business

British Library Cataloguing-in-Publication Data
A catalogue record for this book is available from the British Library

Library of Congress Cataloging-in-Publication Data
A catalog record has been requested for this book

ISBN 13: 978-0-367-58816-8 (pbk)
ISBN 13: 978-1-138-60957-0 (hbk)

Typeset in Times New Roman
by Wearset Ltd, Boldon, Tyne and Wear

For Amrita Devi, my mother

The Goddess granted a boon:
"In just a few days, O king,
you will slay your enemies
and reclaim your throne.
It will be forever yours."
Devī Māhātmya, 18.13–20

Contents

List of illustrations ix
Foreword x
Acknowledgments xii

Introduction: framing ascetics, framing kings 1

Querying the commencement of the Devī Māhātmya *1*
Chapter outline 4
A note on nomenclature 4

1 **Framing the framing: focusing the study of the *Devī Māhātmya*** 6

Frame I: colonial encounters with purāṇic *narratives 7*
Frame II: scholarly encounters with the Devī Māhātmya *13*
Frame III: a matching methodology for thinking in circles 19

2 **Finding the forest hermit: ascetic ideology in the *Devī Māhātmya*** 34

Brāhmaṇism's dharmic *double helix 35*
Encoding the double helix 41
Ascetic ideology in the Devī Māhātmya *53*

3 **Mother of kings: royal ideology in the *Devī Māhātmya*** 60

The womb of royal power 61
The Indian king: divine protector 69
Royal ideology in the Devī Māhātmya *73*

4 Reading the ring: focusing the frame of the *Devī Māhātmya* 88

Focusing the frame of the Devī Māhātmya *89*
Reading the ring of power 102
Framing finale 114

5 Mother of power: focusing the Goddess of the *Devī Māhātmya* 124

Breaking through the breast–tooth binary 124
The ring of wrath 131
Mother of power 136

Conclusion: framing frontier 147

Closing frames, framing closures 147
Frame I: ideology 147
Frame II: methodology 148
Frame III: history of scholarship 152
Framing the future 154

Bibliography *157*
Index *163*

Illustrations

Figure

2.1 Encoding the *brāhmaṇic* double helix 52

Tables

2.1 The constituent strands of the *brāhmaṇic* double helix 41
4.1 The content of the *Devī Māhātmya* 90
4.2 The chiastic structure of the *Devī Māhātmya* 92
4.3 The chiastic structure of the *Bhagavad Gītā* 93
4.4 General narrative ring structure 99
4.5 The *Devī Māhātmya*'s narrative ring structure 100
4.6 Royal-ascetic ideological allocation within the *Devī Māhātmya* 100
4.7 Thematic allocation within the *Devī Māhātmya* 103
4.8 Royal-ascetic thematic allocation within the *Devī Māhātmya* 111
4.9 Proper nouns in the *Devī Māhātmya* (by episode) 113
5.1 Ramanujan's breast–tooth typology 125
5.2 The secondary narrative ring in the *Devī Māhātmya* 133

Foreword

Since the time of its composition over a millennium ago, the *Devī Māhātmya*, a relatively short text of about 700 verses in glorification (*māhātmya*) of the Great Goddess (Devī), has been hugely influential on subsequent Purāṇic myths, ritual action, and iconographic depictions. Only in the last several decades has it begun to receive the sustained attention it deserves by scholars, particularly due to the burgeoning interest in Hindu goddess traditions. Previous studies have focused on the dramatic myths of the martial exploits of the Goddess's destruction of an assortment of demons, since these form the bulk of the text. In *The Goddess and the King in Indian Myth* Raj Balkaran extends his scrutiny to the frame tales in tandem with the text's engaging narratives. As such, he reads the *Devī Māhātmya* synchronically as an integral part of the *Mārkaṇḍeya Purāṇa*, rather than as an independently composed and haphazard interpolation.

Balkaran effectively applies the theory of ring narratives proposed by Mary Douglas to extract novel insights into the scripture. For instance, the theory does well to substantiate why the second mythic episode, namely the Devī's slaying of the buffalo-demon, Mahiṣa, is of central importance even though it occupies only chapters 2 to 4 of the text's thirteen chapters. In what he has termed the "double helix of dharma," Balkaran analyzes how the inextricably intertwined tensions found within the Hindu tradition between the pursuit of this-worldly (*pravṛtti*) and otherworldly (*nivṛtti*) goals of life play out within the *Devī Māhātmya*. Previous studies contend that both are valorized equally, because the Goddess grants a restoration of temporal power to the disenfranchised king Suratha, and knowledge conducive to spiritual perfection to the similarly distraught merchant Samādhi. Others, noting the text's forest setting and that its teachings emanate from a sage in a hermitage, suggest that the bias is toward *nivṛtti* ends. However, Balkaran points out the shortcomings in those analyses, and convincingly argues that the emphasis is actually on world-affirming goals, because these, especially the sovereign's exercise of violence within society, are at times dharmically essential. The Goddess herself engages in such fierce battles with demons not to assume kingship over the divine pantheon for herself, but to restore the gods to their rightful place in the heavens. As such, she embodies the principle of sovereignty itself, combining or transcending the binaries of fierce versus benign, and directs her power in the service of cosmic and social stability.

Although he does not sacrifice any of the rigor expected of an academic work, one is infectiously drawn into his study by the author's evident affection for his material. I, for one, was delighted that even though its focus is on textual analysis, the book includes material culled from ethnographic studies of the Devī and her worship. Solidly researched and eloquently written, *The Goddess and the King in Indian Myth* offers an exciting alternative model for the study of Purāṇic material, and contains a wealth of rewarding insights into the Great Goddess tradition in Hinduism.

Hillary Peter Rodrigues
Lethbridge University

Acknowledgments

The list of conversation partners—friends, strangers, colleagues, students, teachers—who have enriched my thinking throughout the production of this work is *far* too great to reproduce here. I've strived to convey appreciation in each encounter, hopefully successfully so.

I must, however, acknowledge five souls who have indelibly impacted the course of my life, steering it toward the production of this book. Firstly, I offer heartfelt gratitude to my life mentor, K.L. Mantri, for attuning me to my potential, setting me on my path, and serving as a profound example of wisdom in action.

Many thanks to Arti Dhand for being an inspiration at every turn. Enthralled by her teaching style and command of all things Hinduism in my days as an undergrad, I caught a glimpse of what I might aspire after. Many thanks also to Ajay Rao for roping me into graduate studies, and serving as my Master's supervisor while I endeavored to make sense of the *Rāmāyaṇa*. Confounded by the paradox that is Rāma, I see now where my thinking on dharma's double helix began.

Inspired by his book on Durgā Pūjā, I took a trip to Lethbridge to meet with Hillary Rodrigues after the Master's. That was the first of many important interactions, throughout which his mentorship and support have proven invaluable—and for this I am most grateful. He in fact pointed me to Calgary for doctoral study.

My sincere thanks to Elizabeth Rohlman, without whose colossal insight and support this work would not exist. Her profound appreciation for narrative has enriched this enterprise. Beyond serving as my doctoral supervisor, it is my distinct pleasure to benefit from her continued presence in my life as advisor, colleague, and friend.

Introduction

Framing ascetics, framing kings

Querying the commencement of the *Devī Māhātmya*

The Sanskrit narrative text *Devī Māhātmya*, "The Greatness of the Goddess" (henceforth DM), extols the triumphs of an all-powerful Goddess, Durgā, over universe-imperiling demons. The exploits of this formidable figure constitute the first known Sanskrit articulation of a Great Goddess within the Indian subcontinent, indeed the first occasion where the ultimate divine principle is accorded femininity. Believed to have emerged somewhere along the Narmada River circa fifth century CE, the DM is preserved in thousands of manuscripts across India, in remarkably stable fashion. It is recited as liturgy in temples to Durgā, during individual daily spiritual practice, and at temples and homes during the autumnal *Navarātra* ("nine nights") Hindu festival. While the DM equates supreme reality with the feminine Hindu concepts of *māyā*, *śakti*, and *prakṛti*, it posits no systematic theory; instead, it masterfully interweaves these philosophical strands—as only narrative can—into the visage of a feminine divine whose power surpasses that of the Vedic pantheon, and even that of the cosmic *trimūrti* composed of Brahmā, Viṣṇu, and Śiva.

The DM details Durgā's manifestations for the protection of the gods (and cosmic order as a whole) in times of dire calamity, whereby she crushes demonic forces and offers benediction to the devout. More than demon crusher extraordinaire, however, Durgā is simultaneously creation's efficient cause and material cause. At once the clay, the potter, and the pot, she might be best understood as the energy of potting, which is responsible for all manner of manifest pots, existing *in potentia* even while the potter remains at rest. She is power itself, comprising the power innate to the universe and its beings, yet ultimately uncontained by them. Hers is the matrix of power, which mothers all things. As such, none can possibly overpower her; hence, she serves as a prime principle of protection against the most virulent adversaries of order, all the while serving as the font of compassionate care for the imperiled. Our mother of power is a supreme source of salvific refuge for all who invoke her.

The DM details three exploits wherein Durgā manifests for the restoration of cosmic order, exercising colossal martial prowess in doing so. These exploits are embedded in an intriguing frame narrative: a deposed king, Suratha, solicits the counsel of a forest-dwelling ascetic, Medhas, who narrates the tripartite acts of Durgā which comprise the main body of the text (DM1.1–44). Upon doing so, the sage offers esoteric instruction for the worship of Durgā through which the king regains his reign, and is blessed to become the Manu of the next age (DM 13.1–17). This begs the question at the heart of this research: *why are the monumental exploits of the Goddess of the DM framed by an encounter between a forest-dwelling ascetic and a deposed king? What does this have to do with those exploits?*

This study argues that the DM's frame narrative cleverly engages a dichotomy at the heart of Hinduism: the opposing ideals of asceticism and kingship. These ideals comprise two strands of what is referred to herein as the *brāhmaṇic* double helix. *Brāhmaṇic* discourse on *dharma* can dispense with neither the virtues of the world-affirming householder (epitomized by the king), nor those of the world-abnegating renouncer (epitomized by the ascetic). Therefore both strands, however disparate, must be integrated into a shared ideological platform. The *Mahābhārata* (henceforth MBh) voices perhaps the most refined articulation of *dharma*'s dual standing through its bifurcated discourse on *pravṛtti* (world-engaging) and *nivṛtti* (world-eschewing) *dharmas*. In querying the portrayal of the ideals of asceticism and of kingship, this study combs through the text to ascertain which passages support *nivṛtti dharma*, and which support *pravṛtti dharma*. Engaging the tension between the *nivṛttic* moral necessity for nonviolence and the *pravṛttic* sociopolitical necessity for violence, this project deconstructs the ideological ambivalence throughout the DM to demonstrate that its frame narrative invariably sheds light on its core content. Its very structure serves to underscore a theme that prevails throughout the text, one inalienable to the rubric of the episodes themselves: sovereignty on both cosmic and mundane scales, the epitome of *pravṛtti* ideology.

The ascetic shuns society, while the king upholds it, yet both figures are celebrated within the Hindu religious tradition. Nonviolence (*ahiṃsā*) is the duty of the ascetic, while kings are required to implement force in defense and expansion of state. Similarly, Durgā forgoes the *nivṛttic* precept of *ahiṃsā* in order to fulfill her *pravṛttic* cosmic purpose: protection of the universe. It is noteworthy that Durgā manifests for the very purpose of restoring sovereignty to the king of heaven, whose throne had been usurped by demonic forces. Returning to our frame narrative, the king, upon hearing the acts of Durgā, propitiates her and thereby regains his sovereignty through her grace. Ironically, he does so as per the teachings of the sage, who, as emblematic of *nivṛtti* dharma, appears aloof to the concerns of the world. This research demonstrates the extent to which the tripartite tales of the DM—in extolling a vision of divinity that manifests to protect the world while implementing awesome martial prowess to do so—in fact *privileges* the blood-soaked duty of kings over that of nonviolent ascetics. Our text celebrates the sanguinary strand of what I call the *dharmic* double helix.

While the DM is sure to valorize the divergent *dharmas* of ascetics and kings, in glorifying Durgā, it glorifies the ideology of kingship, which she represents without exception. It thereby offers a refreshing rebuttal to the world-denying caricature (as in *mokṣa*-oriented *upaniṣadic* religiosity) too often ascribed to Hinduism as a whole. In the ideological arm-wrestle between *pravṛtti* and *nivṛtti*, ascetic ideals too often win out. Take, for example, Kṛṣṇa's disparaging comment to Queen Gāndhārī in the MBh (11.26.5): "A *brahmin* woman conceives a child destined to asceticism … while the child born to the princess of the warrior class is made to kill."[1] Yet the grandeur of the Goddess lies squarely within the *pravṛttic* ideals of kingship, as evidenced in her forceful penchant to preserve *this* world, and the beings within it. That world is, after all, one that she pervades, the fabric of which is inextricable to her essential nature. By extension, the DM posits that the world—despite its transient trappings—is in no way inferior to supreme salvific reality.

Acknowledging narrative's paramount function of encoding ideology, this project locates the DM ideologically more so than historically, looking to the trajectory of these vying values at the heart of Hinduism. Given that royal and ascetic ideologies are both very much valorized today, this study emphasizes the *current and ongoing* relevance of the DM, given its ability to speak to these lasting ideals. The DM deals with ideals, drawing upon notions of the ideal king, the ideal sage, and the ideal feminine figure required to safeguard existence itself. The text expects familiarity with this ideological ambivalence pervading the Hindu world.

To draw from Umberto Eco's narrative theory, this study argues that the DM's model reader is not only expected to be equipped with the ideological savvy outlined above, but also with a certain structural savvy. The former of these interpretational tools pertains to content, while the latter pertains to form. Regarding the latter, this research demonstrates that the DM possesses a sophisticated narrative ring structure, arguing that familiarity with the mechanics of ring composition is indispensable to engaging the DM on its own terms. In the absence of this awareness, one fails to register the role of the work's enframement in the manner the work anticipates, starkly missing the mark of model readership.

This research argues that, at least in the case of the DM, narrative enframement is an indispensable component of a complex, consciously orchestrated, meaningful narrative structure, one purposefully geared toward encoding ideology and eliciting interpretation through structural cues. It therefore serves as a counterpoint to dissecting Sanskrit narrative texts for "data" they "contain" within them. The methodology adopted herein counters the overwhelming grain of how the DM (and *purāṇic* texts in general) has been previously studied; that is, typically for historicist and philological purposes. Instead, it safeguards the integrity of the DM as an intelligent literary whole. Rather than querying the extent to which the text functions as history masquerading as myth (or even myth masquerading as history), this research approaches the DM qua narrative. It constitutes a synchronic study of the glories of the Goddess, one that necessarily makes sense of the text as a whole, frame and all. In short, it takes its primary direction from the world within the text.

Chapter outline

Chapter 1, "Framing the framing," traces trenchant biases within the field of *purāṇic* studies and how they filter into scholarship on the DM. Drawing on the work of Umberto Eco and Mary Douglas, it discusses the literary methodological approach of this work, emphasizing the novelty of this approach against the pervasive scholarly trajectory, which itself is a scholarly contribution.

Chapter 2, "Finding the forest hermit," defines the vying ideologies entailed in *nivṛtti* and *pravṛtti dharma* as discussed in their *locus classicus*, the MBh. It then proceeds to decode the symbolism of encounters between forest hermits and exiled kings through the lens of the *dharmic* double helix, demonstrating the extent to which this common narrative trope masterfully encodes the ambivalence of *brāhmaṇic* ideology. It concludes by examining the extent to which the DM affirms the ideology of *nivṛtti*.

Chapter 3, "Mother of kings," first reexamines Heesterman's famous rhetoric on the "conundrum of the king's authority" to discuss how the DM undercuts that conundrum. It secondly traces the extent to which the Indian King is conceived of as a divine protector, and thirdly demonstrates the extent to which the DM affirms *pravṛtti* ideology, particularly in its depiction of a royal Goddess who is called to protect imperiled beings.

Chapter 4, "Reading the ring," provides a close analysis of the enframement of the DM, demonstrating its function in encoding the text's primarily *pravṛttic* impetus. It shows that the very configuration of the DM points to the *dharmic* interplay of ascetics and kings, ultimately championing the latter. Its discussion revolves around the discovery that the text exhibits a sophisticated narrative ring structure, which showcases the centerpoint of the work: Episode II, geared squarely toward royal ideology.

Chapter 5, "Mother of power," reexamines the commonly held notion of the Goddess of the DM as a paradigmatic wrathful goddess of the tooth, before reflecting upon the actual Goddess we see within the DM. In demonstrating the extent to which Durgā operates as a cosmic sovereign—and therefore enacts the function of cosmic *preservation*—this work serves as a corrective to scholarship prone to emphasizing the Goddess of the DM's wrathful role as an instrument of *destruction*.

The Conclusion of this project, "Framing frontier," summarizes the argument herein, and suggests avenues for future research, most notably an examination of why the DM should inhabit the *Mārkaṇḍeya Purāṇa* at all. It moreover conjectures upon the utility of the methodology adopted herein toward examining other Sanskrit narrative works in future. As emphasized by its subtitle, this book is not merely about royal ideology in the DM; it is equally about *how to read* that ideology. The exegetical knowhow acquired herein can readily be applied elsewhere.

A note on nomenclature

In this study, I use the proper noun "Durgā" to refer to the specific central character we see within the verses of the DM. While I, at times, refer to "the

Goddess" in a more abstract sense, this research revolves around the principal character portrayed in this intriguing narrative work. "The Goddess" refers to a *that*, while "Durgā" refers to a *whom*. Alternately put, "the Goddess" is an abstract conceptual construct, while "Durgā" is a narrative character whose contours are delineated by what we see in the text. I am studying the DM as a literary entity, and so its principal personality deserves a name, not a label. Moreover, a term such as "the Goddess" proves too generic to signify the multi-faceted figure we encounter in our text.

While there are certainly a great many names in the DM ascribed to its Goddess, relatively few of these refer to the supreme actor of the DM. Of the ones that do, Durgā is foremost. As Coburn notes:

> this famous designation for the Goddess is used in our text on seven occasions, and in all three episodes. It is clearly applied to her supreme form, for four of its appearances are in hymns, one is an epilogue to a hymn, and one characterizes the Goddess who resumes all goddesses into herself.[2]

The epithet actually occurs in only Episodes II and III; and it occurs eight times, not seven. While this number is lower than her most common epithets, Caṇḍikā (occurring on twenty-nine occasions) and Ambikā (twenty-five occasions), the Goddess of our text herself declares that she will be known as Durgā, having slain Durgama (DM 11.46). More crucially, she is *addressed as Durgā* by the demon Śumbha while he challenges her thus: "O Durgā, puffed up with misplaced pride in your own strength of arms, don't be so haughty! It is by relying on the strength of others that you fight, with this inflated sense of your own importance!" (DM 10.2). Her response is critical for our purposes: "I alone exist here in the world; what second, other than I, is there? O wicked one, behold these my manifestations of power entering back into me!"[3] (DM 10.3). The text explicitly informs us that Durgā is the unified Goddess in whom various emanations ultimately reside. It is unsurprising, then, that the Goddess of our text is known throughout the Hindu world as Durgā, and that her exploits are commonly referred to as *Durgāsaptaśatī*, Durgā's Seven Hundred (Verses).

Notes

1 Kate Krosby, *Mahābhārata: Book 10, Dead of the Night. Book 11, The Women*, vol. 1 (New York: New York University Press: JJC Foundation, 2009), 327.
2 Thomas B. Coburn, *Devī Māhātmya: The Crystallization of the Goddess Tradition* (Columbia, MO: South Asia Books, 1985), 115–16. He lists the junctures as follows: 4.10, 4.16, 5.10, 5.66, 9.29, 10.2, 11.22. The last of these actually occurs at 11.23.
3 Coburn, *Encountering the Goddess*, 71.

1 Framing the framing

Focusing the study of the *Devī Māhātmya*

How should we engage the DM? Hindu narrative literature is enormously didactic in nature, functioning to preserve religious ideology across centuries. Therefore, the overwhelming scholarly emphasis on philosophical texts over narrative literature has proven problematic. Recent scholars have argued in favor of locating religious authority within narrative text.[1] This study builds on such work in looking to the DM for ideological importance. This first chapter demonstrates the pitfalls of diachronic dissection of the DM, then goes on to outline a solid strategy for synchronically grappling with the work. It probes the DM in search of the religious ideologies encoded *within* the text through a close synchronic critical analysis of its narrative content. The fact that this study approaches the text as a whole, in and of itself, actively counters three tendencies within current scholarship: firstly, to regard the DM as a late interpolation into the *Mārkaṇḍeya Purāṇa* (henceforth MkP); secondly, to examine the DM through philological and historicist lenses; and, thirdly, to examine the text through the lens of ritual and tantric studies. In approaching the DM as a narrative text in its own right, "flimsy frame" and all, this work guards the DM against historicist, philological, or structuralist reductions.

This chapter traces the scholarly legacy of diachronic dissection, owing to the influence of H.H. Wilson (1786–1860) and his colonial contemporaries. Misguidedly expecting the Purāṇas to function like the Vedas, these individuals were ill-prepared to receive the *purāṇic* corpus. Their disdainful misgivings regarding *purāṇic* engagement resound to this day, echoed by F.E. Pargiter (1852–1927), translator of the MkP two generations later, and prevailing to modern times throughout historicist and philological excavation of *purāṇic* works in tandem with the creation of critical editions of extant Purāṇas. This chapter then proceeds to trace the impact of this legacy upon DM scholarship proper: in addition to historicist and philological dissection of the text, we find it used for the purposes of tantric and ritual studies, along with ethnographic research. In short, the emphasis on the world *behind* the text inaugurated by our colonial forebears is now split between that world, and the world *in front of* the text. The biases driving the trajectory of scholarship on the DM have thus far successfully deterred sustained analysis of the world *within* the text. Geared toward properly probing that world, the final section of this chapter unpacks the tools whereby we may do so, most importantly Umberto Eco's theoretical foundation on the function of narrative, and Mary Douglas' work on narrative ring composition.

Frame I: colonial encounters with *purāṇic* narratives

The inclination to make sense of the DM's framing as integral to its whole counters the trajectory of western scholarship on Indian narrative texts, stemming from the initial reception of *purāṇic* texts by early colonial scholars. In broaching the DM as a literary whole and viewing its frame narrative as inextricable to that whole, this study squarely counters the thrust of nearly two centuries of scholarship on the DM. The overwhelming scholarly assumption, following Eden Pargiter (1852–1927), is that the DM is a late interpolation into the MkP, and that the narrative enframement linking it to this *purāṇic* context is thus a contrived afterthought. What is novel about this research is not only the answers it provides for its research question, but the very stance it adopts in posing that research question, one which acknowledges the indispensability of the DM's enframement to its structural and thematic cohesion. While the DM's enframement has been cast as ancillary to the actual greatness of the Goddess proper, I argue that the DM's frame narrative is in fact a crucial component to the sophisticated structuring of the text, indeed an architectural enterprise undertaken for the very purpose of showcasing its most significant themes. Unpacking its enframement is therefore integral to a proper appreciation of the text, and the principal character it features. Prior to disclosing the specific synchronic methodology adopted herein to broach the DM, we first need to trace the trenchant scholarly legacy that would have us diachronically dissect the text.

Thomas Coburn, modern scholar on the DM, quotes H.H. Wilson (1786–1860)[2] as having referred to the DM in an 1840 lecture as "amongst the most popular works in the Sanskrit language."[3] Coburn clarifies that

> this is not to say, of course, that scholarly scrutiny immediately ensued, for it is only within the past two decades that the Purāṇic corpus, to which the *Devī Māhātmya* belongs (as chapters 81–93, in most editions, of the *Mārkaṇḍeya Purāṇa*) had begun to receive the attention it merits as the fibre of popular Hinduism.[4]

Given the tremendous impact of this text, why was it neglected for so long? In attending to this question, we must unpack the trajectory of western scholarship on the Purāṇas by early Orientalist and later Romantic figures, whose legacy has proven impactful for even modern scholarship on Purāṇas as dominated by weak structuralist analysis, especially by the work of Wendy Doniger. This research squarely counters these earlier waves of scholarship that were keen to dissect them for philological and historicist purposes rather than regard them as intrinsically valuable synchronic wholes.

The Purāṇas differ drastically from Vedic texts. The Vedas (Hinduism's most ancient and most revered scriptures) are marked by fixity of form, constitute the quintessential category of revelation (*śruti*, i.e., that which was heard), and indeed are considered un-authored (*apauruṣeya*) collections of sounds whose semantic meaning is secondary to their precise ritual enunciation. These are primarily acoustic entities, and secondarily semantic ones. These texts are considered unalterable, beyond translation, and ought to be "memorized with meticulous care to their word order, accent, and stress."[5] It is no wonder that a tradition upholding so rigid a class of texts would in tandem need to uphold a complementary class of literature marked by utter fluidity: the Purāṇas.

Unlike the Vedas, the Purāṇas are living, organic, multi-formed entities, which continually adapted to history, geography, class, gender, vernacular language, and local custom. They serve as a means of integrating and propagating religious values, reinterpreting old material, and, overall, renovating religious tradition as needed. Despite their organic fluidity and relevance to daily Hindu life, they boast a unified, exalted origin, compiled by Sage Vyāsa and, in some cases, uttered by the creator, Lord Brahmā; in short, they speak of themselves as indispensable to Vedic understanding. Take, for example, one Purāṇic verse, which reads:

> The *Brāhmaṇ* who learns his four *Vedas* along with their *Upaniṣads* and ancillary texts does not become a learned man until he learns the Purāṇas. The *Veda* has to be expanded with the aid of the Purāṇas. The *Veda* itself fears a man of little learning lest he should hurt it.[6]

Rao argues that the "complementarity of the *Vedas* and the Purāṇas is crucial for an understanding of the text culture of *Brāhmaṇic* Hinduism."[7] He does so by suggesting that the two essential components of language—form and content, that is, the signifying *utterance* and the *meaning* it signifies—are bifurcated and located in two separate groups of texts: the Vedas, which tradition considers *śabdapradhāna* (important for sound, and thus unchangeable and untranslatable), and the Purāṇas, considered *arthapradhāna* (that which is important for its meaning). It is the meaning of these texts (both with respect to the tales they tell and the significance they hold) that persists despite their formal fluctuations across language, time, and place.[8]

The fluidity of this genre, along with its resultant multiformity, posed a major problem in the early history of the western study of these texts. Mistakenly holding them accountable to the characteristics of Vedic texts, early western scholars viewed the Purāṇas as haphazard and disorganized. This misapprehension is unsurprising given the Purāṇas' own claim to a Vedic heritage: that they were composed as a unified whole by Vyāsa who orally transmitted them to his son Romaharṣaṇa, who then orally transmitted them to his six disciples.[9] Romaharṣaṇa was a gifted bard, capable of causing the hairs of his listeners to stand on end. Furthermore, the Purāṇas claim that their genre is distinguished by "five marks" (*pañcalakṣaṇas*) as indicated by the fifth-century Sanskrit lexicon,

Amarakośa. While the *Amarakośa* does not specifically indicate what these five distinguishing features are, several Purāṇas detail the "five marks" to be: *sarga* (creation or evolution of the universe), *pratisarga* (re-creation of the universe after its periodic dissolution), *vaṃśa* (genealogies of gods, patriarchs, sages, and kings), *manvantara* ("Manu-intervals"—cosmic cycles—each of which is presided over by a Manu, a primordial patriarch), and *vaṃśānucarita* (accounts of royal dynasties).[10] However, from what we can tell from the extant manuscripts, discourse along the lines of these five topics occupied a small percentage of the Purāṇic material; according to Kane's estimate, less than 3 percent.[11] This "anomaly" fueled suspicion toward these texts by early Indologists. Yet the staggering number and variety of Purāṇic manuscripts found throughout the subcontinent surely attests to the popularity of this genre, a popularity which can only be born of a widespread acceptance as an intelligible and relevant genre to its audiences, multiformity notwithstanding.

The first wave of scholarship in the colonial period was undertaken by westerners "eager to gather religious and cultural information about the Hindus," but who viewed these texts as artifacts, proceeding with "little direct interaction with the users of the texts and their textual practices."[12] In 1784, Warren Hastings commissioned Radhakanta Sarma to prepare a summary of the Purāṇas,[13] and scholars such as Horace Hayman Wilson (1786–1860), Vans Kennedy (1784–1846), and Eugene Burnouf (1801–1852) spent most of their lives studying Purāṇas and were swept up in the prospect of unearthing their possible Vedic origins, along with identifying the historical processes which allowed for sectarian corruption of a theorized lost Ur-Purāṇa. Despite the fact that the three figures are credited in Maurice Winternitz's (1863–1937) 1907 *History of Indian Literature* as the founding fathers of Purāṇic studies—Kennedy, Wilson, and Burnouf—Wilson was the central figure of this wave of scholarship. Beginning in the 1830s, he set out on an ambitious task to survey the entirety of Purāṇic literature, an enterprise which found "culmination in his monumental translation of the *Viṣṇu Purāṇa* (1840), which he filled with copious notes from his researches into other Purāṇas."[14] Elizabeth Rohlman has effectively traced Wilson's immense impact on subsequent waves of *purāṇic* scholarship.[15]

As alarming as it is that this pioneering Indologist "condemned extant Purāṇic manuscripts as base, sectarian corruptions of a pristine, imagined ideal,"[16] what was enormously problematic was Wilson's methodology: he enlisted the aid of a group of local *paṇḍitas* to convert the extant manuscripts into Sanskrit indexes, recapitulating the content of every page from which they worked. These indexes were then translated into English by another group of Indians conversant in English, which Wilson supervised, correcting both the Sanskrit and English where needed, and himself deciding which of the indexes were worthy of being fleshed out. As Rohlman observes, we have no way of knowing how many of these indexes he personally surveyed, or what his precise criteria were for deciding which sections warranted attention. What we do know about his methodology was that he engaged the manuscripts with an attitude of distrust. He writes in his preface to the *Viṣṇu Purāṇa* that "we are far from being in possession of that knowledge which the authentic writings of the Hindus alone can give us of their religion, mythology, and historical traditions."[17] Yet one is left wondering at how "authentic" his "translation" of the "text" could be given the indelible influence of his prejudicial editorial presence within the work.

Wilson was convinced of the existence—at some point in history long past—of either eighteen pristine Mahāpurāṇas, unadulterated by sectarian interpolation; or, which would prove enticing to the second wave of Romantic-era Victorian scholars, one single Ur-Purāṇa—mother to them all. His idealistic bias toward the "old" and the "universal" would remain forever at odds with the fabric of the Purāṇic texts: how can one neatly fold textual entities which insist on billowing with the winds of culture change? Incapable of appreciating the Purāṇas' dance through tradition, he perceived them as flighty, and thus unreliable. He therefore writes that:

> [I]t will be evident that in their present condition they must be received with caution as authorities for the mythological religion of the Hindus at any remote period. They preserve, no doubt, many ancient notions and traditions; but these have been so much mixed up with foreign matter, intended to favour the popularity of particular forms of worship or articles of faith, that they cannot be unreservedly recognised as genuine representations of what we have reason to believe the Puránas originally were.[18]

Under the sway of his own disillusionment, Wilson thwarted future study of the Purāṇas.[19] His legacy has proved indelible, succeeding in influencing both French and German scholarship, through Eugene Burnouf and Christian Lassen (1800–1876) respectively. Rohlman calls to our attention the fact that Wilson's view of Purāṇas and resultant theorizing to account for their supposed fall from grace have led

> scholars for over a century to assume three things: that the Purāṇas are necessarily late compositions, that the current manuscripts are merely haphazardly assembled collections of interpolation and accretion, and that those Purāṇas most riddled by "sectarian biases" are necessarily later than those that are not.[20]

This attitude fueled prevalent colonial disdain for the DM as a late, highly sectarian entity, haphazardly interpolated into the MkP.

While this first wave, through their search for the Ur-progenitor of the Purāṇa family, at least paid attention to the narratives proper, the second wave of scholarship dissected texts in search of historical and mythological data, abandoning regard for their literary status. Attention to these condemned texts was revived when Vincent A. Smith (1848–1920) demonstrated that the *vaṃūānucarita* of the *Matsya Purāṇa* accurately recorded the historical *Āndhra* dynasty. Pargiter, one of the early champions of turning to the Purāṇas for the sake of historical data,[21] established the historical validity of the texts, followed by R. Morton Smith. These scholars were classically trained and accustomed to engaging Greek and Latin texts, which were very different entities in contrast to the ways of the Purāṇic tradition, where texts interacted with their living oral milieus, an interaction which was viewed as corruption via interpolation and forgery. This persisted even in 1927 with Winternitz who writes: "compilers of the Puranas who worked haphazardly" still managed to "include in their texts some dialogues reminiscent of the *Upanishads*" and hence, "even in the desert of the Purāṇa-literature there is no lack of oases."[22] Pargiter's impulse later flourished in the work of Rajendra C. Hazra who demonstrated the significance of the Upapurāṇas in the reconstruction of ancient Indian history. However, in emphasizing their historical dimension, Hazra ignored the extent to which the Purāṇas voice current religious themes. He read the texts as "historically descriptive rather than religiously prescriptive," adopting Pargiter's predilection toward redactive reading derived from approaches to Biblical Studies at the time, and condensed into works such as Pargiter's 1922 *Ancient Indian Historical Traditions* wherein he constructed an Ur-Purāṇa.[23]

The Purāṇas floundered amid a first wave of scholarship, which overlooked them in an attempt to discover a posited Ur-ancestor, and then almost drowned in the second wave, which focused on their historical and mythic data. The first approach was based on the assumption that the text no longer exists (and probably never did), and the second resorted to dissecting the text which does exist. Both processes—the former akin to a séance contrived to conjure the ghosts of Purāṇa past, the second akin to death by dismemberment for the sake of scientific research—view the Purāṇic corpus as a field of corpses: both waves fail to recognize that they constituted an organic, *living* textual tradition. What about more modern scholarship on the Purāṇas?

The tides begin to change in the third wave of purāṇic scholarship, as exemplified in the sage summation of Greg Bailey:

> When reading the Purāṇas, what we find is a collection of texts filled with symbols of the past mixed easily with startlingly new literary and cultural material. Whether any tension was felt by reciters and audience about what is, in truth, a juxtaposition of the traditional and the new seems unlikely, yet the presence of such a juxtaposition compels us to interpret the Purāṇas as a textual process successful in transforming whatever was new, and potentially radical, into a form acceptable to the present. This corresponds to a very ancient indigenous perception of the Purāṇas in which they are defined as preserving the old while constantly coming to terms with the new. Never should they be seen as static relics of a past frozen into the present.[24]

Bailey identifies the 1986 publication of Ludo Rocher's *The Purāṇas* as the inauguration of this wave of modern scholarship. Rocher's publication emerged one year after an important conference on the Purāṇas at the University of Wisconsin, Madison, which united several key scholars in Hindu Studies. The fruit of this conference, *Purāṇa Perennis*, published in 1993, showcases methods of literary criticism, structural analysis, and an appreciation of sociocultural contextualization of Purāṇic works.

The modern epoch of study is also marked by an international group of philological scholars who have faithfully applied principles of text-criticism to produce critical editions of the Purāṇas, including the *Mahābhārata* and the *Rāmāyaṇa*. Another noteworthy initiative of our time is the fact that the Mahārājā of Kāśī, V.N. Singh, has sponsored the formation of the All-India Kashiraj Trust, which has begun critically editing the Purāṇas and also published the scholarly journal *Purāṇam* from 1959–2009. Text-criticism employs a philological approach, which

> assumes that there was a single author for each of the Purāṇas who produced a single text which was then transmitted through a wide area over a long period of time during which the text acquired scribal errors, textual attritions, not to mention deliberate interpolations by motivated anonymous authors.[25]

Yet this stance has not escaped critique. Rocher writes, e.g.,

> I too have been trained in classical philology in Europe. I too have learned how to prepare critical editions, comparing manuscripts and reconstructing the original text—the archetype. But I am prepared to forget all that when it comes to Purāṇas.[26]

Inaugurated by the twin auspices of literary criticism and structuralism, this third wave of scholarship has nevertheless been somewhat preoccupied with mining the Purāṇas for mythological motifs. The most significant figure in this enterprise is Wendy Doniger, who has spent nearly half a century plucking mythic moments from across vast spans of time and boundaries of genre and region to bring them into conversation within the rubric of structuralist discourse. Does this enterprise, too, not remain soaked in the legacy of the scholarly waves of her predecessors? Rohlman observes the striking corollary between Romantic attitudes to the Purāṇas and modern scholarship on the material: for example, Doniger remarks upon their "strong sectarian bias," and that they were "subject to frequent interpolations over a period of many centuries."[27] Given this view, it is no wonder that she did not opt toward synchronic analysis of the works she studied. Similarly, J.A.B. van Buitenen and C. Dimmit remarked that the Purāṇas gathered accretions "as if they were libraries to which new volumes have been continuously added, not necessarily at the end of the shelf, but randomly."[28] Early encounters with purāṇic narratives have bequeathed a hermeneutic of distrust, stemming from the suspicion that they are fragmented and corrupted versions of once-pristine cohesive texts. Rao notes that despite (and perhaps because of) the fact that Purāṇas are "ideologically closed," promoting a specifically *Brāhmaṇic* ideology, they are "functionally open," occasioning their assimilation of various religious material into the scope of that ideology.[29] Therefore, rather than look to the imagined background of what the cohesive text "originally might have been," why not look to the concrete foreground of a specific narrative, such as the DM, and understand why it is construed as it is? Though more than *seventeen decades* have elapsed since Wilson's pronouncement on the enormous popularity of the DM, this is among the first research to acknowledge it as the intricate and engaging literary whole that it is.

Frame II: scholarly encounters with the *Devī Māhātmya*

While Pargiter writes of the MkP that "the general character of this Purāṇa has been well summed up by Prof. Wilson in his preface to his Translation of the *Viṣṇu Purāṇa*,"[30] he is quick to clarify that Wilson's summation "hardly applies to the *Devī-māhātmya*."[31] Despite the fact that the DM is by far the most popular component of the MkP, it is viewed as the most sectarian and therefore most recent portion thereof, which both affront the sanctity of Wilson's pronouncement on the MkP as among the oldest and most important of the extant Purāṇas. Banerjea, who first edited and translated the MkP into English, had divided the MkP into five sections as early as 1855. In the words of Pargiter:

> The Purāṇa is clearly divisible (as Dr. Banerjea noticed) into five distinct parts, namely: 1. Cantos 1–9, in which Jaimini is referred by Mārkaṇḍeya to the wise Birds, and they directly explain to him the four questions that perplexed him and some connected matters. 2. Cantos 10–44, where, though Jaimini propounds further questions to the Birds and they nominally expound them, yet the real speakers are Sumati, nicknamed Jaḍa, and his father. 3. Cantos 45–81: here, though Jaimini and the Birds are the nominal speakers, yet the real speakers are Mārkaṇḍeya and his disciple Kraustuki. 4. Cantos 82–92, the Devi-mahatmya, a pure interpolation, in which the real speaker is a ṛṣi named Medhas, and which is only repeated by Mārkaṇḍeya. 5. Cantos 93–136, where Mārkaṇḍeya and Krauṣṭuki carry on their discourse from canto 81. The 137th canto concludes the work; it is a necessary corollary to the first part.[32]

This fivefold feature of the *purāṇa* was implicated to bolster claims regarding the historical development of the text, wherein three overarching strata were posited to account for its five narrative sections.

The scholarly trajectory established by this diachronic thrust has proven most influential. Winternitz, for example, follows Pargiter in taking as the oldest the parts of the Purāṇa where Mārkaṇḍeya is the narrator proper (instructing his pupil Krauṣṭuki), as in 45–81 and 93–136, dating these presumably most ancient sections to 300 CE or earlier. These conclusions are reinforced by R.C. Hazra in 1975 who writes that "the above conclusion about the date of the chapters under discussion agrees remarkably with the view of Pargiter."[33] Hazra directly quotes Pargiter as follows:

> The *Devī-māhātmya*, the latest part, was certainly complete in the 9th century and very probably in the 5th or 6th century A. D. The third and fifth parts (i.e. chaps. 45–81 and 93–136 respectively), which constituted the original Purāṇa, were very probably in existence in the third century, and perhaps even earlier; and the first and second parts (i.e., chaps. 1–9 and 10–44 respectively) were composed between those two periods.[34]

This legacy of historicizing the Purāṇas infiltrates even modern scholarship as C. Mackenzie Brown quotes both Pargiter[35] and Hazra[36] in his 1974 publication *God as Mother* to assert that the DM was dated "later than the ninth century AD and probably from the fifth or sixth."[37] This legacy is so trenchant that Ludo Rocher invokes it in the very first line of his introduction to the MkP, which: "consists of 137 *adhyāyas*; the *purāṇa* proper is interrupted by the thirteen chapters (81–93) of the *Devīmāhātmya*."[38] He again reiterates its status as an "interruption," writing a little later in his discussion that the MkP "proper is interrupted by thirteen chapters (81–93) which form the Devimahatmya."[39] He later more fully unpacks the DM's mismatched status as follows:

> Even though the *Devīmāhātmya* has, more often than not, been recognized as an originally independent composition, its date and the date of the Mārkaṇḍeya [Purāṇa] have, in most cases, been examined simultaneously. The general idea is that the *māhātmya* is a later work which, at a certain moment, has been inserted into the already existing purāṇa. As indicated earlier, the description of the consecutive Manus is interrupted after chapter eighty, and resumes in chapter ninety-four with the same interlocutors, Mārkaṇḍeya and Krauṣṭuki; the interruption occurs on account of the eighth Manu, Sāvarṇi, an incarnation of king Suratha who, after hearing the exploits of the Devī becomes a worshiper of the goddess. This "obviously very flimsy" connection implies, then, that the purāṇa is older than the *māhātmya*.[40]

The issues of the dating are not intellectual alone; later implies less authentic, which has historically inspired intense disdain for works such as the DM. The "obviously very flimsy" remark, quoting Agrawala,[41] is a correlate of the prejudice with which the work was originally received by our scholarly forebears. The general attitude that Purāṇas were sloppy, grammatically erroneous, and generally unsophisticated works would have held sway for *Māhātmya* literature as well. He describes them as "texts which are composed with the specific purpose of proclaiming the 'greatness' of a variety of things: a place, an auspicious time, a deity, a ritual activity such as *tirthayātrā* (pilgrimage) or *dāna* (donation), etc."[42] Hence, they also ensured the prejudice directed at Purāṇas in general. Moriz Winternitz (1863–1936) writes in his *History of Indian Literature*:

> The majority of the Māhātmyas which are connected with or included in the Purāṇas and the Upapurāṇas, is, on the whole, inferior literature. They arose

> as hand-books for the Purohitas of the Tīrthas praised in them, and tell legends which in part belong to the tradition, and in part are inventions, with the purpose of proving the holiness of these places of pilgrimage.[43]

Owing to this disdain, scholarship on the DM has proven quite scant over the centuries. This is particularly problematic given the work's *tremendous* sway in the life of Hinduism, past and present, across *Śākta*, tantric, and mainstream devotional lines. It was first translated into English in 1823,[44] immediately followed by an analysis with excerpts in French in 1824,[45] and a translation into Latin in 1831.[46] However, interest dwindles after Wilson's dire pronouncement on the inferiority of these texts in 1840 in the introduction to his translation on the *Viṣṇu Purāṇa*. Barring Galanos' Greek translation in 1853 (who had been a resident of Benaras for multiple decades at the time), the DM is not again addressed until Wortham's English translation in 1885. This brings us to Pargiter's 1904 English translation of the MkP (inclusive of the DM), in the introduction to which we find perhaps the most vividly voiced disdain for the DM:

> The Devī-māhātmya stands entirely by itself as a later interpolation. It is a poem complete in itself. Its subject and the character attributed to the goddess show that it is the product of a later age which developed and took pleasure in the sanguinary features of popular religion. The praise of the goddess Mahā-māyā in canto 81 is in the ordinary style. Her special glorification begins in canto 82, and is elaborated with the most extravagant laudation and the most miraculous imagination. Some of the hymns breathe deep religious feeling, express enthusiastic adoration, and evince fervent spiritual meditation. On the other hand, the descriptions of the battles abound with wild and repulsive incidents, and revel in gross and amazing fancies. The Devī-māhātmya is a compound of the most opposite characters. The religious outpourings are at times pure and elevated: the material descriptions are absurd and debased.[47]

The DM has also been discussed within histories of Indian literature,[48] and has been translated into European languages a dozen or so times over the last two centuries: into English by Sinha in 1922, Agarwala in 1963, Shankaranarayanan in 1968, Jagadisvaranada in 1972, Varenne (into French) in 1975, Coburn in 1991, Saraswati in 1998, and Kali in 2004. Most of these translations are quite obscure, and the only two generally referenced in modern scholarship are Agarwala's and Coburn's, most notably the latter. As the most rigorous scholarly translation, Coburn's is used throughout this study unless otherwise stated.

While studies demonstrating the role of the DM within Śākta traditions abound,[49] studies on the DM itself do not. There has even been research on the artwork accompanying DM manuscripts,[50] along with brief articles on the topic, most notably Mirashi's dating argument based on a Nepal manuscript,[51] and Tiwari's note on a variant reading of *devyāstanau* (from *devyāḥ tanau* to *devyāḥ stanau* at DM 10.6),[52] and even a study of the DM's role in the modern Indian comic book *Amar Chitra Katha*.[53]

Cynthia Hume's 1990 doctoral dissertation examines the extent to which the DM "is imbedded in a living religious tradition in north India, the Vidhyācal Temple, and the effect of historical change on the role and interpretation of the text."[54] Her interest in the role of the DM in contemporary religious life is further explored in book chapters in 1997 and 2000. Furthermore, Hillary Rodrigues has produced an exceptional study on the liturgical aspect of the DM within a modern ritual context since then. Indeed, a number of scholars have focused on the ritual and sociological applications of the DM,[55] rather than on the narrative itself. Moreover, scholars who do focus more on the narrative fabric of the work follow suit with how purāṇic narratives have been studied in the west in general: David Kinsley's 1978 article therefore dissects the DM in order to delimit the various goddess traditions of which he finds traces within; and Renate Söhnen-Thieme's insightful 2002 article likewise concludes by slicing up its myths along historicist and sectarian lines. A similar approach can be found in the work of Yuko Yokochi, albeit in a more complex register, engaged below in greater detail.

Two Master's theses directly pertain to this study, constituting, to my knowledge, the only other research projects engaging the DM primarily *as narrative*. Firstly, Elizabeth Cecil's Master's work reads the DM within its MkP context to suggest that the presence of prominent feminine mythological figures elsewhere in the MkP might account for the DM's presence within the greater work. She further suggests that this endeavor might constitute a preliminary step toward reading the MkP itself as a literary whole. While this avenue of investigation falls beyond the narrower scope of this current research, its thrust pertains to the work at hand, and shall therefore be addressed in the concluding chapter of the present research. Secondly, the Master's work of Kendra Marks directly pertains to this current project in that it centers around the character of Kālī as seen in the DM. On the other hand, the fact that Marks' research isolates Kālī as a character separate from Durgā ultimately departs from the inclination of this research, which views Kālī as a personified aspect of the ultimate mother of power featured in the DM. This predilection stems from the Goddess's own declaration within the text that all of the entities emerging from her are no more than projected portions of her own singular power; hence, they are necessarily folded back into her throughout the text, operating as personified sides of a complex personality while manifest.

Thomas Coburn makes the most substantive contribution to the scholarship on the DM. He provides a rationale for broaching the DM independent of the MkP given that it has been enormously popular, circulating as an independent, self-contained work which, furthermore, has attracted numerous commentaries: no fewer than sixty-seven. Even when its manuscripts are included as part of the MkP, there is often commentary only on the DM portion of the text. However, he claims that the significance of the text is not derived from its *purāṇic* context, and that "the fact that the DM also occurs as a portion of the MkP is practically irrelevant."[56] This cannot be the case given that the DM invokes *Mārkaṇḍeya* as its expounder in every known manuscript at both beginning and ending even while circulating independently. It is in fact Mārkaṇḍeya's account of the story of Suratha, Samādhi, and Medhas that proves crucial to contextualizing the themes of the DM. Medhas does not only expound the glories of the Goddess; he is an essential character of the DM himself.

Coburn's first book, *Devī Māhātmya: The Crystallization of the Goddess Tradition*, explores the extent to which the DM results from the cross-pollination of Aryan and non-Aryan religions, arguing that it unifies an amalgamation of various local *devīs* into one supreme *brāhmaṇic mahādevī*. His second book, *Encountering the Goddess*, comprises a translation of the DM, along with a demonstration of its vitality in the religious lives of modern practitioners.[57] Coburn aims at overcoming the prevalent nineteenth-century historicist bias by looking to the contemporary significance of the DM to the religious lives of devotees of Durgā.[58] This research, much like Coburn's second book, aims to shift the focus away from historicism, but we each shift it in different directions: he is concerned with the religious *application* of the DM, while I am concerned with the narrative *content* of the DM. While this research may well shed light on religious application such as the ritual invocation of Durgā, and particularly on rituals of kingship, it is primarily concerned with what we find in the world *within* the DM, and concerned secondarily with the ideological resonance of that world with the world in front of the text.

Yuko Yokochi's research draws on textual, epigraphic, and iconographic evidence in order to develop a historical narrative about the rise of Goddess worship in early India, a narrative that entails dissecting the DM into constituent themes in concordance to her mode of inquiry. She argues that separate *Mahiṣāsuramardinī* and *Vindhyavāsinī* myth cycles were integrated into the resultant "Warrior Goddess" of the DM, occurring "around the early eighth century."[59] Partaking in the legacy of colonial scholarship on the Purāṇas, she laments "sound philological studies based on critical editions have not matured in the research into [Purāṇas], thus hampering plausible assessments of literary sources and synthesization with the archaeological sources."[60] She moreover lauds as an important cornerstone of her research "the correct evaluation of the text as the original Skandapurāṇa by Adriaensen, Bakker and Isaacson (1994)."[61] She dates "the" Skandapurāṇa at the sixth century, from which she draws upon the eighteen-chapter *Kauūikī-Vindhyavāsinī* myth cycle. Based on her assessment, this text is an important bridge between *Vindhyavāsinī* in the *Harivaṃœa* and the DM.[62] She attributes the absence of sound critical editions as "responsible for a tendency related to the idea of the Goddess: many scholars tend to presuppose this concept ahistorically without taking it as a historical product."[63] It appears inconceivable to Yokochi that the notion of a "Great Goddess" could have existed prior to the evolution of the *Vindhyavāsinī* and *Mahiṣāsuramardinī* myth cycles.

Her study is premised upon three sorts of goddesses, "the Warrior Goddess, the Consort Goddess and the Supreme Goddess."[64] Given that "in the Devīmāhātmya, the Warrior Goddess attains the status of Supreme Goddess, absorbing the latent Consort Goddess, Pārvatī, into herself,"[65] it is clear that her study is interested in dissecting and excavating the text for historicist purposes, rather than examining it as a whole. She dismembers the vision of the feminine divine found in the DM in order to disambiguate constituent elements which conform to *Mahiṣāsuramardinī* iconographical sources and *Vindhyavāsinī* textual sources.

Convinced of the lateness of the DM, she appears unable to register the full significance of the *Taittirīya Āraṇyaka* 10 verse (ascribed with a *terminus ad quem* of the third century BCE[66]), which hails Durgā as follows: "*tām agnivarṇām tapasā jvalantīm vairocinīm karmaphaleṣu juṣṭām, durgāṃ devīṃ œaraṇam ahaṃ prapadye sutarasi tarase namaḥ,*" which Coburn translates:

> In her who has the color of Agni, flaming with ascetic power (tapas), the offspring of Virocana (*vairocani*) who delights in the fruits of one's actions. In the goddess Durgā do I take refuge; O one of great speed, (well) do you navigate. Hail (to you)![67]

This verse is duplicated verbatim in *Ṛg Vedic Khila, Rātrī Sūkta* (4.2.13).[68] Yokochi concludes that it is "very likely that the goddess Durgā was originally not a demon-slaying, warlike goddess [and] it may well be that this goddess was absorbed into the nascent Warrior Goddess by the sixth century and the epithet Durgā as well,"[69] cautioning that we "not confuse three subjects: the goddess Durgā in the *Vedas*, the origin of Mahiṣāsuramardinī (or, that of the myth of a goddess slaying a buffalo), and the rise of 'the Warrior Goddess,' "[70] the latter on which her thesis centers. Yet, the DM knows no such distinctions.

Can we really think the authors of the DM to be ignorant of the ancient *Taittirīya Āraṇyaka* verse hailing Durgā as protectress? Do we really think there is a stark divide between a "protector" goddess and a "warrior" goddess given that the *sine qua non* of *kṣatriya dharma* is protection? If there was a need, they most certainly have capitalized on textual precedent in order to establish the demon-battling Durgā of the DM with the flaming protectress of the *Taittirīya Āraṇyaka.* That the authors of the DM make no explicit reference to this verse is telling: doing so is obsolete. Do we think it took 700 years between the recitation of this verse to Durgā and others to follow in the DM? Clearly the DM is the result of a compositional process incorporating known hymns to Durgā, or at the very least presenting new hymns of attributes of a Goddess already established. As the DM so successfully houses those hymns within its narrative fold, we do not find them occupying other texts. Furthermore, given the radical thematic thrust of the content of the DM, coupled with its seemingly uncontested inclusion within the *Brāhmaṇic* fold via its adoption into the MkP, it is not unreasonable to conjecture a compositional period of centuries before it arrived at its current state. Hence, it is problematic to speak of it as indicative of any one moment of purāṇic religious time separate from another moment of late Vedic religious time.

As my project is not historical in nature, I do not problematize Yukochi's thesis with a mind to necessarily refuting her dating of the DM. It could well be that the middle episode of the DM was composed, as she concludes, in the ninth century based on the medieval iconographical representation found at Ellora. Or, it could have been adapted then for that purpose. Or, neither of these could be true. What I problematize is her methodology, one which has prevailed throughout the history of western scholarship on the Purāṇas and the DM. Is this work worth nothing more than an avenue of historical excavation? Even if so, do we not wish to closely examine its fabric *before* cutting it to shreds? Yokochi is an example of the dominant impulse to unravel the tapestry of the text so as to trace elusive historical threads throughout, an impulse stemming from the dynamics of our very first scholarly encounters with these text, as outlined above.

Given the absence of variants of either its current form, or any sort of discrepancy or dissent about its current purāṇic juncture, I am inclined to speculate that both of these aspects were established *in tandem* during the final stages of the DM's compositional evolution. That is to say, it was, in the end, given its current form *so as to* occur in the *Manvantara* discourse of the MkP. As to the thematic threads tying it to the MkP, this is a question for another day, the parameters of which are to be laid out in the concluding chapter of this study; for now, we seek only a better understanding of the thematic threads holding it together, frame and all. The world behind the text necessarily remains murky, but we can bring into focus the world within the text. The approach proposed herein is not dissimilar to Simon Brodbeck's approach to the MBh:

> I want to set aside history and approach the Mahābhārata as fiction ... my research relates to thinking about the Mahābhārata insofar as this is constrained by the Mahābhārata itself: I discuss possibilities and their ramifications within the text's imaginary world.[71]

Let us therefore delve into the world of the DM. Yet while we have located this project against the historical trajectory of how the DM (and *purāṇic* texts in general) have been traditionally studied, and have established the imperative of studying the text as a whole, we must still attend to a most important question: how *does* one study the DM as a literary entity?

Frame III: a matching methodology for thinking in circles

This section outlines the methodological and theoretical considerations entailed in approaching the DM as religious narrative. I should note that the approach adopted herein was not hatched overnight—it resulted from prolonged exposure to the text over an extended period of time. In the words of Terry Eagleton: "it is a matter of finding out, not of assuming from the start that a single method or theory will do."[72]

On the level of narrative studies, this project aligns with the thinking of Umberto Eco. In his *Six Walks in the Fictional Woods*—lectures delivered at Harvard in 1992 and 1993—Umberto Eco argues for the implied presence of a "model reader," which the text creates through its very structure. Eco posits that "the main business of interpretation is to figure out the nature of this reader, in spite of its ghostly existence."[73] The model reader must

> tacitly accept a fictional agreement, which Coleridge called "the suspension of disbelief." The reader has to know that what is being narrated is an imaginary story, but he must not therefore believe that the writer is telling lies. According to John Searle, the author simply *pretends* to be telling the truth. We accept the fictional agreement and we *pretend* that what is narrated has really taken place.[74]

Eco writes that "what actually interests us is not the ontology of possible worlds and their inhabitants … but *the position of the reader*."[75] Indeed the possible worlds arising through the act of interpretation are ideally functions of the interpreter coming to the text: ideally, she is able to resonate with the manner in which the text expects to be engaged. Given that knowledge of one's audience is crucial for the act of writing, indication of what that audience is presumed to know is embedded within the text. The text itself encodes parameters for the type of audience it expects.

In accepting Eco's proposition of the primacy of model readership, one readily accounts for the jarring manner in which *purāṇic* narratives were received by our colonial forebears. Meeting with texts that utterly defied their expectations, they were simply unable to sufficiently suspend their disbelief to live up to the model readership required of the Purāṇas. This was only exacerbated by the suspicion with which they regarded these texts based upon the biases implicit in their agenda to uncover India's unsullied Vedic past. That *purāṇic* narratives "defy ready description, classification, authorship, or dating"[76] is a direct corollary of the fact that they do not expect this of their readers. Imagine one encountering Rushdie's *Midnight's Children*[77] centuries from now without ever having been exposed to magical realism as a genre—the work, in such readers' eyes, would seem suspect, to say the least, particularly if viewed through a historicist lens. But the model reader readily acquiesces Rushdie is neither liar nor lunatic. His artistry is only acknowledged once one understands one's role as reader, and refrains from scrutinizing the miraculous powers ascribed to his children of midnight on empirical terms. He is writing neither a travel guide, nor an historical chronicle, and looking to his work to fulfill either of these functions would result in frustration for the seeker, and utter neglect for the artistry of the work. Appreciation for artistry can only arise once one receives a work in general accordance with its expectations.

This research therefore adopts as its foundation Umberto Eco's narrative theory, particularly his thinking on model readership. In accepting Eco's paradigm that a text's primary function is to elicit interpretation, it asks, following Eco, after what specific sort of cooperation the DM expects of its reader. It asserts that the DM's model reader requires two important intellectual tools in order to most fruitfully engage the text on its own terms: firstly, one requires structural orientation (familiarity with the work's form) and secondly, one requires ideological orientation (familiarity with the worldview embedded within the work's content). The first of these can be greatly enhanced by careful examination of the manner in which the DM's enframement framing contributes to its textual architecture as a whole, particularly through the lens of Mary Douglas' insightful analysis of the phenomenon of narrative ring composition.[78] The DM was in fact crafted in the form of the narrative ring structure theorized by Douglas, and while she of course does not address the DM per se, it bespeaks both the prevalence of this compositional form in the ancient world, and the incisiveness of her analysis, that her work might readily assist in grappling with the DM. Furthermore, the fact that, as Douglas asserts, the function of ring composition is ultimately a hermeneutic one adds credence to the impetus of this work to closely examine the DM's frame in order to interpret the text as a whole. This theme is discussed in greater detail below.

The second intellectual tool the DM's model reader requires is familiarity with the ideological tension at the heart of the Hindu world, between householder and renouncer ideologies. We look at the MBh's discussion of *pravṛtti dharma* versus *nivṛtti dharma* as the tradition's most comprehensive, and most pervasive, discursive synthesis of these vying ideologies. This knowledge is vital for interpreting the common narrative trope of forest encounters between exiled kings and forest-dwelling ascetics as occurring throughout the MBh, and, more importantly, in the frame of the DM. The first of these hermeneutic tools (knowledge of narrative ring structures) uncovers the mechanics whereby the DM's frame serves to color the work as whole, and the second of these hermeneutic tools (knowledge of the *pravṛtti-nivṛtti* tension) establishes the specific ideological shades the work employs to do so. Both of these are therefore vital for understanding the portrait of the Goddess painted by the DM.

One of the prime functions of narrative is to encode ideology. Furthermore, it does so in such a manner as to guide interpretation of that ideology. Given the precious little we know about the world behind the text, much less to say about the extent to which the text reflects those worlds, we are wise to position ourselves *within* the text in order to understand it through the lens of what it expects of its audience. We must spend a fair bit of time within that world before we attempt to decode it. In short, we must take seriously the work of becoming model readers. Just as driving signs expect us to know the rules of the road and musical scores expect knowledge of pitch and rhythm, we must come to know the kind of cooperation enframed texts such as the DM expect of us. In doing so, we are wise to look to the interpretational cues embedded within the structure of the work.

Hermeneutic tool I: reading a ring—knowledge of narrative structure

It will prove useful here to delve more deeply into the work of Mary Douglas on narrative ring composition, which she describes as a pervasive, worldwide mode of ancient composition, one not just stemming from the ancient near east. She notes that

> ring composition is used for ceremonial speeches, victory odes, funeral orations, and joyful celebrations. It is also the common form for solemnly reciting myths of origin, or for entertainment by wandering bards. It is very old, and it is extant still in different parts of the world.[79]

Narrative rings follow the essential chiastic A-B-C-B′-A′ structure, assuming five components, but this number is variable. They comprise "a form that pervades the Bible and other famous archaic texts,"[80] where each side of the ring takes as its reference point the middle turn (C). The middle turn signals a change of direction occurring in the narrative. Sequence one (AB) leads to the mid-turn, and sequence two (B′-A′) leads back to the beginning. Also, this bidirectional motion results in pairs of parallel narrative analogies, such that A will necessarily correspond to A′, as will B to B′, constituting formal parallelism. One can readily recognize the mid-turn based on the function it serves for the work as whole. Since the ring structure returns to its narrative point of origin, its ending will necessarily be anticipated in its very beginning, and the mid-turn will signal that return, defining the composition's symmetry. Furthermore, the mid-turn will thematically interlace with the end and the beginning: C will shed light on the A-A′ complex, and vice versa.

Two things are crucial to note here. Firstly, Douglas explicitly remarks that "a ring is a framing device. The linking up of starting point and end creates an envelope that contains everything between the opening phrases and the conclusion."[81] Intriguing for our purposes is that literary works containing frame narratives, such as the DM (and an extremely common maneuver within South Asian narrative literature), comprise *prime fascia* de facto narrative rings. The end of the tale necessarily returns to where it began. What we may not have noticed is the literary parallelism that governs the text above and beyond its initial enframement, rendering it an authentic ring composition. The rules she establishes in her ring theory all apply to the DM, discussed in detail in Chapter 4.

Secondly, narrative rings guide interpretation. Their purpose is providing hermeneutic support. Douglas writes:

> I am more concerned to emphasize ring composition's exegetical function. It controls meaning, it restricts what is said, and in doing so it expands meanings along channels it has dug. Though it never completely escapes ambiguity, writing in a ring puts various strategies at the writer's disposal; when he chooses one path or another he ties the meaning into a recognizable, restricting context.[82]

By extension, we can apply this feature to Sanskrit narrative framing devices: they function to guide interpretation of the central text. In short, they may be considered as inbuilt guidelines for model readership, which can facilitate our grappling with ancient texts on their own terms. These structural initiatives serve to orient—even create—an audience that is willing and able to heed their interpretive cues. Texts such as the epics and Purāṇas have proven an incredible mechanism for the inculcation of cultural values by virtue of the ideologies they encode, and the interpretive strategies implicated in their very structures toward this end. Narrative enframement is a superbly effective tool for facilitating model readership across generations. Enframed texts as such expect that we (consciously or subconsciously) know the significance of their structure. We run into trouble when we don't.

Dorsey (on whose work on chiasmus Douglas builds) outlines basic steps in studying literary structure. This methodology has been adopted herein. It consists of "(1) identifying the composition's constituent parts, (2) analyzing the arrangement of those parts, and (3) considering the relationship of the composition's structure to its meaning (i.e., identifying the structure's role in conveying the composition's message)."[83] We all too often fail to properly do this with Sanskrit narrative texts, and we are not alone in our area of specialization. Douglas was in fact inspired to write on ring composition by the fact that she was able to use it to make sense of the seemingly disorderly appearance of the Book of Numbers, and rebut its modern commentators' disdainful remarks. These remarks closely parallel the disparaging sentiments toward *purāṇic* narratives noted above. As Douglas writes,

> there are many instances of misunderstanding, of a scholar despising or rejecting an antique text because of its alleged lack of order and syntax … the various cases of error are either due to the critic having missed altogether the internal structure of alternating parallels or due to their having missed the central place where the keys to the main theme are gathered together.[84]

What Dorsey writes of Hebrew Bible scholarship might therefore well apply to scholarship on *Purāṇas*:

> Modern scholars sometimes question the integrity of books or passages within the Hebrew Bible on the basis of what seems to be chaotic organization or unevenness in the text … explaining the unevenness with theories involving long, complex processes of accretions, insertions, careless editing, and the like. Structural analysis may sometimes reveal an alternate and more plausible explanation for this so-called unevenness.[85]

In like fashion, Douglas remarks:

> Writings that used to baffle and dismay unprepared readers, when read correctly, turn out to be marvelously controlled and complex compositions. Learning how they were constructed is like a revelation, with something of the excitement of hidden treasure. Now is a good moment for the effort of rereading. Various disciplines are taking up the task.[86]

Hence its present application within the field of Hindu Studies.

This work is not the first to look to ring composition in studying Sanskrit text, though such works are scant indeed. Matthew Orsborn, for example, has recently demonstrated its profound utility in grappling with the Mahāyāna Buddhist genre *Prajñāpāramitā*.[87] He aptly points out, however, that work of this sort in Indic texts is still in its infancy, despite Brereton's observation that chiastic structure has prevailed in Indic texts, "both earlier and later than the *Upaniṣad*s [and that] this form of composition does not appear only in poetic or even only in literary works."[88] Joel Brereton's essay, *Why is a sleeping dog like the Vedic Sacrifice? The structure of an Upaniṣadic Brahmodya*, is in many ways "similar to Douglas' analysis of the Hexateuch as structurally modeled on the shape of the Jewish tabernacle, which in turn is based on that of Mount Sinai."[89] Also, Minkowsky demonstrates the interplay between the principles of embedding adopted in Vedic sacrificial rites and the narrative of the *Mahābhārata*, itself being relayed at a *sattra*, "the most elaborate and hypotactic of Vedic rites."[90] Most notably is Safavi and Weightman's work on the supremely complex structure of the Sufi text, Mathnawī.[91] The current work contributes to the scant work on the ring composition within Sanskrit literature.

The present study therefore emphasizes the nature of the DM's frame narrative as a consciously contrived device, incorporated with an eye to thematically framing the work as a whole. While the individuals responsible for transmitting the DM would surely have registered the "uneven" texture and distribution of its narrative, it is, to my knowledge, only we scholars who seem to take issue with this. Furthermore, the distinction of a "sectarian" versus "nonsectarian" spirit, as originally advanced by Wilson and Pargiter, is an altogether imposed category. The tradition appears oblivious that the DM might in any way present as an intruder within the MkP. Traditional commentaries exhibit no angst whatsoever that the face of Durgā should peek out from the fabric of the MkP. This might well be attributed to their appreciation for the mechanics of narrative enframement which we are only beginning to understand.

Interpolation or not, by virtue of the sophistication of its structural orchestration (as demonstrated in this work), the DM invites us to take its fabric at face value, promising deep insight in doing so. Its very contours serve to coax us into model readership so that we can turn our attention toward the direction to which it points. For example, the DM as is cannot be rightly read as a work "in which the real speaker is a ṛṣi named Medhas, and which is only repeated by Mārkaṇḍeya."[92] In regarding the text as proper to Medhas introduced in verse 29, we miss out on the rich introduction provided by Mārkaṇḍeya, which serves to ideologically orient the reader to receive the glories of the Goddess, setting up the parameters of the ring structure governing the work as a whole (discussed in detail in Chapter 4). Mārkaṇḍeya's narrative about the restoration of Suratha's sovereignty is a quintessential component of the DM; hence, it is consistently included within the DM in its thousands of extant self-circulating manuscripts. This research helps us to understand the glories of the Goddess in light of the tremendous hermeneutic import to be found in the intrinsic enframement of those glories.

Given that the text expects us to know the value of its enframement, this research places great value on the forest encounter between the sage and the king spawning the glories of the Goddess. It regards this as a lens with which to focus the themes of the work. Frame narratives are not dissimilar to methodological and theoretical apparatuses: both aim at orienting the object of study for the sake of intelligibility. Frame narratives may be viewed as inbuilt hermeneutical aids, serving to orient the reader toward an angle whereby the text may be "properly" viewed, and in so doing, serve as an essential feature of what they frame. For this reason, rather than being dismissed, they ought to be emphasized.

We might look to the work of Hiltebeitel as an exemplar of the sort of methodology adopted herein. He writes of his approach to the MBh as follows: "I have looked at the *Mahābhārata* mainly as story—not, however, taking its narrative content as prior to its didactic, but as a story in which didactic intentions must always have been included."[93] Furthermore, what Hiltebeitel says of the story of Vyāsa and Śuka and its relation to the MBh as a whole directly aligns with how this research regards the frame story of Suratha and the DM as a whole. He writes, upon presenting the story of Śuka,

> What do we do with these literary facts? First, I think it is simply uninteresting and probably false to explain them as the result of textual oversights or interpolations. Rather, risky as it is, we should be willing to consider doing what the story of Śuka invites us to do: to read the "main story" from the vantage point of *this* story.[94]

Similarly, we read the exploits of the Goddess from the vantage point of the fate of Suratha. Whatever else our methodological approach, we cannot deny the DM its literary dignity, frame and all. The text expects no less. Now that we have a method and theory about *where* to look, let us discuss how to see *what* we find there.

Hermeneutic tool II: ideological import—the **dharmic** *double helix*

The function of frame narratives is not the only thing the text expects us to know in order to fruitfully interpret it: we need to understand the ongoing ideological tension that frame narrative engages. This tension persists today, and with it, the pertinence of voices which speak to it, such as those encoded within the DM. We can tentatively disambiguate three worlds: that behind the text, that within it, and that in front of it. Yet a closer examination reveals that these boundaries are provisional, perspectival, and easily smudged. Like the three dimensions of physical space, none can exist without the other two. While the entire picture ultimately comprises all three, there is great utility in provisionally focusing one's attention on "height" versus "width" versus "length."

A text resides within a world of its own, derived from, but fundamentally independent of, historical reality. This particularly applies to narrative works of the imagination. As Arti Dhand writes, referring to the MBh, "text has limits for what light they can shed on history, and we need to be cautious in extrapolating evidence of lived reality from interpretations of text."[95] This difficulty is exacerbated while grappling with texts as geographically, historically, and culturally removed from our present as the DM. Seeking to interpret the DM through the lens of its historical background is not only encumbered by the nebulous dating accorded to the DM, but more importantly, it relegates as an afterthought the reason for which the text has survived for centuries: the relevance of the ideology it *presently* encodes to the world we inhabit. Arguably, this feature is the measure of literary greatness: the greater a work of literature, the greater its historical, geographical, and cultural sphere of relevance. But this is not to say that we can outright ignore the historical horizon giving rise to the DM; only that we should not ignore the fact that it is a literary work in and of itself, and, as such, constitutes is own inherent structure, worthy of attention.

Despite the fact that the text inhabits a world of its own, for us to engage it in the manner it intends us to, we must know something of the world behind the text. As Umberto Eco puts it:

> [I]n order to read a work of fiction, one must have some notion of the economic criteria that rule the fictional world. The criteria aren't there—or rather, as in every hermeneutic circle, they have to be presupposed even as you are trying to infer them from the evidence of the text. For this reason, reading is like a bet. You bet that you will be faithful to the suggestions of a voice that is not saying explicitly what it is suggesting.[96]

In the case of the DM, we must know the ideological tension at the heart of Hinduism, and at the heart of its quintessentially lasting narratives. Before examining this specific ideological tension, let us reflect on what we mean by ideology in a general sense.

While Eagleton specifies six successively more narrow definitions of ideology, the broadest best pertain to our purposes. Ideology comprises, in short, a worldview: viz. it involves a society's production of ideas, beliefs, and values, and the complex of signifying and symbolic processes alluding to individual enactment thereof. Important for our purposes is to note that

> the rationalist view of ideologies as conscious, well-articulated systems of belief is clearly inadequate: it misses the affective, unconscious, mythical or symbolic dimensions of ideology; the way it constitutes the subject's lived, apparently spontaneous relations to a power-structure and comes to provide the invisible colour of daily life itself.[97]

Therefore, following Dhand, this work takes stock of "the political and social ramifications of the ways in which narrative is constructed[, for] narrative, as Eagleton suggests, is inherently ideological; in its apparently naive meanderings is encoded a worldview, a perspective, a way of thinking and being."[98] Ideological subtlety is perhaps most powerfully, and unassumingly, encoded in narrative works such as the DM, which tell us not necessarily how ascetics and kings actually live, but how they were *imagined* to ideally live; and whence could these ideals emerge but from the leanings of individuals in history? The text encodes ancient ideals, ideals which persist to this day.

Narrative can be broadly conceived of as an account (whether spoken or written) of events connected by a plot; it is, in short, a story. When we apply the term "literature" to a narrative tale, we implicitly engage social ideology. As Terry Eagleton demonstrates, literature does not exist in an objective sense, but is constituted by historically variably value-judgments, which "themselves have a close relation to social ideologies ... They refer in the end not simply to private taste, but to the assumptions by which certain social groups exercise and maintain power over others."[99] Classifying something as literature is ultimately an ideological act, both in the sense that it results from the conditions of a particular ideology and that it perpetuates the ideology encoded within that narrative work.

Eagleton notes that one could not tell if a statement was an "ideological" statement without its context: "Ideology is less a matter of the inherent linguistic properties of a pronouncement than a question of who is saying what to whom for what purposes."[100] While he is referring here to the world behind the text—that is, who was writing the text and for whom—this very much applies to the world within the text as well: the *brāhmaṇa* speaks to the king. Hence the work derives its ideological authority from within itself. This is not to say we don't need to rely on a *brāhmaṇic* context to recognize or make sense of that authority; of course we do. What this says is that the DM is crafted such that its *brāhmaṇic* ideology is inalienable to its fabric: it is spoken by a *brāhmaṇa* even when being recited by a *mleccha*.

Eagleton argues that one cannot define literature ontologically, or methodologically, but strategically, which

> means asking first not *what* the object is or *how* we should approach it, but *why* we should want to engage with it in the first place. The liberal humanist response to this question, I have suggested, is at once perfectly reasonable.[101]

Literature is that which engages core human experiences, facilitating reflections on ideas, ideals, issues of meaning, and the navigation of the labyrinth of life. Literature teaches us about ourselves, and about what we value. For, if we did not value its themes, it would not be deemed worthy of the appellation "literature." Literature, then, can be described broadly as narrative which speaks to our lasting values and desires as human beings. As Eagleton put it, "the study of ideology is among other things an inquiry into the ways in which people may come to invest in their own unhappiness."[102] Interestingly, the DM presents two divergent paths to happiness in its conclusion, and purposefully so. It thus readily serves as an object of literary analysis.

The DM anticipates a model reader who knows more than the configuration of a ring composition and how to decode one. It anticipates a reader intimately familiar with the interplay of two divergent religious ideologies: one fundamentally world-embracing, the other fundamentally world-denying. We might refer to the former as householder ideology, and the latter as renouncer ideology. Given that the king symbolizes the quintessence of householder ideology, as does the ascetic the quintessence of renouncer ideology, this book broadly speaks of the tension between royal and ascetic ideologies.

The text has so internalized these divergent strands that it richly encodes their interplay without even explicitly naming them. Doing so is obsolete by the time our text is composed, at a point when these vying ideological strands have been successfully assimilated into the one *dharmic* double helix at the heart of the Hindu world. Hence, in one breath, Durgā unflinchingly grants two divergent boons at the culmination of our text: one granting liberation from worldly affairs, and the other granting lordship over them. I've opted for the imagery of the double helix to describe *dharma*'s overarching strands, given that though they are disparate, they are interwoven such as to appear as a singular *dharmic* entity. The double helix encoded by Durgā's boons ultimately represents a singular, albeit contradictory, *brāhmaṇic* ideology: she grants them during a vision before two characters, each a personification of one of *dharma*'s strands, the characters having been collectively schooled by the *brāhmaṇa* sage.

The king, longing to govern and protect the social sphere, is the paragon of world-affirmation, while his merchant counterpart, who requests release from worldly existence, personifies world-abnegation. The *brāhmaṇa* who instructs them both must remain ambivalent in order to ambiguously encapsulate the ideologically double helix. Referred to in the MBh as *pravṛtti dharma* versus *nivṛtti dharma*,[103] these vying ideological religiosities are made to cooperate, working in tandem as if wheels on a single chariot. Narratives such as the DM invite the reader into cleverly crafted vehicles of *dharma*,[104] promising the most complex, contradictory, and colorful of journeys amid monumental commemorations of ascetics and kings.

Sanskrit narrative literature thus overwhelmingly celebrates these two divergent figures: the ascetic and the king. The ancient Indian king upholds society (stationed at its very center), while the ancient Indian ascetic shuns society (poised at its periphery). As such, the former is a paragon of worldly pursuits, while the latter serves as the epitome of all things otherworldly. The dichotomy between the ideologies of kingship and asceticism might be understood as distinct expressions of power: the king wields *outer* power, which he employs to control others and regulate the mundane world, while the ascetic commands *inner* power, which he hones through ardent control of self and rejection of the world. Furthermore, *ahiṃsā* (nonviolence) is the imperative of the ascetic, while kings are required to implement force in protection of subject and state. Yet each of these figures—ascetic and king alike—is venerated as a virtuoso of his respective realm. Their interaction comprises a literary trope that encapsulates a lasting ideological tension within the Hindu world: the tension between the divergent duties of (world-denying) renouncers and (world-affirming) householders, synthesized as *pravṛtti* and *nivṛtti dharmas* by the time of the MBh. This typology is being used as a literary, and not historical, lens. As Dhand notes with regard to the "data" within the MBh, "[i]f we have references to characters and narratives about women, to what extent can we take them as literary hyperbole, and to what extent should we assume they reflect historical reality?"[105] This poignant consideration equally applies the material we examine in the DM on kingship and asceticism. Royal and ascetic ideals are at the very heart of the *pravṛtti-nivṛtti* divide, since the king is the emblematic apex of *pravṛtti*, while the ascetic is *nivṛtti*'s emblematic apex.

The tension between these opposing paragons, and their opposing orientations toward the sphere of human enterprise, is poignantly preserved in the narrative motif of kings who are (temporarily) sentenced to forest exile where they commingle with, and often mimic, ascetic figures from whom they receive social and moral instruction. The most famous examples of these are the heroes of both Sanskrit epics, who inevitably quit the aristocracy to roam the forest in ascetic garb. Though the forest-teachings received by these figures often promote an ethos of ascetic detachment and introspection, these experiences paradoxically enrich the royal pupils' capacity to rule. That ascetics and kings are so often brought into conversation in Hindu narrative works such as the DM bespeaks of the need to reconcile the ideological tension between the two, a tension which must necessarily reside within a Goddess representing existence itself. As this study emphasizes the literary, and not historical, dimensions of the text, we may embrace the full import of the narrative tropes as literary hyperbole, indicative of the cultural imagination authoring them. These texts are spun to encode and communicate cherished ideals, irrespective of the extent to which those ideals were historically enacted. The consideration of whether kings or ascetics as described in these works actually graced the soil of the Indian subcontinent is subordinate to the salient fact that individuals holding such ideals most certainly did. Moreover, the DM expects its model reader to be well acquainted with this trope.

Possessing knowledge of how frame narratives function, and knowledge of the ideological tension showcased in this particular trope, we can now proceed to intelligibly engage the DM in a manner befitting its expectations.

Notes

1 Cheever Mackenzie Brown, "Purāṇa as Scripture: From Sound to Image of the Holy Word in the Hindu Tradition," *History of Religions* 26, no. 1 (August 1, 1986): 68–86; Arti Dhand, "The Dharma of Ethics, the Ethics of Dharma: Quizzing the Ideals of Hinduism," *The Journal of Religious Ethics* 30, no. 3 (October 1, 2002): 347–72; Thomas B. Coburn, "The Study of the Purāṇas and the Study of Religion," *Religious Studies* 16, no. 3 (September 1, 1980): 341–52; McComas Taylor, "What Enables Canonical Literature to Function as 'True'? The Case of the Hindu Purāṇas," *International Journal of Hindu Studies* 12, no. 3 (December 1, 2008): 309–28.

2 Wilson was among the colonial founding fathers of the western study of the Purāṇas, having published his monumental and copiously annotated translation of the Viṣṇu Purāṇa in 1840. See: Horace Hayman Wilson, trans., *The Viṣṇu Purāṇa: A System of Hindu Mythology and Tradition* (Calcutta, India: Punthi Pustak, 1961).

3 Thomas B. Coburn, "Devi: The Great Goddess," in *Devī: Goddesses of India*, ed. John Stratton Hawley and Donna Marie Wulff (Berkeley, CA: University of California Press, 1996), 31.
4 Thomas B. Coburn, "The Devī-Māhātmya as a Feminist Document," *Journal of Religious Studies* 8, no. 2 (1980): 1–11 fn. 1.
5 Velcheru Narayana Rao, "Purāṇa," in *The Hindu World*, ed. Sushil Mittal and Gene R Thursby (New York: Routledge, 2004), 97.
6 Rao, 98.
7 Rao, 98.
8 Rao, 98.
9 These disciples were Sumati Ātreya, Akṛtavraṇa Kāśyapa, Agnivarcas Bhāradvāja, Mitrāyu Vāsisiṣṭa, Sāvarṇi Saumadatti, and Suśarman Śāṃśapāyana.
10 Coburn, *Devī-Māhātmya: The Crystallization of the Goddess Tradition*, 21. It is worth noting that Willibald Kerfel estimates that only 2–3 percent of all Purāṇic materials actually deal with the *pañcalakṣaṇa. Devī-Māhātmya: The Crystallization of the Goddess Tradition*, 21.
11 Ludo Rocher Gonda, Jan, *The Purāṇas* (Wiesbaden: Harrassowitz, 1986), 29.
12 Rao, "Purāṇa," 115.
13 Rocher, *The Purāṇas*, 2.
14 Elizabeth Mary Rohlman, "Textual Authority, Accretion, and Suspicion: The Legacy of Horace Hayman Wilson in Western Studies of the Purāṇas," *Journal of the Oriental Institute* 52, no. 1–2 (2002): 57.
15 Rohlman, "Textual Authority, Accretion, and Suspicion: The Legacy of Horace Hayman Wilson in Western Studies of the Purāṇas."
16 Rohlman, 56.
17 Wilson, *The Viṣṇu Purāṇa: A System of Hindu Mythology and Tradition*, i.
18 See: Wilson, lviii.
19 Wilson, lxxiv–lxxv.
20 Rohlman, "Textual Authority, Accretion, and Suspicion: The Legacy of Horace Hayman Wilson in Western Studies of the Purāṇas," 62.
21 Pargiter has translated the Mārkaṇḍeya Purāṇa in its entirety, and all translations herein of the Sanskrit text are his. See: F. Eden Pargiter, *Mārkaṇḍeya Purāṇa* (Calcutta, India: Asiatic Society of Bengal, 1904).
22 Moriz Winternitz, *A History of Indian Literature. 1, 1* (New Delhi: Oriental Books Repr. Corp., 1972), 507; also cited in Rao, "Purāṇa," 110.
23 Rohlman, "Textual Authority, Accretion, and Suspicion: The Legacy of Horace Hayman Wilson in Western Studies of the Purāṇas," 65.
24 Greg Bailey, "The Purāṇas. A Study in the Development of Hinduism," in *The Study of Hinduism*, ed. Arvind Sharma (Studies in Comparative Religion) (Columbia, SC: University of South Carolina Press, 2003), 139–40.
25 Rao, "Purāṇa," 110.
26 Rocher, *The Purāṇas*, 72.
27 Wendy Doniger, ed., *Hindu Myths: A Sourcebook Translated from the Sanskrit* (London; New York: Penguin, 2004), 15, 16.
28 Rohlman, "Textual Authority, Accretion, and Suspicion: The Legacy of Horace Hayman Wilson in Western Studies of the Purāṇas," 69; originally cited in Cornelia Dimmitt and J.A.B. van Buitenen, *Classical Hindu Mythology: A Reader in the Sanskrit Purāṇas* (Philadelphia, PA: Temple University Press, 1978), 3.
29 Velcheru Narayana Rao, "Purāṇa as Brahaminic Ideology," in *Purāna Perennis: Reciprocity and Transformation in Hindu and Jaina Texts*, ed. Wendy Doniger (Albany, NY: State University of New York Press, 1993), 94.
30 Pargiter, *Mārkaṇḍeya Purāṇa*, iii.
31 Pargiter, iii.
32 Pargiter, iv.

33 R.C. Hazra, *Studies in the Purāṇic Records on Hindu Rites and Customs* (Delhi: Motilal Banarsidass, 1975), 13.
34 Hazra, 13. Originally quoted in Pargiter, *Mārkaṇḍeya Purāṇa*, xx.
35 Pargiter, *Mārkaṇḍeya Purāṇa*, xx.
36 Hazra, *Studies in the Purāṇic Records on Hindu Rites and Customs*, 12.
37 Cheever Mackenzie Brown, *God as Mother: A Feminine Theology in India: An Historical and Theological Study of the Brahmavaivarta Purāṇa* (Hartford, VT: Claude Stark & Co., 1974), 149.
38 Rocher, *The Purāṇas*, 191.
39 Rocher, 193.
40 Rocher, 195.
41 Rocher, 195. See fn. 258 where Rocher cites Agrawala for this phrase: Vasudeva Sharana Agrawala, *Devī-Māhātmyam: The Glorification of the Great Goddess* (Varanasi: All-India Kashiraj Trust, 1963), 832.
42 Rocher, *The Purāṇas*, 70. He credits Diana Eck for this in fn. 13: Diana L. ECK: A Survey of Sanskrit Sources for the Study of Varanasi, Pur 22, 1980, 81–101 at 81–2.
43 Cited in Rocher, 11. See Winternitz, *A History of Indian Literature. 1, 1.*
44 Kavali Venkata Rāmaswami, *The Supta-Sati or Chundi-Pat: Being a Portion of the Marcundeya Purana* (Calcutta, India: Columbian Press, 1823).
45 Eugene Burnouf, "Analyse Et Extrait Du Devi Mahatmyam, Fragmens Du Markandeya Pourana," *Société Asiatique* 1, no. 4 (1824): 24–32. Burnouf gives a brief sketch and a translation of the DM's opening frame herein.
46 Ludwig Poley, *Markandeyi Purani Sectio Edidit Latinam Interpretationem Annotationesque Adiecit Ludovicus Poley* (Berolini: Impensis F. Duemmleri, 1831).
47 Pargiter, *Mārkaṇḍeya Purāṇa*, vi–vii.
48 Rocher, *The Purāṇas*, 193–6. See Jan Gonda, *A History of Indian Literature. Volume II, Fasc. 1* (Wiesbaden: O. Harrassowitz, 1977), 281–2; J.N. Farquhar, *An Outline of the Religious Literature of India* (London; New York: H. Milford, Oxford University Press, 1920).
49 See Coburn, *Devī-Māhātmya*, 53–8.
50 See, e.g., Tryna Lyons, "The Simla 'Devī Māhātmya' Illustrations: A Reappraisal of Content," *Archives of Asian Art* 45 (January 1, 1992): 29–41; K.M. McDonald, "The Sacred Aesthetics of Scriptural Illustration: An Analysis of the Devi Mahatmya" (University of Wisconsin-Madison, 1997).
51 V.V. Mirashi, "A Lower Limit for the Date of the Devī-Māhātmya," *Purāṇa* 10, no. 1 (January 1968): 179–86.
52 J.N. Tiwari, "An Interesting Variant in the Devī-Māhātmya," *Purāṇa* 25, no. 2 (1983): 235–45.
53 Karline McLain, "Holy Superheroine: A Comic Book Interpretation of the Hindu Devī Māhātmya Scripture," *Bulletin of the School of Oriental and African Studies* 71, no. 2 (2008): 297–322.
54 Cynthia Ann Humes, "The Text and Temple of the Great Goddess: The Devī-Māhātmya and the Vindhyacal Temple of Mirzapur (Volumes I and II)" (The University of Iowa, 1990), 1.
55 Jeffrey J Kripal, *Kālī's Child: The Mystical and the Erotic in the Life and Teachings of Ramakrishna* (Chicago, IL: University of Chicago Press, 1995); David R. Kinsley, *Hindu Goddesses: Visions of the Divine Feminine in the Hindu Religious Tradition; with a New Preface* (Berkeley, CA: University of California Press, 1997); Sarah Caldwell, *Oh Terrifying Mother: Sexuality, Violence, and Worship of the Goddess Kāḷi* (New Delhi; New York: Oxford University Press, 1999); Rachel Fell McDermott and Jeffrey J. Kripal, *Encountering Kālī in the Margins, at the Center, in the West* (Berkeley, CA: University of California Press, 2003); Rachel Fell McDermott, *Revelry, Rivalry, and Longing for the Goddesses of Bengal: The Fortunes of Hindu Festivals* (New York: Columbia University Press, 2011).

56 Coburn, *Devī-Māhātmya*, 53.
57 Coburn, *Encountering the Goddess*. Given the merits of this rendition, all translations in this study are Coburn's, unless otherwise stated.
58 Thomas B. Coburn, *The Conceptualization of Religious Change: And the Worship of the Great Goddess* (Canton, NY: St. Lawrence University, 1980), 10.
59 Yuko Yokochi, "The Warrior Goddess in the Devīmāhātmya," *SENRI Ethnological Studies* 50 (1999): 90. She changes this to possibly early ninth century in her 2005 dissertation. For a fuller account of the epigraphic, manuscript, and iconographic evidence she uses for her argument, see Yuko Yokochi, "The Rise of the Warrior Goddess in Ancient India: A Study of the Myth Cycle of Kauśikī-Vindhyavāsinī in the Skandapurāṇa" (University of Groningen, 2005), 21–3 fn. 42.
60 Yokochi, "The Rise of the Warrior Goddess in Ancient India," 7.
61 Yokochi, 10.
62 Yokochi, 11.
63 Yokochi, 7.
64 Yokochi, 12.
65 Yokochi, 21.
66 Thomas B. Coburn, "'Scripture' in India: Towards a Typology of the Word in Hindu Life," *Journal of the American Academy of Religion* 52, no. 3 (September 1, 1984): 118 fn. 109.
67 Coburn, 119.
68 Coburn, 119 fn. 112.
69 Yokochi, "The Rise of the Warrior Goddess in Ancient India," 18.
70 Yokochi, 8. See fn. 14.
71 Simon Brodbeck, *The Mahābhārata Patriline: Gender, Culture, and the Royal Hereditary* (Farnham, UK; Burlington, VT: Ashgate, 2009), 10.
72 Terry Eagleton, *Literary Theory* (Oxford: Blackwell, 1983), 184.
73 Umberto Eco, *Six Walks in the Fictional Woods* (Cambridge, MA: Harvard University Press, 1994), 16.
74 Eco, 75.
75 Eco, 107.
76 Rao, "*Purāṇa*," 97.
77 Salman Rushdie, *Midnight's Children* (New York: Knopf, 1981).
78 Mary Douglas, "Writing in Circles: Ring Composition as a Creative Stimulus," *Dwight H Terry Lectureship, Yale University*, 2005, http://terrylecture.yale.edu/previous-lectureships.
79 Mary Douglas, *Thinking in Circles: An Essay on Ring Composition* (New Haven, CT: Yale University Press, 2007), 27.
80 Douglas, 2.
81 Douglas, 1.
82 Douglas, 13.
83 David A. Dorsey, *The Literary Structure of the Old Testament: A Commentary on Genesis-Malachi* (Grand Rapids, MI: Baker Books, 1999), 16.
84 Douglas, *Thinking in Circles: An Essay on Ring Composition*, 10.
85 Dorsey, *The Literary Structure of the Old Testament*, 43–4.
86 Douglas, *Thinking in Circles: An Essay on Ring Composition*, 1.
87 Matthew Bryan Orsborn and University of Hong Kong, *Chiasmus in the Early Prajñāpāramitā: Literary Parallelism Connecting Criticism & Hermeneutics in an Early Mahāyāna Sūtra*, 2012.
88 Joel Brereton, "Why Is a Sleeping Dog Like the Vedic Sacrifice?: The Structure of an Upaniṣadic Brahmodya," in *Inside the Texts, Beyond the Texts: New Approaches to the Study of the Vedas*, ed. Michael Witzel (Harvard University, 1997), 5. Cited in Orsborn and University of Hong Kong, *Chiasmus in the Early Prajñāpāramitā*, 27.
89 Orsborn and University of Hong Kong, *Chiasmus in the Early Prajñāpāramitā*, 28.

90 C.Z. Minkowski, "Janamejaya's Sattra and Ritual Structure," *Journal of the American Oriental Society* 109, no. 3 (1989): 421.
91 Seyed Ghahreman Safavi and S.C.R. Weightman, *Rūmī's Mystical Design: Reading the Mathnawī, Book One* (Albany, NY: SUNY Press, 2009).
92 Pargiter, *Mārkaṇḍeya Purāṇa*, iv.
93 Alf Hiltebeitel, *The Ritual of Battle: Kṛṣṇa in the Mahābhārata* (Ithaca, NY; London: Cornell University Press, 1976), 13.
94 Alf Hiltebeitel, *Rethinking the Mahābhārata: A Reader's Guide to the Education of the Dharma King* (Chicago, IL: University of Chicago Press, 2001), 317.
95 Consisting of the prima facie narrative, the metaphorical struggle between good and evil, the level of metaphysical principles, or the search for human meaning. Arti Dhand, *Woman as Fire, Woman as Sage Sexual Ideology in the Mahābhārata* (Albany, NY: State University of New York Press, 2008), 15.
96 Eco, *Six Walks in the Fictional Woods*, 75.
97 Terry Eagleton, *Ideology: An Introduction* (London: Verso, 1991), 221.
98 Dhand, *Woman as Fire, Woman as Sage Sexual Ideology in the Mahābhārata*, 17.
99 Eagleton, *Literary Theory*, 14.
100 Eagleton, *Ideology: An Introduction*, 9.
101 Eagleton, *Literary Theory*, 183.
102 Eagleton, *Ideology: An Introduction*, xiii.
103 This ideological culling of the DM within this thesis is modeled after the work of Arti Dhand (Dhand, *Woman as Fire, Woman as Sage Sexual Ideology in the Mahābhārata.*), who establishes the potency of the *pravṛtti-nivṛtti* heuristic as a means of making sense of the world within the text. This methodological strategy will be discussed in greater detail in the following chapter.
104 The semantic range of the term *dharma*, however broad (ranging from decree to law, ordinance, virtue, morality, merit, righteousness, essential nature, and prescribed duty), consistently pertains to social ideology.
105 See Dhand, *Woman as Fire, Woman as Sage Sexual Ideology in the Mahābhārata*, 92.

2 Finding the forest hermit

Ascetic ideology in the *Devī Māhātmya*

Why do Indian kings so frequently find themselves in forest exile in *purāṇic* literature? Why do they invariably encounter forest-dwelling ascetics while there? This chapter examines the forest-dwelling hermit figure appearing throughout epic and *purāṇic* literature through the lens of Hinduism's dual religious inheritance as articulated in the MBh: one leaning toward world-affirmation, termed *pravṛtti dharma*, the other leaning toward world-abnegation, termed *nivṛtti dharma*. It is the latter of these bents to which I broadly refer herein when speaking of ascetic ideology. The MBh is invoked as the prime juncture where these two strands of the ensuing *dharmic* double helix are clearly demarcated, and tacitly synthesized. Probably composed in the centuries following the last phases of the epic's composition, the DM has internalized the bifurcation: while it refrains from naming or disambiguating between two types of *dharma* per se, the double helix yet at the heart of Hinduism is expressed through Durgā's divergent boons. Indeed, even when these ideologies are explicitly discussed, "it is always as though there was scarcely a need to define [them] in an extensive manner, that they were so obvious as to be known by the learned audiences of the texts."[1] Moreover, that Durgā's divergent boons are procured through an encounter between a forest sage and an exiled king itself bespeaks the interplay of these *dharmas*. Therefore, in unpacking the thematic import of such fateful forest encounters, one acquires the ideological savvy to register the significance of a forest-dwelling sage relaying the acts of Durgā to an exiled king.

This chapter argues that the forest-dweller's ideological evasiveness is intentional, preserved in narrative works so as to embody a religious tension: he simultaneously stands in for *brāhmaṇa* householder, emblematic of *pravṛtti dharma*, and ascetic renouncer, emblematic of *nivṛtti dharma*. He therefore represents the ambivalence innate to *brāhmaṇic* ideology itself. Similarly, the exiled king, paragon of *pravṛtti dharma*, enters the forest, a *nivṛtti* environment, in order to receive *nivṛtti* teachings, all the while maintaining *pravṛtti* social caste duties, and indeed destined to return to the sphere of *pravṛtti* for the sake of its preservation. The complex ideological tension between (*pravṛtti*) householder and (*nivṛtti*) renouncer is moreover compounded through the interaction between king and sage during these fateful forest exchanges: they simultaneously engage as would *brāhmaṇa* and *kṣatriya* householders in society, and as would pupil and teacher in forest renunciation. This narrative trope thereby masterfully intertwines both ideologies, symbolically encoding the *dharmic* double helix at the heart of *brāhmaṇic* ideology. Upon deconstructing this symbolism, this chapter goes on to note the presence of *nivṛtti* religiosity within the DM, in anticipation of the examination of *pravṛtti* religiosity in the DM occurring in the following chapter.

Brāhmaṇism's dharmic double helix

Scholarly narratives about the origins of Indian asceticism abound. The need for such narrative stems from the fact that Vedic religion is premised, at its core, upon progeny, prosperity, and an affirmation of interdependent, communal *life in the world*. It thus presents as antithetical to the ascetic impulse. In searching for the origins of this impulse, which began being absorbed into the *brāhmaṇic* fold in the middle of the first millennium BCE with the composition of *upaniṣadic* literature, scholars have implicated various disparate cultural relics: from seals from the Indus Valley civilization (2600–1900 BCE) to the *Ṛg Veda* X.136[2] "Keśin" verse, composed circa 1500 BCE. Some argue for ascetic impulses originating from Vedic sacrifice itself,[3] while others argue for both Vedic and non-Vedic origins.[4] While such historical narratives proceed to occupy the scholarly imagination, it is the Hindu religious imagination that concerns us here, as enshrined within lasting literary works such as the DM. As evidenced in such works, whatever their historical origin or trajectory, it is clear that ascetic virtues are eventually embraced into the Vedic fold such that classical Hinduism is itself marked with a valorizing of stoic rejection of worldly pursuits in favor of supreme knowledge.

Greg Bailey notes that while there is just cause to categorize ancient Indian religious traditions into three separate strands—Hinduism, Buddhism, and Jainism—"the level of differences between the three major religious traditions are less than their similarities,"[5] and therefore "a study of the basic teachings embodied in the early Buddhist and Jain texts, and the Upaniṣads, reveals many basic similarities which cohere to such an extent as to suggest a common source out of which these teachings came."[6] Indeed, what we now call Jainism, Buddhism, and *upaniṣadic* religion are entities that crystallized circa the sixth century BCE from the same religious revolutions that were occurring across the Indian subcontinent in the centuries prior, if not (more silently) as far back as the time of the *Ṛg Veda*. Resulting from undoubtedly complex historical interactions occurring throughout the millennia before classical Hinduism emerged, the MBh encapsulates a bifurcated religious ideology whereby *dharma* is spun into a double-helical figure, intertwining both an ethos of world-affirmation with one of abnegation. This latter ideology, notes Bailey,

> centers upon renunciation of the social world and advocates an adoption of an ascetic life-style. This ideology is given a positive face in the Upaniṣads, parts of the Hindu epics and Purāṇas and generally in Buddhist and Jain

> literature. Its most famous exemplars are the Buddha, Mahāvīra ... and the countless ascetics who figure so prominently in the myths of the epics and the Puranas.[7]

It is these literary figures around which this discussion revolves. Following the nomenclature established in the MBh, this study refers to the ideology enacted by these figures as *nivṛtti dharma*; while its counterpart, *pravṛtti dharma*, is that strand of the *dharmic* double helix stemming from world-affirming Vedic religiosity, which emphasizes the goals and practices of the married householder. The opposition of these two ideologies is no mere imposition of the analyst, but rather "an opposition found unanimously in the indigenous literature" itself.[8]

The MBh has much to say on each of these vying ideologies; indeed, one could argue that the epic revolves around their very reconciliation. It is arguably "the most important early Indian text signaling a transition between Vedic and post-Vedic culture"[9] wherein the "integrity and coherence [of these ideological stances] is assumed rather than demonstrated."[10] Therefore the epic's *Śāntiparvan* serves as the *locus classicus* for exposition on *pravṛtti* and *nivṛtti* ideologies.[11] The deep ambivalence in the epic between these two paths is attributed to its ambitious attempt to straddle these divergent ideologies. It capitalizes on its contradictory religious heritage, meandering between the two in order to advocate the best of each, paradox notwithstanding. Its process necessarily results in contradiction. Yet the structural opposition innate to these ideologies functions as complementarity more than mutual exclusion: indeed, *pravṛtti* and *nivṛtti dharmas* make sense "only in relation to each other, offering a total world view consisting of two related, if opposite, perceptions of how the world and the person operated."[12] Therefore, much can be learned by embracing the *pravṛtti-nivṛtti* heuristic as a means of model readership, grappling with the epic on its own terms. Dhand notes its profound utility in broaching sexual ideology within the text, disentangling the inconsistencies residing within the text. While this methodology proves equally useful in grappling with the DM, we must register an important difference: Dhand traces the problem *sexuality* presents to ascetic ideology, affronting its commitment to chastity, while this work traces the equally rich problem *violence* presents to that ideology, affronting its commitment to nonviolence.

Violence is the central point of controversy to have "irked the first Jains and Buddhist, namely, the use of animals in sacrifice, the worldly orientation of the sacrificial religion";[13] hence the epic's ongoing anxiety around its own legitimization of social violence. After all, violence must be legitimized, being an indispensable aspect of *pravṛtti dharma*. Nonviolence is a stringent *nivṛtti* precept in the MBh, arguably even more so than chastity: while even celibate ascetics are called upon to bear children in the MBh, they are never called upon to bear arms; hence they rely upon royal figures for protection. The bifurcation between *pravṛtti* and *nivṛtti dharma* is a clear indication of the dual religious heritage at play within the classical Hindu world, one stemming from Vedic orthodoxy, and the other primarily originating from outside of that orthodoxy, eventually folded into it so as to assimilate a tension which is fundamentally irreconcilable. Yet to do otherwise would be to choose between world-affirmation, articulated in *pravṛtti* religion, and affirmation of lofty ideals articulated in its *nivṛttic* counterpart. Let us take a closer look at the distinctive features of *pravṛtti* and *nivṛtti dharmas*.

Pravṛtti is geared toward regulating worldly activity, as its etymology suggests, derived from the verbal root *vṛt*, which connotes to occur, to proceed, to grow, to increase, indeed even to exist. Apte gives, "active life; taking an active part in worldly affairs."[14] *Pravṛtti dharma* entails immersion in ordinary life embraced by the vast majority of humans on the planet, providing stringent prescriptions for social engagement and ritual performance. It "prescribes the attitudes that are appropriate for human beings to this relationship—reverence, honor, methodically precise worship"[15] along with precepts whereby "human beings maintain their commitment to the divine by executing with scrupulous care the rituals of the sacrifice."[16] It advances sophisticated social and ritual imperatives designed to regulate the flow both of the "lateral" interdependence among persons, and the "vertical" interdependence between humanity and the gods, the latter of which constitutes a reciprocal exchange which ensures not only the proper regulation of the cosmos, but the fulfillment of human desires, and amelioration of life on earth. One of the interesting aspects of *pravṛtti dharma* is the fact that "a universal ethics is decidedly absent"[17] therein; rather, ethics remains perspectival, ever dependent upon gender, caste, and (depending on the historical horizon) one's stage of life. This is not to say that ethics are subjective in the sense of being based upon opinion: they are situational, and objectively prescribed for various subjective situations. How one is to conduct one's life is strictly situational, and dependent not upon categorical ethical imperatives, but on the dictates of one's specific *dharma*.

Etymologically speaking, that the term *nivṛtti* replaces *pravṛtti*'s affirmative prefix *pra* with the negative prefix *ni* is in no way misleading. *Nivṛtti* represents an emphatic rejection of the aspirations, methodologies, and very locus of *pravṛtti dharma*, replacing these with a radically different mentality geared toward one's personal spiritual achievement of liberation from all things worldly; a pursuit which occurs in isolation, away from worldly habitation. Indeed, "the term connotes disappearance, cessation, abstinence from work, inactivity, resignation, discontinuance of worldly acts or emotions, separation."[18] It is used idiomatically in the MBh to invoke a rejection of worldly life and the hierarchical social and ritual systems inextricable to *pravṛtti* religion. Its orientation toward life in the world is radically different, and therefore its religious methodology and goal diametrically opposes those of *pravṛtti*. As Dhand summarizes:

> It diagnoses this life as fundamentally flawed, a wholly unsatisfactory place of entrapment, and earnestly seeks release from it. *Nivṛtti dharma*, therefore, is vitally premised on *Upaniṣadic* views of existence. The world (*saṃsāra*) is seen as a place of suffering and anxiety that are perpetuated by one's

> actions (*karma*, both of a moral and a ritual nature). One's participation in this realm of pleasurable distraction is endlessly rehearsed through rebirth. The only worthy goal of human striving is to emancipate oneself from the shackles or birth and death (*punarjanma*), and achieve lasting peace, permanent happiness (*mokṣa*). In defiance and repudiation of all social convention, *nivṛtti* directs itself to the goal of *mokṣa*, which also represents freedom from the cyclical enclosures of birth and death. *Nivṛtti dharma*, therefore, is frequently used as a synonym for *mokṣadharma*, the religion of freedom.[19]

Such is the quintessence of ascetic ideology. Furthermore, while the masses overwhelmingly operate within the realm of *pravṛtti* from the moment of their very birth, the path of *nivṛtti* is *far* less trodden. It requires extraordinary rigor, isolation, focus, and care; it is the path of the razor's edge, which can alone lead to emancipation from bondage of cyclical, interdependent, communal, embodied existence. The lifestyle of such a soul typically entails:

> (1) cutting social and kinship ties; (2) living an itinerant life without a fixed home; (3) mendicancy associated with the abandonment of socially recognized economic activities and the ownership of property, especially of food; (4) abandoning ritual activities customary within society; and (5) celibacy.[20]

Alternately termed *parivrajaka* or *saṃnyāsin*, this study refers to the renouncer embracing this arduous *nivṛttic* path as the ascetic, emblematic of ascetic ideology, for which the forest hermit readily proxies.

Are *nivṛtti* and *pravṛtti dharmas* compatible? The tension between *pravṛtti* and *nivṛtti dharma* is tantamount to the tension between world-denial and world-affirmation at the heart of Hinduism, which, as several scholars argue, has never been resolved. One can understand *dharma* then as two-tiered, entailing one's personal *dharma*, and a loftier universal *dharma*, which can conflict, for example, "in cases where one's specific duty involves injury and thus violates the injunction of non-injury."[21] However, as evidenced by the *mokṣadharma* section of the MBh, the ideological superiority of *nivṛtti* is emphatically affirmed, perhaps surprisingly, even to the point of outright chastising the use of violence. There are several affirmations of *ahiṃsā* to be found in the MBh. Christopher Chapple lists several key ones as follows:

> One should never do that to another which one regards as injurious to one's self. This, in brief, is the rule of *dharma*. Yielding to desire and acting differently, one becomes guilty of *adharma*.
>
> (XIII: 113: 8)

> Those high-souled persons who desire beauty, faultlessness of limbs, long life, understanding, mental and physical strength, and memory, should abstain from acts of injury.
>
> (XIII: 115: 8)

> *Ahiṃsā* is the *dharma*. It is the highest purification. It is also the highest truth from which all *dharma* proceeds.
>
> (XIII: 125: 25)

> *Ahiṃsā* is the highest *dharma*. *Ahiṃsā* is the best austerity (*tapas*). *Ahiṃsā* is the greatest gift. *Ahiṃsā* is the highest self control. *Ahiṃsā* is the highest sacrifice. *Ahiṃsā* is the highest power. *Ahiṃsā* is the highest friend. *Ahiṃsā* is the highest teaching.
>
> (XIII: 116: 37–41)

> The purification of one who does *ahiṃsā* are inexhaustible. Such a one is regarded as always performing sacrifices, and is the father and mother of all beings.
>
> (XIII: 115: 41)[22]

Despite the MBh's acceptance of it as a "higher" path, *nivṛtti* nevertheless presents a problem to the majority of inhabitants of the planet since it is an ascetic religious strand. While the commonly held ethical precepts of *nivṛtti*—*ahiṃsā, satya, asteya, brahmacarya, dama, kṣamā, aparigraha*: noninjuriousness, truthfulness, nonstealing, celibacy, self-restraint, forgiveness, nongrasping—are overall not dissimilar to the ideals of Vedic religion, two of those precepts pose as fundamentally incompatible categorical imperatives: *ahiṃsā* and *brahmacarya*. *Brahmacarya* poses a major problem not only because its universal adoption would result in the end of our species, but also because it thwarts the theological imperative to repay the debt to the ancestors through the begetting of progeny; particularly important to the sway of *pravṛtti* is royal progeny, the absence of which constitutes a crisis of succession. While injuring other beings causes negative karma in the *nivṛtti* model, *ahiṃsā* presents as an impossibility for even ascetics to entirely uphold,[23] much less householders who must harm other beings to eat, produce food, and maintain society through defense and punishment. This *nivṛttic* imperative is particularly problematic for the warrior in general, and the king in particular, whose use of violence is paramount for safeguarding the social sphere. Ironically, it is this very social sphere which produces the *nivṛttic* adherent, and he is thus dependent upon it: for the ascetic to do his *dharma*, the king must first do his.

While *nivṛtti dharma* is predicated upon world-eschewing ascetic practices entailing the renunciation of human relationships, one of the most paradoxical ironies of the world-effacing rhetoric of *nivṛtti* is that it calls the adherent to transform himself into one who is full of care for others, irrespective of social standing. The adherent of *nivṛtti dharma* is characterized by calmness, compassion, equanimity, and kindness. Therefore such a one is considered the refuge of all creatures. Ironically, despite *nivṛtti*'s utterly anti-communal leanings, it calls its adherent to a psychology which befits that of a king, he who is the very center of communal affairs. Therefore, both he who is responsible for policing *pravṛtti dharma* and he who utterly rejects it ideally serve as the refuge of all creatures.

Ironically, *nivṛtti dharma* is more egalitarian than *pravṛtti dharma*, theoretically collapsing caste *dharma* in favor of a loftier *dharmic* enjoinment of categorical nonviolence, truthfulness, restraint, and care for all beings. One should be mindful, though, that *nivṛtti dharma* is not *directed* toward other beings. It is entirely self-directed, toward the individual achievement of *mokṣa*. Its psychological "side-effect" is compassion, which results in care for other beings, should they chance upon the path of the refined recluse. Yet, what role can compassion serve while one resides in isolation of others?

That *brāhmaṇic* ideology is necessarily a *social* ideology; it must combine onto one platform the mandates of *pravṛtti* and *nivṛtti* alike. Let us not forget that the ascetic depends upon the very social structure he shuns. The rhetoric of *nivṛtti*'s moral supremacy makes for a convenient association between renouncer and *brāhmaṇa*, who, as Olivelle notes, serves as "a suitable candidate for being homologized with the renouncer,"[24] given that he earned his livelihood through religious activities (sacrificing and teaching), rather than other economic activity, and was the only caste authorized to receive gifts. However, the extent to which the *brāhmaṇa* could appropriate the path of *nivṛtti* was ultimately curtailed by the fact that renunciation was fundamentally antistructural, and by definition could never be fully folded back into the structure of Hindu society.

On a pragmatic level, the assimilation of ascetic ideology was facilitated by the implementation of the *maṭha*, monasteries established across India, credited to the eighth-century philosopher Śaṅkara. Additionally, the *āśrama* system itself was adopted as a means of folding in the two religious ethoses: one esteeming the married householder, and the other esteeming the celibate renouncer. However, the clash between the two was never resolved, and "old battles had to be fought over and over again throughout the Middle Ages and down to modern times even after the *āśrama*s had become part of the mainstream of *Brāhmaṇical* theology."[25]

Another poignant means whereby ascetic ideology was folded into a vital component of the *dharmic* double helix comprising *brāhmaṇism* was through narrative works. As Wendy Doniger writes,

> theological texts such as the *Gītā* offer sophisticated and not altogether satisfactory answers to the problem; but as it is the primary task for mythology to resolve irreconcilable conflicts, it is in Hindu myths that the most dramatic examples of the conflict may be found.[26]

It is unsurprising then that the most cherished and influential tale to pervade the Indian subcontinent—i.e., the story of Rāma—masterfully dovetails royal penchant for justified bloodshed[27] and ethical imperative of ahiṃsā alike.[28] Rāma embodies Hinduism's *dharmic* double helix bar none. The *pravṛtti-nivṛtti* tension is skillfully preserved in narrative texts, particularly in a recursive figure throughout Indian lore: the ideologically elusive forest-dwelling sage.

Encoding the double helix

This section examines the manner in which the disparate religious strands of *brāhmaṇic* ideology (laid out in Table 2.1 below) are collectively encoded in the figure of the forest-dweller. In so doing, it firstly examines the structurally opposed imagery of two important spheres occurring in the Indian religious imagination, *grāma* (village) and *araṇya* (wilderness), along with the tensions between village householder and forest householding hermit. It then examines the various permutations of forest-dwellers we see in the MBh in order to engage how they relate to the double-helical model proposed. Lastly, it draws the exiled king into the fold, arguing for a symbolic symbiosis between him and the forest-dwelling hermit, serving to masterfully encode the ideological ambivalence constituting the *brāhmaṇic* double helix.

Village and wilderness in the religious imagination

What does the forest symbolize in the Indian religious imagination? The religion of the householder and that of the renouncer partake in stringent structural opposition, one which the forest-dweller is able to skillfully straddle. The opposition between these two ideologies is tantamount to the opposition innate to the associations of two spheres, *grāma* and *araṇya*, village and wilderness.

The nomadic lifestyle of the earliest adherents of Vedic religion within the subcontinent gave way to urbanization beginning with the use of the plough circa the ninth century BCE. The cultural centers resulting from this process of cultivation comprised the sphere of the *grāma*, against which *araṇya* culture was pitted. While the ancient Vedic Aryan maintains ritual and communal ties in the absence of ties to the land (being nomadic), the village culture that evolved engaged the same ritual and communal associations, while becoming tied to the land.

Table 2.1 The constituent strands of the *brāhmaṇic* double helix

	Strand I	*Strand II*
Origin	Renouncer Traditions	Vedic Tradition
Locus Association	Forest, Wilderness	Settled Community
Methodology	Contemplation	Ritual Sacrifice
Social Structure	Caste Disintegration	Stringent Caste Hierarchy
World Orientation	World Abnegation	World Affirmation
Reproduction	Celibacy	Progeny
Life Goal	Self-Realization	Prosperity
Ethics of Violence	Categorical Nonviolence	Situationally Sanctioned Violence
Cosmology	Illusion, Self, Cycle of Rebirth	Earth, Heaven, Hell
Divine Agency	Principle of Karma	Gods, Fate
Soteriology	Liberation	Heaven

Olivelle notes that

> asceticism in India found expression in two distinct but interrelated forms: the sedentary hermit and the itinerant mendicant. The former is celebrated in myth and epic, but became obsolete at least by the early centuries of the common era. The latter has continued to persist until today in some form or other as the central institution of holiness in nearly all Indian religious traditions.[29]

The renouncer renounces ritual, community, and even dwelling, becoming a wandering mendicant. He severs kinship ties, leaving the family and caste into which he was born. He refrains from economic activity, even food gathering or production, and therefore begs for his daily bread. Of great significance is the fact that he refrains from sacrificial rites, rejecting the central religious activity of Vedic culture as the impetus for *saṃsāra* itself. Renunciation defines itself in direct opposition to society, both spatially and ideologically, challenging the validity and foundation of the Vedic world. The sedentary forest hermit pervading epic and *purāṇic* literature, on the other hand, is able to appropriate ascetic ideology, intimating the *saṃnyāsin* proper, all the while affirming the sacrificial householder ideology so central to Vedic religion.

Moreover, while renunciation depends upon established culture as both a concept and an institution, this cannot be said of the forest hermit who establishes a parallel forest social structure. The ideological beauty of the forest-dweller within the religious imagination (occasioning his long-lived preservation within Indian religious narrative) is his ability to simultaneously embody the religious impulses of renouncer and householder, rejecting the specific sphere of the village, without rejecting the core elements of villager religion. He therefore, unlike the renouncer proper, retains fire for the sake of ritual practice. Therefore Olivelle's conflation with the forest hermit and the anti-civilizational renouncer (who is to be defined in opposition to cultured village life and associated with forest beasts) is problematic.

Most importantly, the forest hermit generally *lives in dwellings*, and *maintains Vedic ritual*. While he rejects social bonds with village life, he maintains them within the social microcosm of his hermitage through engagement with pupils, and sometimes wife and children. He thus becomes a sort of renouncer-householder hybrid, which, though ideologically ambiguous and religiously obsolete, is apt in preserving the tension between *pravṛtti* and *nivṛtti* religiosity in works of literature. While the renouncer is in absolute dependence on society and culture, the forest hermit is not. He inhabits a parallel society, upholding Vedic religiosity, while occupying the locale of renunciant ideology. Ritual sacrifice is at the core of Vedic religiosity. Given the centrality of sacrifice within the Vedic theological framework, *śramaṇa* religion unsurprisingly critiques it as an emblem of culture they reject. Hence the following pair of passages occurring in several Upaniṣads[30] which draws on the imagery of village and the wilderness to contrast their respective religious associations:

> Those who know thus and those here who, [living] in the wilderness, worship with the thought "Faith is [our] austerity," pass on to the flame, and from the flame to the day, from the day to the fortnight of the waxing moon, from the fortnight of the waxing moon to the six months when the sun moves north, from [these] months to the year, from the year to the sun, from the sun to the moon, from the moon to lightening. There is a person there who is not human. He leads them to Brahman. This is the path leading to the gods.
>
> But those who, [living] in the village, worship with the thought "Sacrifice and good works are [our] gift," go to the smoke, and from the smoke to the night, from the night to the latter [that is, dark] fortnight, from the latter fortnight to the six months when the sun moves south. These do not reach the year. From [these] months to the world of the fathers, from the world of the fathers to space, from space to the moon … Having dwelt there until the exhaustion [of their merits], they returned by the same course along which they went.
>
> (*Chāndogya Upaniṣad* 5.10.1–5)[31]

As Olivelle notes, we may infer a trenchant dichotomy of associations at play on the following basis:

> Village is the human habitat, the locus of Vedic culture, a place of purity and safety. Wilderness is the antithesis of village. It is a place of danger, impurity, and desolation, the habitat of wild beasts, barbarians, and evil spirits. It is where people dispose of their dead. Asceticism inverts the accepted value of these symbols.[32]

Further, the divide within the above passage

> sees the practices of the Vedic culture as inextricably bound to the *saṃsāric* process, and the ascetical practices as the gateway to *mokṣa*. Culture and village represent *saṃsāra*; anti-culture and wilderness symbolize *mokṣa*. … A deeper opposition cannot be found within the framework of Hindu thought.[33]

The MBh's shorthand for talking about this divide is "*pravṛtti*" versus "*nivṛtti*" religion, which the forest hermit happily straddles, domesticating the forest as it were, as a place of purity, auspiciousness, and Vedic culture, enhanced by the air of detachment, composure, and sagacity implicated in forest-dwelling ascetic life.

It is significant that "the hermit gives up totally all products of culture, *except the use of fire*,"[34] the *sine qua non* of Vedic religion. Insofar as he inhabits a dwelling, and perpetuates Vedic domestic ritual, he coopts and ideologically domesticates the setting of *nivṛttic* religion for the purposes of *pravṛtti* religiosity. Indeed, the only manner in which the sacrificing hermit householder might be disambiguated from the sacrificing village householder is in his geographical setting. Because of this suspicious similitude, tradition toils to distinguish the forest hermit householder from his villager householder prototype through the often-repeated injunction that the former shall not step on ploughed land, the domain of the latter. Ploughed land separates village and wilderness geographically and symbolically alike, since "the plough symbolizes man's dominance over and his manipulation of nature."[35] This injunction enables the forest hermit to retain his hybrid ideological import: were he to step foot on village soil, how would his religiosity differ from that of the village sacrificer?

Anxiety about disambiguating the two is expressed not only in injunctions about locale, but also about behavior. Olivelle notes the association in Indian ascetic literature between living in the wilderness *among* animals and living *like* animals. He cites, for example, *Baudhāyana Dharmasūtra* 3.2.19 as follows: "Moving about with wild beasts,/And dwelling with them alone,/Living a life just like theirs—/Clearly that's the way to heaven."[36] Despite the ambiguity in the textual sources, Olivelle argues that "it is very likely that celibacy, vegetarianism, and anti-ritualism were not central themes in the original hermit ideology"[37] given that "a return to nature and the imitation of wild beasts do not require the first two,"[38] and furthermore, anti-ritualism "never became a part of the hermit life style."[39] This line of thinking should be reversed: it cannot be such that forest hermits were *literally* meant to emulate wild beasts because they generally retained their seed, thwarting the most animal impulse within them from expression. The sporadic manner in which hermits reproduce (if at all) seems a telling sign that celibacy was a crucial means for disambiguation from ordinary "village life." If it is a twice-born's duty to approach his wife during her season, we can suppose that even married hermits practiced chastity given the paucity or absence of hermitage progeny. The state of marriage then might serve a ritual rather than procreative function, given Vedic religion's emphasis that the married householder perform rituals.

Moreover, while one could make an argument either way regarding vegetarianism—forest hermits are usually associated with (herbivorous) deer, and not (carnivorous) tigers—the extent to which forest hermits can be likened in the Indian mythic imagination to "wild animals" is tempered by the fact that these hermits are compared to animals that *forage*, and never animals that *hunt*. Forest hermits were therefore probably conceived as vegetarians, hence why the hunter serves as so different a symbol in Indian cultural imagination. Indeed the latter is often used as a foil to the former, as most famously the forest-dwelling Vālmīki cursing the hunter's violence, which spawns that fateful inaugural verse of Sanskrit poetry.

Therefore in Olivelle's assertion that "although he follows nature's way, the hermit paradoxically continues to use fire, a prime symbol of culture, both within and outside the ritual,"[40] it is only paradoxical if one takes the forest hermit as literally mimicking beasts, which clearly he does not. In fact, beasts mimic him, often becoming tame in his presence.

When can one live in the forest? *Vanaprasthya* is construed as a stage of life in the classical *varṇāśrama* system. Olivelle writes of the classical *āśrama* system as an innovation stemming from pre-classical religious ideology sanctioning four *dharmic* life styles for an adult male as follows: (1) student (*brahmacārin*), (2) householder (*gṛhastha*), (3) hermit (*vānaprastha*), and (4) renouncer (*parivrājaka*). In this model, the *āśramas* are lifelong occupations, rather than periodic stages of life. He notes that "all the authors of the early *Dharmasūtras* present the four *āśrama*s as alternate and parallel vocations open to a young adult male who has undergone Vedic initiation and completed the period of study that follows."[41] It is noteworthy that all vocations, other than householder, demand chastity of its adherent. Olivelle notes that

> though many boys underwent Vedic initiation, it is doubtful whether, apart from Brāhmaṇs, many ever went through the long period of Vedic study in a teacher's house. At the practical level, therefore, we are back to the householder and the renouncer.[42]

It is these two enterprises (householding and renouncing) which provide the ideological tension that the *varṇāśrama* system itself aims to address. This same tension likewise informs the parallel development of the *pravṛtti-nivṛtti dharmic* complex outlined above.

It is important for our purposes to note that the third *āśrama* became obsolete at an early age as something to be avoided in the current epoch (*kali yuga*). The forest-dweller (*vānaprastha*) stage "seems to have become obsolete in the first few centuries of the Common Era."[43] Indeed, the *Yājñavalkya Dharmaśāstra* (3.56) even permits a man to undertake the stage of *saṃnyāsa* to bypass *vānaprastha*. Yet "its memory [is] preserved in legend, poetry, drama, and works on *dharma* which still discussed it up to medieval times."[44] Why is this so? The absence (or paucity) of actual forest hermits would have afforded license for the authors of *itihāsa* to freely conjure their forest hermits, without being hindered by the manner in which the hermits of their conjuring might conflict with actual religious realities. The forest-hermit motif provides a safe space for the literary intertwining of householder and renouncer, of *pravṛtti* and *nivṛtti dharmas*. The imagery of the forest-dweller apparently provided great fodder for encoding the double-helical *dharmic* ideology at the heart of *Brāhmaṇism*; it is therefore a *brāhmaṇic* literary imagination, and not necessarily a "memory," which we find in the pages of the epics and *Purāṇas*. Let us unpack the *vānaprastha* as evidenced in the MBh, and examine how they hold up to my double-helical model.

Forest hermits in the Mahābhārata

Arti Dhand identifies four broad types of *asceticism* in the MBh, distinct from each other by virtue of their religious methodology, as well as their soteriological goals. The four types of asceticism are: *brahmacarya*, *vanaprasthya*, *saṃnyāsa*, and *mahāvrata*. The two that concern us most here are the *mahāvrata*, and to a much greater extent, *vanaprasthya* varieties of asceticism. Therefore, upon briefly treating *mahāvrata*, the remainder of this discussion focuses on *vanaprasthya*.

The *mahāvrata* form of asceticism is extremely common in the MBh. It is generally aimed at particular ends, such as offspring, invincibility, or, most important for our purposes, sovereignty. As its name suggests, it entails adhering to a strict vow either binding one to, or barring one from, specified conduct. It commonly entails appealing to a particular deity prior to undertaking such ascetic vows; for example, standing on one leg in a river for months on end. The *mahāvratin*'s acts are geared toward winning the favor of a deity, and thus earning a desired boon. This type of asceticism is practiced by all variety of beings in the MBh, e.g., *rākṣasa, dānava, asura,* human, animal, and bird, and is even adopted by the heroes of the text.[45] Unsurprisingly, then, the *mahāvrata* brand of asceticism is undertaken mostly for *pravṛttic* pursuits; as Dhand writes,

> while this kind of asceticism is generally practiced for the attainment of worldly goals, it may also be practiced in the spirit of *bhakti*, seeking not a temporal end but a spiritual one. This is suggested, for example, in the lengthy *Śāntiparva* hymn offered to the god Śiva.[46]

This is, in fact, the type of asceticism practiced by the merchant and the king in the terminal frame of the DM, in order to obtain their respective boons. The fact that the king asks for sovereignty while the merchant asks for *mokṣa* already suggests the marginalization of the merchant and his aim, due to the motif of *mahāvrata* being used primarily for worldly pursuits. This discrepancy between the standings of the two boons shall be discussed in detail in Chapter 4. Let us now turn to *vanaprasthya*. While we endeavor to bring into greater focus the composed, wise, forest-dwelling ascetic figure inhabiting the frame of the DM and countless epic and *purāṇic* junctures, his religious profile necessarily remains blurred. We can only ever see him with our peripheral vision, because the texts only ever present him in their periphery.

The religious *modus operandi* of forest hermits is murky, and intentionally so. The Indian literary imagination harnesses the nebulousness of the forest so as to populate it with a hybrid creature. The threat that *nivṛtti dharma* poses to caste, as embodied by the renouncer who by his very act of renouncing collapses the caste hegemony, is neutralized by the forest hermit's paradoxical retention of caste, and *brāhmaṇic* caste duties. He remains a *brāhmaṇa*, and enacts his caste duty in advising (displaced) kings as a good *brāhmaṇa* should. The *nivṛttic* ideal of the renouncer is thus appropriated by *brāhmaṇa* ideology in the guise of an ascetic who nevertheless upholds Vedic sacrifice, and even at times reproduces, though doesn't otherwise waste his seed. The forest hermit partakes in a clever literary trope. While the *brāhmaṇa* and the *kṣatriya* are both displaced in the forest, they find themselves there in order to honor ascetic ideals: one to teach it, and the other to learn it. The hermit harnesses *nivṛtti*'s precepts to govern himself, and the king does so to govern others. This is ironic, for do sages and kings not *both* serve as refuge of all creatures?

Given that the *vanaprasthya* is a hotly contested figure in discussions of Indian asceticism, the MBh unsurprisingly presents variations on this figure. While it is clear that *vanaprasthins* dwell in forest hermitages in seclusion and simplicity, we really do not know to what end: for example, "is the *vanaprasthin* the model of the *pravṛtti* actor, who is conscious of his dues to society and its ritual world, but is mentally and spiritually attuned to soteriological goals?"[47] I suggest the ambiguity is purposeful, allowing the forest hermit to straddle both *pravṛtti* and *nivṛtti* worlds. Commenting upon a description of the *vanaprasthin* at MBh XII.236, Dhand concludes "it would seem that *vanaprasthin*s should be understood as supporting *pravṛtti* ideals, as is apparent from their maintenance of the minimal accouterments of the Vedic tradition—the household fire, veneration of *devas* and *pitṛs*, and some household rituals."[48] However, *vanaprasthins* quite often commingle *pravṛtti* means with *nivṛtti* ideals. So crucial is this ambivalence that it accompanies the most prominent of epic sages: Vyāsa himself. Rather than asking which of the two ideologies he represents, it proves more fruitful to ask why the very author of the MBh himself is to be shrouded in such ambiguity.

Other than being without wife, Vyāsa is an orthodox *brāhmaṇa* who dwells in an *āūrama* maintaining Vedic rituals. Indeed he

> may rightly be taken to epitomize the *pravṛtti* tradition. He offers priestly services to people (for instance, at Yudhiṣṭhira's *rājasūya* and later, at his *aśvamedha*), and later, admonishes Yudhiṣṭhira sternly on his worldly duties. As Bruce Sullivan has pointed out in his work on Vyāsa, the sage replicates the priestly role of Brahmā in the world, where Brahmā is archetypally a Vedic deity, epitomizing *pravṛtti* functions.[49]

However, Vyāsa, like most forest hermits we meet, is a staunch advocate of *nivṛttic* soteriological ideals: he refers Dhṛtarāṣṭra to the *nivṛtti* progenitor Sanatsujāta for spiritual counsel on the eve of war; and, more prominently, he grants his son a stringently *nivṛttic* education such that Śuka seeks *mokṣa*, and not enjoyment in the world. Dhand takes Vyāsa to represent one archetype of *vanaprasthin*:

> Although they themselves do participate in certain Vedic functions, and thus cannot be considered antistructural in the same way as the ideals of *nivṛtti* hold, at the level of ideas, they espouse the philosophies and ethics of *nivṛtti*, explicitly denouncing the ritual and social preoccupations of *pravṛtti* and advocating the radical ethics and teleology of *nivṛtti*. This kind of *vanaprasthin* represents the inherent religious ambivalence of the text as a whole, intensely inspired by renunciant ideals yet also dialectically committed to maintaining order in the world. One way to read them may be as figures rehearsing toward liberation and counseling others on *nivṛtti* ideals, but not yet accomplished enough to achieve it themselves. This would seem to be the case with Vyāsa, who coaches his son Śuka on *nivṛtti* ideals but later,

> lamenting his loss and seeking to follow his itinerary through the high heavens, discovers to his embarrassment that he is not advanced enough to replicate Śuka's success.
>
> (XII.320.29–30)[50]

It is only fitting that the author of the MBh embodies a religious ambivalence that pervades the epic itself. More to the point of this study, the MBh's author is sure to imply that *nivṛtti*'s lofty aims are ultimately "for the birds," confining himself to a range of motion conforming to *pravṛttic* cosmology; indeed confining himself to the very epic world he creates. Vyāsa performs *pravṛtti*, but expounds *nivṛtti*; as does the MBh as a whole and the principal characters with it. Hence, our epic heroes ultimately attain *svarga*, not *mokṣa*.

Vyāsa is representative of one of three *vānaprastha* archetypes in the MBh. The second one is essentially the same as the first, with the addition of a wife. It seems to be that the married forest-dweller represents the archetype in full, and Vyāsa's unmarried version appears to be a variation thereof. The sage of the DM is presumably of the first type: the text is clear in telling us that he and his students study the *Vedas*, yet makes no mention of a wife. While it is curious that Vyāsa is without wife, this lacuna creates the opportunity for him firstly to inject his seed into the patriline without the complication of an existing consort, and also allows him to father Śuka with an *apsara*-cum-bird, for the sake of symbolic parroting. His otherwise retention of semen further associates him with the *nivṛttic* ideal. The complete *vanaprasthin* archetype (essentially Vyāsa with wife) is therefore unsurprisingly the most common type of *Vanaprasthin* in the MBh, arguably because it bears the most affinity with the Vedic householder. He is described as

> the *bhāhmaṇa* who marries and then sets up a home away from the presses of the village. He is thus both householder and *vanaprasthin* simultaneously. This is the most common variety of *vanaprasthin* encountered in the Mbh. The famous seven sages of Vedic lore might be said to represent this type: all the Bhārgavas, Agastya, Vasiṣṭha, Viśvamitra, and others make their homes in the forest, living a simple eremitic existence while engaging in their duties as priests and Vedic teachers. Intimately involved in the intrigues of the gods and the *asuras*, they often operate as advisers or counselors to one or the other side in the battle for universal sovereignty. These figures are most obviously modeled on the *ṛṣis* of ancient Vedic lore. Most often, they reinforce Vedic paradigms rather than *śramāṇika* ones and are cited as the progenitors of the *pravṛtti* traditions, exemplifying Vedic values. They are idealized as forest-dwelling creatures, eking subsistence out of the simple fare of the forest, often suffering pecuniary hardship.[51]

It is significant that these reclusive forest-dwellers strive to serve the interests of universal sovereignty. It demonstrates their importance at the upper echelons of *pravṛtti* ideology. Insofar as one is not contributing to the "loftier" *dharma* of *nivṛtti*, consisting of complete severance from worldly affiliations, one might as well be of use to the most impactful level of *pravṛttic dharma*: sovereignty.

The third type of forest-dweller occurring in the MBh

> retires to the forest in the third stage of life, after having lived a rich life in society. This *vanaprasthin* is almost always aged, and almost always *kṣatriya*; Dhṛtarāṣṭra, Bṛhadaśva, Yayāti, Śibi, and various other kings all retire to the forest in the twilight of their royal careers. *Brāhmaṇas* in the *MBh* are most often *originally* forest-dwellers and do not undertake *vanaprasthya* as a stage of life. Exceptions are those who serve as ministers and advisers to kings, figures such as Kṛpa or Dhaumya, who accompany their lieges wherever they go.[52]

The emphasis on the "life stage" aspect of *vānaprastha* might have been useful rhetoric to appease kings inclined to shirk their royal responsibility, and renounce in their prime. In addition to these three types of forest-dwellers, Dhand notes the added presence of anomalous figures "such as kings deprived of their kingdoms, exiled heirs, and disenchanted others: figures such as Nala, Satyavat, and the Pāṇḍavas themselves are almost always *kṣatriya*." This class of forest inhabitant pertains directly to the exiled king of the DM.

One might then understand the four varieties of forest-dwellers in the MBh not only as individually, but collectively, symbolic of the *nivṛtti-pravṛtti* tension. Let us treat the two types of *brāhmaṇa* forest-dwellers as, for our purposes, interchangeable. With or without wife, they appear to consistently engage in the *pravṛttic* paradigm of Vedic ritual, functioning as self-composed forest-dwelling householders. Vyāsa himself is incapable of achieving *mokṣa*. Furthermore, let us set aside the kings who resort to the forest as a life stage, once their careers are over, for this trope tends to occur at the end of a narrative, as a sort of "happily ever after," and does not generally play a significant role in the advancement of a plot, or the conflict to be resolved.[53] It is the exiled king around which the plot revolves. One might therefore divide forest-dwelling figures into two basic groups: *brāhmaṇa* forest-dwellers, permanently stationed there, and *kṣatriya* forest-dwellers, temporarily stationed there.[54] It is significant that the latter *invariably* encounter the former as a means of advancing the plot; for, in finding the forest hermit, the exiled king is able to contribute toward a clever symbolic symbiosis.

Finding the forest hermit: tracing the fate of the exiled king

The Indian literary imagination frequently conjures not only forest-dwelling hermits, but interestingly, kings who more often than not wind up in the forest so as to engage such hermits. Why is this? This is a particularly evocative trope given the opposition between *grāma* (settled community) and *araṇya* (wild jungle) in the Indian religious imagination: the first of these is home to civilization and revolves around the king, while the latter of these is home to the mystical and the wild. Heesterman, who argues that the authority of the Indian king is precarious at best (to be discussed in the following chapter), draws on the structural opposition of village and wilderness to assert that the "dilemma of kingship can then be expressed in terms of the basic paradigm: the king must belong to the *grāma*, but his authority must be based in the alien sphere of *araṇya*."[55] Hence, Indian tradition has established an alternating *grāma-araṇya* cycle as part of its rituals of royal investiture. Heesterman intriguingly suggests that this cycle is responsible for the royal exiles in both Indian epics. The same might be said to apply to the king of the DM, except his *araṇya* sojourn is not implicated in his royal investiture.

Charles Malamoud, too, notes the use of both *grāma* and *araṇya* animals during the *aœvamedha*. The specific usage of these animals underscores themes which are fundamental to Vedic ideology, such as

> the opposition between village and forest; the dual nature of the sacrifice (or at least of royal sacrifice) which, while it essentially remains a village affair, attempts to encompass the forest as well; the link between wholeness and the forest, and between violence and the village and non-violence and the forest; and, lastly, the place reserved for humans in the succession of animal species.[56]

Regarding the interplay of violence and nonviolence, he writes:

> While the forest is the locus of violence in its most elementary form, that violence symbolized by the gods Rudra and Vāyu, it is also that locus within which the ideal of non-violence (*ahiṃsā*) is most fully developed. And, while the village may have no qualms about inflicting the violence of the hunt upon the forest populations, it strives at the same time to draw it, as little as possible, into the violence of the sacrifice. For the sacrifice, that supreme form of village activity, is, once again, fundamentally violent; and while this is a regulated violence that sacrificers and sacrificial priests seek, through their practical knowledge, to channel, dissimulate and compensate, it is a violence they can never do away with completely.[57]

The violence of the *kṣatriya*, ideologically grounded in the social village context as necessary, is exposed in forest exile where it affronts the sensibilities of non-violent forest life, and proxies for the basest form of violence found in the forest, that of hunters and beasts. But more than merely entering the forest, weapons and all, the kings of which we speak are in some manner or another dethroned—indeed displaced—and it is under these grim auspices that they are made to sojourn into the *araṇya*. What does this exiled king represent?

Exile is the other, the structural opposite, of sovereignty. While an innumerable number of points might be located in a circle, only one of them can claim to be its center. And while these various points within might relate to each other in a myriad of ways, the center takes both its means of definition, and means of opposition, from the circle's circumference. As center and circumference serve to define one another, so too might sovereignty and exile within the sphere of society. The king in exile represents involuntary social, vocational displacement. This also proxies for an existential displacement, which the ideology of *pravṛtti* must, too, confront when faced with the sobering ideals of *nivṛtti*, which never forgets that nothing is lasting, not even royal power. Thus, not only are these warriors in the woods exiled, they find comfort in the refuge of forest-dwelling hermits, who, in fine *nivṛttic* fashion, can school them on the mechanics of world-induced human suffering.

A clever inversion takes place between ascetic and exiled king. The ascetic voluntarily restrains his desire to engage the world, while the exiled king has the world restrain his engagement within it. The ascetic undergoes self-imposed renunciation, while the exiled king undergoes world-imposed exile. The ascetic has renounced relationship, and is therefore able to socially stand alone. The king, on the other hand, remains in relationship through dependence, and possesses no ability to be socially independent: his very definition relates him to the entire citizenry. The king has the ability to command all others, except for the (true) ascetic who has opted out of the social contract, so to speak, such that he is sovereign over a state of one, a state which is, ultimately, boundless. Yet the forest-dwelling ascetics of our texts retain their caste and retain their classification as subjects of the king. Also, the exiled king carries with him his consecrated kingship and warrior duty and enacts his role upon the pseudo-societal settings he finds in the forest. He is never really secluded while in exile. Why? He and his *brāhmaṇa* pseudo-subject (the forest hermit) together remotely enact their proper social function, all the while mimicking a state of renunciation.

The king and the ascetic are both masters, both exerting supreme control: the first over the outer and over others, the second over the inner, over the self. The ascetic is the hero of the inner struggle, against lust, rage, etc., while the king might be said to represent the hero of the outer battle, against enemies, demons, etc. The self-composed slayer of the enemy represents the pinnacle wherein both of these modes of heroism coincide, exhibiting control over inner and outer alike. The king's *dharma* is to outwardly restrain (others), and he is made to inwardly restrain (himself) as a means of properly doing so. Of what use is outward social power when one is powerless against one's own mental and emotional compulsions? How can the king rightfully lord over others when he is but a slave to his own impulses? Great power is born from commanding one's self, and that power might be harnessed to command others.

Upon entering the liminal domain of the forest, imagined as the locus of the mysterious, hazardous, and otherworldly, we witness key exchanges between the *brāhmaṇa*-cum-ascetic permanently forest-dwelling guru and his *kṣatriya*-cum-ascetic temporarily forest-dwelling disciple. The hermit clings to his *brāhmaṇa* caste and the exiled king similarly retains his *kṣatriya* penchant for violence. Moreover, the social interdependence of their caste duties is necessarily retained, evidenced through their enactment in the forest of the same *kṣatriya-brāhmaṇa* interdependence occurring in the world: the *brāhmaṇa* advises the king in forest exile just as he would advise the king at his court, and the *kṣatriya* performs the acts of violence necessary to communal existence, so the *brāhmaṇa*'s hands might remain unsullied qua *nivṛttic* moral necessity. Given the king's function here, he does not merely represent necessary violence of his caste, he represents the violence necessary to the social system itself, indeed to communal life as a whole, even while in forest exile.

These two figures work in tandem: *brāhmaṇas* dwell in the forest *so as to* advise displaced kings, and kings become displaced *so as to* receive counsel from and protect forest-dwelling *brāhmaṇas*. The symbiosis between these symbols masterfully weaves the disparate *pravṛtti-nivṛtti* ideological strands into a narrative representation of hybrid ideology comprising *brāhmaṇism* at large. These constituent strands are structurally opposite one another, but once paradoxically interwoven as only narrative can, collectively comprise a singular double-helical entity. Figure 2.1 below maps the encoding of this hybrid ideology.

The exiled king represents a lopsided hybrid ideology, overall leaning toward *pravṛtti*: though exiled, he remains a king. The forest-dwelling hermit represents a complementarily lopsided hybrid, overall leaning toward *nivṛtti*: though householder, he is nonviolent, composed, and usually chaste. Moreover, there is a noteworthy asymmetry between the royal and ascetic ideologies comprising the *brāhmaṇic* double helix: ascetic ideology necessarily applies to isolationist tendencies and so governs only one person; yet royal ideology applies to an individual who governs the collective. As such, while we might loosely consider ascetic ideology as synonymous with *nivṛtti dharma*, royal ideology is a specialized subset of *pravṛtti dharma*, pertaining to the headquarters of the social beast, which ensures the crucial function of preserving the very sphere of *pravṛtti* as a whole. Enacted by the Indian king, royal ideology is that specific aspect of *pravṛtti dharma* geared toward what is expected of him, along with what he

Strand I	**Strand II**
Śramaṇa Religion	Vedic Religion
→ *Nivṛtti Dharma*	*Pravṛtti Dharma* ←
→ Ascetic Ideology	Royal Ideology ←
→ Ascetic	King ←
→ Forest Hermit	Exiled King ←

→ Forest-Hermit + Exiled King ←

Hybrid Ideology

Double Helix

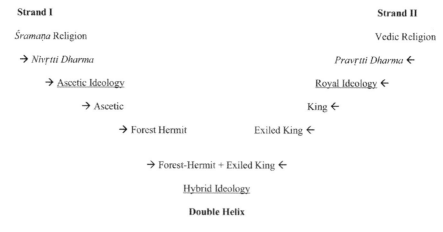

Figure 2.1 Encoding the *brāhmaṇic* double helix.

represents. Hence the structural opposition between *pravṛtti* and *nivṛtti* at large is personified by the structural opposition between ascetic and king.

Sanskrit narratives bridge this opposition by casting the ascetic as a pseudo-householder, granting him a Vedic cottage in the woods, and exiling the king to the forest. The symbiosis between the forest-dweller and exiled king therefore engages the *pravṛtti-nivṛtti* tension at the heart of Hinduism in two important ways. Firstly, it addresses the problem of violence, evidenced through the *brāhmaṇa-kṣatriya* division of labor so crucial to *brāhmaṇic* ideology. That the king represents the legitimization of violence is evident. However, he typically fulfills this function *while in the world*. Hence, secondly, the symbolic symbiosis between forest hermit and exiled king more pronouncedly assuages to the problem renunciation itself poses to *brāhmaṇism* qua social ideology. Sanskrit narrative works therefore repeatedly displace royal paragons of worldly life, sentencing them to pseudo-ascetic forest exile where such sovereigns pay homage to ascetic ideology not only through their own pseudo-ascetic displacement, but particularly through momentous encounters with self-composed sages. Such encounters represent a clever synthesis: since the ideological dance cannot be danced alone, exiled kings throughout the epics and *Purāṇas* are bound to find hermit sages, as with the frame of the DM. Sanskrit literature prides itself in celebrating such ethically impeccable figures, the DM being no exception. Not only is ascetic ideology embodied by the self-composed sage serving as the mouthpiece of the DM, it pervades the work as a whole.

Ascetic ideology in the *Devī Māhātmya*

The DM commences with Suratha's loss of sovereignty, after which he, like countless kings before him, enters the forest. He does so under the pretext of hunting. It is crucial that the king isn't actually going hunting because anyone who is familiar with South Asian narrative knows that danger lurks when kings go hunting, which proves to be the case for so many of the patriarchs in the MBh, for example. Unlike any of his royal literary correlates, however, this king only *pretends* to go hunting (DM 1.8). This is significant for two interrelated reasons. The hunt is a common trope to draw kings into the forest and occasion the commingling of *pravṛttic* and *nivṛttic* ideals through the exchange of ascetic and king. However, in order to advocate through suggestion the ethical supremacy of nonviolence, the king more often than not winds up in trouble when embarking upon his hunt. That Suratha only *pretends* to hunt is significant then in indicating that he is en route to resolution, rather than conflict, through his forest encounter. Secondly, through pretending to hunt, he himself becomes a symbol of nonviolence particularly in the pervasiveness of actual hunting as a royal pastime. And of course his movement into the forest is the impetus for his encounter with nonviolence personified: the self-composed sage.

It is the insightful sage Medhas, paragon of forest-dwelling ascetic life, who relays the glories of the Goddess. He is one who so embodies the precept of *ahiṃsā* that the beasts of the forest become tame (*praśānta*) in the presence of his hermitage.[58] Upon entering the thick of the forest, the king finds refuge, however temporarily, at the hermitage of the contented sage. Shortly thereafter, thoughts of his loss begin to plague him and he (along with his equally plagued merchant companion) opts to approach the sage for advice (DM 1.27–8), in full confidence that the sage would possess the knowledge and skill to guide them beyond their suffering. The king approaches the sage in order to address a perennial human concern: suffering. He complains of an unrestrained mind, one succumbed to grief, ensnared in his attachment. He likens his plight to that of his merchant companion who continues to be fettered by affection to wife and children, who have ruthlessly ousted him from his own home. Athirst for discrimination, the king asks after the nature of the delusion which has overtaken them both, drawing them toward objects of sense which cause only suffering (DM 1.29–33). The rhetoric of the king's appeal fits directly within the ethos of *nivṛtti*, which taken to its logical extreme demands that we realize that *all* sense objects and *all* social relationships ultimately produce suffering.

The reply the sage gives, unsurprisingly, is equally affirmative of the ethos of *nivṛtti*. He likens humans without transcendental awareness to birds and beasts, only to be pushed and pulled by sensory instinct (DM 1.34–7). During his exposition, the sage compares the unwise to birds incessantly striving to feed their young, all the while afflicted by hunger themselves. They toil due to the misguided perception that they may eventually attain gratification through offspring (DM 1.38–9), the *sine qua non* of *pravṛttic* existence. The sage then proceeds to attribute the delusion of creatures to the Goddess as Mahāmāyā, who constitutes the slumber of Viṣṇu (DM 1.40–2), and further equates that blessed Goddess with supreme knowledge, crediting her with the power to sever the bonds of mundane existence (DM 1.43). Upon completion of the Sage's exposition about delusion, the king then asks him after the nature of Mahāmāyā, referring to him as a knower of Brahman (DM 1.45–6). And thus begin the acts of Durgā proper. It is the ascetic who counsels the king and the king who propitiates that ascetic. King Suratha regains his earthly sovereignty as per the teachings of Sage Medhas, who ironically is aloof to worldly affairs.

The motifs established in this encounter between sovereign and sage pervade the acts of Durgā themselves. The DM advances a distinct association between Durgā and *brāhmaṇa* ritual culture. Not only is fire sacrifice a means of pleasing Durgā (DM 12.10), but the text explicitly equates her with Vedic incantation and the Gāyatrī mantra itself (DM 1.54–5; 4.9; 11.21). She is presented as Vedic recitation itself, through which all rituals are properly performed (DM 4.7). As the *nivṛtti* rhetoric conflates *brāhmaṇa* and ascetic, so too is Vedic sacrifice associated with ascetic austerity. And the *brāhmaṇa*-cum-ascetic aspect is of course integral to even our wrathful Goddess, to be sure: in the previous episode, when she emerges from the *Śakti* of all of the gods and is gifted with various weapons and adornments, Brahmā gifts her with an ascetic water jar (DM 2.22b). So stringent a strand of religiosity is Vedic ritualism that even among the gory band of seven mothers who emerge in Episode III, we find the ever-tame Brahmāṇi, conveyed by swans and carrying a rosary and an ascetic water pot (DM 8.14). Even amid the carnage, Brahmāṇi appears to maintain her ritual purity, fighting with mantras (DM 9.36) and sanctified water (DM 8.32), presumably sprinkled by her *kuœa* grass.[59] One also wonders if she partakes alongside her gory sisters when, at the end of the episode, we hear that the band of mothers danced about, intoxicated by blood. Given the gory nature and function of the band of mothers at large, it is a significant appeal to *nivṛtti* ideology that this water-pot-wielding goddess is the very *first* among them to emerge. As noted elsewhere in this study, first implies foremost.

Supreme knowledge is not merely something Durgā grants; it is something she *is*. She is lauded as great knowledge and great insight (DM 1.58; 4.10; 11.22), in tandem with being equated with occlusion of that knowledge (DM 11.30). She is furthermore intrinsically tied to the disposition required to attain that knowledge. The first thing she says during the *phalaœruti* chapter is that she will destroy the misfortune of those who praise her with composed mind (DM 12.1), and shortly thereafter calls for mental composure and singleness of mind (DM 12.2–6). Her praises themselves result in an auspicious mental state (DM 12.23b–24a). For it is she who controls the senses within all creatures (DM 5.33). This contented detachment marking *nivṛtti* religious praxis is, most intriguingly, manifest within the very nature of our wrathful Goddess. She is equated with modesty, contentment, tranquility, forbearance (DM 1.60b), and compassion, even toward her enemies (DM 4.20–1). She furthermore exhibits benevolence even in battle. The *Śakrādi Stuti*, for example, hymns her as driven to purify her opponents, delivering them to heaven by slaying them in battle (DM 4.17–18), all the while soothing them with her compassionate disposition (DM 4.20). Her outward severity in battle, according to this hymn, coincides with an inward disposition of serene compassion (DM 4.21).

Paradoxically the universal source of delusion also serves as the universal source of emancipation: when one is lost in a sentient labyrinth, the labyrinth itself, if petitioned, might grant insight into the way out. The DM repeatedly informs us that Durgā is the cause of liberation from the cycle of rebirth:[60] it is she who liberates the sages who, having restrained their senses and adhered to the principle of truth, repeat her name, intent on liberation (DM 4.8). Her miraculous exploits inspire not only the king, but indeed fill even the sages with wonder (DM 10.18–19). Thus heavenly seers praise her (DM 3.41a), she who is wholly "worthy of worship by all gods and great seers."[61] Invoked by the sages, she will come into being in the future to relieve the earth of drought (DM 11.42), looking upon them with a hundred eyes (DM 11.43). And she will also incarnate in the future for the very purpose of protecting the sages, who will lower their bodies in praise to her (DM 11.46b–47). She is therefore intimately tied to the ideals of *nivṛtti* religion, both in soteriology and in praxis. And it is the very *nivṛttic* praxis of the sages that the king adopts for his own ends. Once hearing the exploits of Durgā, the king pays homage to the austerities-practicing seer and practices severe austerities of his own. Both he and the merchant alternate between fasting completely and fasting partially, for three years straight, minds composed in self-restraint all the while; and indeed it is this devout austerity which earns them Durgā's favor (DM 13.4b–11).

The ascetic methodology adopted at the end of the DM befits the *nivṛttic* goal of the merchant who chooses transcendental knowledge, and attains liberation from the cycle of rebirth (DM 13.12b–13a), a boon which Durgā graciously grants (DM 13.15b–16a). The disenfranchisement-driven merchant has been properly oriented by the ideology of *nivṛtti* so as to wish to do away with notions of "I" and "mine" (DM 13.12b–13a). Asking such of Durgā, she graciously complies, bestowing his *nivṛttic* boon. If we take the merchant's fate as exemplary, one might understand the aims of *nivṛtti* as ultimately dominating those of *pravṛtti*. Yet the DM, as shall be demonstrated in the following chapter, preserves the ambivalence while cleverly articulating an ideological reversal. The text's esteem for royal ideology is seeded in its very frame narrative. Indeed, the king's forest exile serves as a training ground whereby he might be schooled in the ways of *nivṛtti dharma*, both didactically and experientially, learning nonpossession, celibacy, self-restraint, etc. However, it is crucial to note that his forest retreat never succeeds in instilling in him the *nivṛttic* virtue of nonviolence, nor does it even aspire to. He embodies the spirit of the *mahāvrata* described in the MBh, devoting his austerities to a specific deity for the purpose of attaining a *pravṛttic* goal: the destruction of his enemies and reinstatement of his royal power.

The forest is the place of the animal and the esoteric, a place of both brute and higher impulses. What is a warrior in the woods, if not a hunter? For this reason, the king of the DM only pretends to hunt, for, in so doing, he refrains from serving as an expression of cultural anxiety about "legitimated" violence whereby he proxies for the hunter, and becomes an unwitting menace to holy forest-dwellers such as so many kings before him. The king of the DM is not schooled in the perils of violence; on the contrary, he receives teachings utterly glorifying righteous bloodshed for the sake of protecting the world. Despite the anxiety-encapsulating parity between forest-roaming warrior and forest-dwelling hunter, the king's violence is sanctioned even while in exile. He and the forest hermit contribute to a symbolic symbiosis, which addresses both the problem of violence (absolving the *brāhmaṇa* from staining his hands by virtue of their caste interplay), and the problem of renunciation. Their exchange richly encodes the *dharmic* double helix persisting within the Indian literary imagination.

It is vital for us to register that just as the exiled king is never ultimately taught nonviolence, he likewise cannot remain within the forest, for, at the end of the day, he must occupy the middle ground between the never-violent forest-dwelling sage and the wantonly violent forest-dwelling hunter. He must regain his place as justifiably violent world-governing king. The pseudo-ascetic *brāhmaṇa* is stationed in the forest not only to evoke *nivṛtti* ideology, but, ironically, *so as* to point the king back toward the world, partaking in *pravṛtti* ideology in doing so. Furthermore, as paragon of the pervasive ideological double helix, the *brāhmaṇa*'s ambivalence *must* ensue; hence, the DM calls upon the *mokṣa*-seeking merchant and the sovereignty-seeking king to represent the tradition's divergent ideological strands, absolving the *brāhmaṇa* from either pronouncing judgment on which path is to be followed, or from ultimately committing to either path himself. He remains contentedly suspended in the forest, neither in the world, nor liberated from it. The literary trope of the forest-hermit-exiled-king encounter thus details an exchange that cleverly pays homage to *nivṛttic* religiosity, while serving the ultimately *pravṛttic* interests of *brāhmaṇic* ideology. Thus, it is paradoxically through finding the forest hermit, and engaging in ascetic ideology, that the exiled king derives a means whereby to regain royal power. Let us now turn to the extent to which the DM encapsulates royal ideology.

Notes

1 Greg Bailey, "The Pravṛtti/Nivṛtti Project at La Trobe University. With Notes on the Meaning of Vṛt in the Bhagavadgītā," *Indologica Taurinensia* XIX (2006): 3.
2 Cited in Karel Werner, "The Long Haired Sage of *Rg Veda*, 10.136," in *The Yogi and the Mystic: Studies in Indian and Comparative Mysticism* (Hoboken, NJ: Routledge, 1995), 33–53.
3 J.C. Heesterman, *The Broken World of Sacrifice: An Essay in Ancient Indian Ritual* (Chicago, IL: University of Chicago Press, 1993).
4 Johannes Bronkhorst, *The Two Sources of Indian Asceticism* (Bern; New York: P. Lang, 1993).
5 Greg Bailey, *Materials for the Study of Ancient Indian Ideologies: Pravṛtti and Nivṛtti* (Torino: Ed. Jollygrafica, 1986), 9.
6 Bailey, 9.
7 Bailey, 10.
8 Bailey, 22.
9 Bailey, "The Pravṛtti/Nivṛtti Project at La Trobe University. With Notes on the Meaning of Vṛt in the Bhagavadgītā," 4.
10 Bailey, 4.
11 Interestingly, Chapters 27–45 of the MkP itself (Banerjea's Bibliotheca Indica 1862 Calcutta edition) provide nine chapters on each of these ideologies, and "As such these chapters constitute one of the few extended self-conscious treatments of the subject." Greg Bailey, "The Pravṛtti/Nivṛtti Chapters in the Mārkaṇḍeyapurāṇa," in *Epics, Khilas and Purāṇas. Continuities and Ruptures*, ed. P Koskikallio (Zagreb: Croatian Academy of Arts and Sciences, 2005), 19. This connection shall be taken up in a subsequent research project investigating why the DM should be located within the MkP at all.
12 Bailey, "The Pravṛtti/Nivṛtti Project at La Trobe University. With Notes on the Meaning of Vṛt in the Bhagavadgītā," 2.
13 Dhand, *Woman as Fire, Woman as Sage Sexual Ideology in the Mahābhārata*, 52.
14 Apte (1965, 669–70). Cited in Dhand, 28.
15 Dhand, 28–9.
16 Dhand, 28–9.
17 Dhand, 30–1.
18 Dhand, 33.
19 Dhand, 31.
20 Dhand, 70.
21 Wendy Doniger and J. Duncan M. Derrett, *The Concept of Duty in South Asia* (New Delhi: Vikas Publishing House, 1978), 97.
22 Christopher K. Chapple, "Otherness and Nonviolence in the Mahābhārata," in *Nonviolence to Animals, Earth, and Self in Asian Traditions* (Albany, NY: State Univ. of New York Press, 1993), 16–17.
23 MBh XII.15.26 points out that minute beings are killed by the hundreds by our very breathing, eating, and sleeping.

24 Austin B. Creel, Vasudha Narayanan, and J. Patrick Olivelle, "Village Vs. Wilderness: Ascetic Ideals and the Hindu World," in *Monastic Life in the Christian and Hindu Traditions: A Comparative Study* (Lewiston, NY: Edwin Mellen Press, 1990), 150.
25 Patrick Olivelle, *The Āśrama System: The History and Hermeneutics of a Religious Institution* (New York: Oxford University Press, 1993), 4.
26 Doniger and Derrett, *The Concept of Duty in South Asia*, 97.
27 Raj Balkaran and A. Walter Dorn, "Violence in the 'Vālmīki Rāmāyaṇa': Just War Criteria in an Ancient Indian Epic," *Journal of the American Academy of Religion* 80, no. 3 (September 1, 2012): 659–90.
28 Raj Balkaran, "The Sarus' Sorrow: Voicing Nonviolence in the Vālmīki Rāmāyaṇa," *Journal of Vaishnava Studies* 26, no. 3 (Spring 2018): 25–36.
29 Creel, Narayanan, and Olivelle, "Village Vs. Wilderness: Ascetic Ideals and the Hindu World," 132–3.
30 Cf. *Bṛhadāraṇyaka Upaniṣad* 6.2.15–16; *Kauśītakī Upaniṣad* 1.1–7; *Muṇḍaka Upaniṣad* 1.2.9–11; *Praśna Upaniṣad* 1.9–10. See J.F. Sprockhoff, "Āraṇyaka und Vānaprastha in der vedischen Literatur," *Wiener Zeitschrift für die Kunde Südasiens*, 25 (1981): 51 and note 86 for additional secondary literature.
31 Creel, Narayanan, and Olivelle, "Village Vs. Wilderness: Ascetic Ideals and the Hindu World," 130–1.
32 Creel, Narayanan, and Olivelle, 131.
33 Creel, Narayanan, and Olivelle, 132.
34 Creel, Narayanan, and Olivelle, 133. Emphasis my own.
35 Creel, Narayanan, and Olivelle, 133.
36 Cf. MBh, 5.118.6–11, 1.109; Majjhima Nikāya I.79; Jātaka I.390; Aśvgahoṣa, Buddhacarita, 6.59–62. Cf. Patrick Olivelle, "Beast and Ascetic: Animal Motifs in Indian Asceticism," paper presented at the annual meeting of the American Oriental Society, March 22, 1983.
37 Creel, Narayanan, and Olivelle, "Village Vs. Wilderness: Ascetic Ideals and the Hindu World," 134.
38 Creel, Narayanan, and Olivelle, 134.
39 Creel, Narayanan, and Olivelle, 134.
40 Creel, Narayanan, and Olivelle, 134.
41 Olivelle, *The Āśrama System: The History and Hermeneutics of a Religious Institution*, 74.
42 Creel, Narayanan, and Olivelle, "Village Vs. Wilderness: Ascetic Ideals and the Hindu World," 146.
43 Matthew Clark, *The Daśanāmī-Saṃnyāsīs: The Integration of Ascetic Lineages into an Order* (Leiden; Boston, MA: Brill, 2006), 5 fn. 17.
44 Clark, 5 fn. 17.
45 "Kṛṣṇa is seen to practice it, for the birth of a son (XIII.15.4–6); Arjuna practices it for the acquisition of weapons (III.39.10ff.); Viśvāmitra practices it to become a *brahmarṣi* (I.165.40ff.), and Mataṅga practices it to become a *brāhmaṇa* (XIII.129.1–16). Different sages routinely practice it, as do the *asura*s." Dhand, *Woman as Fire, Woman as Sage Sexual Ideology in the MBh*, 72.
46 Dhand, 73.
47 Dhand, 66.
48 Dhand, 67.
49 Dhand, 68.
50 Dhand, 68–9.
51 Dhand, 69.
52 Dhand, 69.
53 A glaring exception to this is the murder of Dama's father in the MkP which takes place in the forest, once he has renounced his kingdom.

54 Dhand, *Woman as Fire, Woman as Sage Sexual Ideology in the MBh*, 69–70.
55 J.C. Heesterman, "The Conundrum of the King's Authority," in *Kingship and Authority in South Asia*, ed. John F. Richards (Delhi; New York: Oxford University Press, 1998), 24–5.
56 See Charles Malamoud, *Cooking the World: Ritual and Thought in Ancient India* (Delhi; New York: Oxford University Press, 1996), 74–5.
57 See Malamoud, 83.
58 DM 1.9: *sa tatrāśramam adrākṣīd dvijavaryasya medhasaḥ | praśāntaśvāpadākīrṇaṃ muniśiṣyopa-śobhitam* || Oddly, Coburn translates *praśānta* as "domesticated": "There he saw the hermitage of Medhas, best of the twice-born,/Crowded with wild beasts that had been domesticated, resplendent with disciples of the sage." Coburn, *Encountering the Goddess*, 32. Yet, according to Monier-Williams, *praśānta* comes to possess two sets of meanings by the time of the MBh, firstly "tranquillized, calm, quiet, composed, indifferent," and secondly "extinguished, ceased, allayed, removed, destroyed, dead." Monier-Williams et al., "Monier-Williams Sanskrit-English Dictionary (2008 Revision)," 2008. Clearly, the text literally refers to the first of these two, probably indicating that the beasts were tamed by the very vicinity of the self-composed master, Medhas.
59 She is specifically invoked in the *Nārāyaṇī Stuti* as doing so. See DM 11.12.
60 This occurs on four occasions, three detailed in this note, and another detailed in the following note. DM 11.6; DM 11.7; DM 13.4.
61 DM 4.2. Coburn, *Encountering the Goddess*, 48.

3 Mother of kings

Royal ideology in the *Devī Māhātmya*

The DM is not only framed by the plight of a deposed king; it culminates in the restoration of that king's power, through Durgā's grace. Why is this? This chapter focuses this book's overarching line of questioning by examining the centrality of royal ideology to the Goddess of the DM. Royal and ascetic ideologies represent two arms of the *brāhmaṇic* body, yet, however lofty the latter, it is the former that guards them both. Though the latter piously remains unstained by blood, it owes this luxury to its armed counterpart. Unsurprisingly, our weaponry-wielding Goddess serves as the font of royal power, beseeched by a royal figure to restore his royal post. It is telling that she unflinchingly blesses him to forcefully overthrow his enemies, just as she overthrows her own; for each of these are enemies of *dharma*. She protects king Suratha's terrestrial sovereignty, as she protects Indra's on the celestial sphere. Moreover, protection is the *sine qua non* of Indian kingship. Durgā therefore not only physically safeguards earthly and heavenly kings, but, as supreme reality personified, she ideologically safeguards the very ethos of world-affirmation. She sanctions the bloodshed of kingship in the face of *nivṛtti*'s nonviolent ideals. She thus raises *brāhmaṇism*'s royal arm to a status beyond the reproach of its ascetic counterpart.

Building on the ideological foundation established in the previous chapter, this chapter reexamines Heesterman's rhetoric on the allegedly precarious nature of Indian kingship, rhetoric since internalized by decades of scholarship on Indian kingship. Owing to romantic notions of renunciation originating in Vedic sacrificial culture, he conflates *brāhmaṇic* ideology with ascetic ideology, fallaciously pitting it *against* royal ideology. He therefore overemphasizes the (necessarily worldly) king's spiritual dependence upon the (supposedly otherworldly) *brāhmaṇa*. Yet the DM, for example, advances a Goddess who serves as a singular font of both ascetic and royal power, to be accessed directly, sans intercessor. This chapter proceeds to examine the *sine qua non* of the Indian king: the function of protection, itself an inalienable attribute of both *pravṛtti* ideology and constructions of the divine. The Indian king is thus construed as divine protector, paragon of *pravṛtti dharma*, who must not only stringently follow its dictates for the sake of his own *dharma*, but who is charged with the preservation of the sphere of *pravṛtti* itself. He represents the full-fledged pravṛttic arm of the *brāhmaṇic* ideological body, without which *brāhmaṇism* qua social ideology would crumble due to the gravity of renunciatory religiosity. Lastly, this chapter examines the extent to which *pravṛtti* ideology in general, and royal ideology in particular, pervades the DM. The text's royal themes are epitomized in the very function of the Goddess, who is explicitly associated with the Indian king, by virtue of her capacity to protect.

The womb of royal power

Despite the disappearance of actual Hindu kingships since Indian independence, the institution of kingship remains of central importance throughout the Hindu world. How can we characterize that institution? Whence does the king's power arise?

J.C. Heesterman, arguably the most influential scholar on the trajectory of western scholarship on Indian kingship, famously laments the absence of a unified theory of Indian kingship amid the copious kingly discourse we find in ancient Indian texts.[1] His work is crucial for our purposes not only because of its impact, but because it speaks to the ambivalent ideological heart of Hinduism. He repeatedly writes of the "conundrum" of the king's authority in the Indian context. While he draws primarily from the Brāhmaṇas (late Vedic ritual texts), he theorizes about the overarching nature of "Indian kingship" *as is*, failing to factor in later works such as the DM. This neglect is crucial, for the "evidence" of such works would be primarily in the form of narrative, the best vehicle for integrating the tensions preserved in the late Vedic period. One cannot integrate by way of injunction the subtleties, nuances, and contradictions afforded by narrative encoding. Description more powerfully instructs than prescription proper, skillfully imparting tension rendered contradictory by overt pronouncement.

Indeed, we have at our disposal material on Indian kingship spanning from *Ṛg Vedic* to medieval times. Arguably, there can be no unified "theory" uniting the social and religious needs of so vast a span of time. While attempts have been made to trace the divergent views on the subject with respect to chronology,[2] the lacuna on the institution of the Indian king remains,[3] and perhaps necessarily so. Heesterman therefore concludes that:

> The religious aspect of kingship cannot be denied. All the parts seem to be available, but the texts do not try to put them together. They remain isolated and disparate pieces of evidence spread over different contexts. What is lacking is a consistent overall scheme that would give substance to a consolidated theory of sacral kingship. As it is, however, kingship remains even theoretically suspended between the sacral and the secular, divinity and mortal humanity, legitimate authority and arbitrary power, dharma and adharma.[4]

It should come as no surprise that the phenomenon of Indian kingship would register as incongruent to imposed binaries, for example the sacral–secular and divinity–humanity divides. Equally unsurprising is the "absence" of a consolidated traditional theory of kingship: it is only the presumption of the scholar that such a unified theory is necessary, desirable, or even possible. While traditional sources on kingship preserve various tensions, to be sure, the *conundrum* of the king's authority is a function of the western scholarly lens, hence the absence of traditional material lamenting such a lack.

This section proceeds to deconstruct Heesterman's perspective of Indian kingship, given its profound influence, paying particular attention to the sacred–secular and immanent–transcendent dichotomies he imposes on his data; it then turns to Ronald Inden's work on rituals of kingship as an important corrective, one apropos to what we see in the DM.

Heesterman's conundrum is dependent upon his understanding of the underlying ideological tension at the heart of Hinduism, which, by the time of the MBh, finds voice as *pravṛtti* and *nivṛtti dharma*. He refers to this inner conflict of tradition as born of "… two diagonally opposed principles of organization, the one based on hierarchical interdependence and the other on separation and independence, represented respectively by the king (or the dominant caste) and the brahmin."[5] While the *pravṛtti-nivṛtti* double-helical tension is fundamentally one existing between householder religion and renunciant religion, Heesterman conflates the householding *brāhmaṇa* with the renouncer; however, this is only one strand of the ideological double helix. The rejection of social relations is proper to the renouncer, not the householding *brāhmaṇa*. Therefore, while Heesterman locates the "pivot of Indian tradition in the irreconcilability of 'brahmin' and 'king,' who yet are dependent on each other,"[6] it is more appropriate to attribute this pivot to the tension between householder and renouncer at the heart of *brāhmaṇic* ideology, more clearly expressed between the tension between king and ascetic, rather than king and *brāhmaṇa* proper.

This conflation of *brāhmaṇa* and renouncer (upon which his conundrum of the Indian king depends) stems from Heesterman's theory that the ideology of renunciation stems from within Vedic religion itself.[7] Rather than acknowledge the innate ideological friction occurring between asceticism and Vedic ritual, he views Vedic ritual as progenitor of the ethos of renunciation, hence the problem for him lies between the *brāhmaṇa* and the king. If the *brāhmaṇa* is concerned with retaining his freedom from social relations (which is actually the impulse proper to the renouncer), then why does he enter into a relationship as the ritual officiant to begin with? If we accept Heesterman's theory that the interiorization of the sacrifice is the logical consequence of Vedic ritual, then why does outward ritual sacrifice persist at all, particularly in lieu of harsh *œramaṇic* critique? Should it not have become obsolete under the sway of its own evolution?

That the dichotomous impulses toward world-renunciation and toward Vedic world-affirmation originate from separate religious traditions is not only evident from their divergent ideological trajectories but evidenced by the fact that Aśoka's rock edicts (circa 250 BCE) encourage reverence for the *œramaṇa and* for the *brāhmaṇa*: for the ideology of the former had yet to be appropriated by the latter through the didactic and symbolic tropes we find in the MBh. Furthermore, it is clear that the precept of nonviolence (central to *œramaṇa* religion) in this era is yet at odds with *brāhmaṇic* ideology, else why would Aśoka need to turn to *śramaṇa*-born Buddhism to assuage his blood-soaked guilt? He had the luxury to embrace nonviolence at the height of royal power, condemning Vedic animal sacrifice: yet one imagines that the number of animals ritually sacrificed in the Vedic fires to ordain his victorious conquest was proportionate to the tens of thousands of lives sacrificed on the battlefield to secure that conquest.

Heesterman nevertheless idealizes the *brāhmaṇa* as a pure ascetic actor, due to his self-contained social independence. In doing so, he tends to gloss over the *brāhmaṇa*'s priesthood, and the social and karmic exchange incurred by that priesthood. He relegates to a single footnote the crucial fact that the *brāhmaṇa* is typically *not* a renouncer,[8] yet proceeds to theorize based on a conflation of the two. While the *brāhmaṇa*'s *sine qua non* is priestcraft, Heesterman argues that a *brāhmaṇa* cannot be both preeminent and a priest, since his priesthood renders him in service of king and community, which would "jeopardize his claim to represent ultramundane authority."[9] Even though "the diffusion of power and authority with the ever-renewed sacrificial contest as the mediating and organizing institution would seem to call for a clearly defined priesthood to manage the central institution,"[10] he advises we not look to the obvious—the *brāhmaṇa*—for fulfilling this role on the grounds that *brāhmaṇas*, as a closed caste, was a "late construct," which "has no clear counterpart in the old-Iranian evidence but is a specifically Indian development."[11] He bolsters this trajectory by invoking *upaniṣadic* religious concepts, stating that the *brāhmaṇa* "in the Vedic texts is the bearer or representative of the impersonal *bráhman*."[12] Astonishingly, he argues that even the *purohita* (the *brāhmaṇa* ritual specialist "placed before" the king for the very purpose of performing royal rituals) does not serve this purpose since the *purohitas* were charioteers "in olden times," similar to the *sūtas* we see in the epics.[13] Irrespective of Heesterman's line of argumentation, by the time of the DM, it is clear that the function of ritual incantation might be fulfilled not only by the king, but by any twice-born male.

Judging by what we see in the MBh, while the *brāhmaṇa* becomes an expounder of renunciant ideologies—probably for reasons of survival—his priestly and instructional functions nevertheless render him enmeshed in the social world. That the priestly function is not essentially associated with renunciation is evidenced in the BhG's disdainful attitude toward *pravṛtti* ritual religion in general (BhG 2.42–3). Given that, as Heesterman writes, the *brāhmaṇa* "is the exemplar of the irresolvable tension that is at the heart of Indian civilization,"[14] why locate the conundrum in the authority of the king, and not in the authority of the *brāhmaṇa* himself in the face of renunciant ideology? Heesterman argues that the price for establishing a transcendent authority was alienation of the social world, and with it, the king, apex of that world.[15] But the *brāhmaṇa* is equally a part of the social world, and equally prey to the tensions of any transcendent authority, as manifests between the vying ideologies of *pravṛtti* and *nivṛtti dharmas*. He thus superimposes the conundrum inherent in the *pravṛtti-nivṛtti dharmic* double helix onto the institution of the Indian king.

Heesterman was heavily influenced by Dumont who, drawing on the Brāhmaṇas, argued that the Indian king became "secularized" after the Vedic period since he does not retain ritual supremacy as in other cultures. One of the mandates of Indian kingship, therefore, was to secure the services and counsel of a skilled court ritualist, the *purohita*, whose function it was to uphold the prosperity, (spiritual) protection, and victory for the king. Therefore, the king himself did not primarily fulfill a ritual function, despite his common role as celebrant in public rites and festivals. That the primary magico-religious aspect proper to the king in other societies is retained only by the *purohita* in the Indian case indicates for Dumont (and subsequently Heesterman) that the king loses his hierarchical pre-eminence in favor of the priest. Dumont, therefore, dismisses the obvious divine status accorded to Indian kings as somehow the product of (lowly) popular Hinduism. As Inden remarks:

> One could see the priest and king related in a hierarchic but complementary fashion, as together forming a complex agent. But there is difficulty here. The king stands between the Brahman and the world of the Indian village. Dumont cannot, however, let the king stay there because he is committed to seeing the world through a metaphysics of mutual exclusion. Either the king is going to be classed with the Brahman in the realm of hierarchy, or he is going to be classed, along with the state, with the villagers. Dumont vacillates, but on the whole tends to class the king with the villager. The dichotomous thinking in which he is enmeshed thus leads him to this conclusion, that "the function of the king has been *secularized*" (293). The embarrassment of the Hindu king's divinity he explains away by attributing it to a "popular mentality" that somehow lurks below the level of Brahminical thought.
>
> (297–9)[16]

However crucial the role of the *purohita*, one cannot reduce the Indian king to a "secular" entity given that he is considered the embodiment of the essences of various deities. While the use of categories such as secular can, at times, be useful tools to analyze the data, they can also serve as blinders, particularly in the case of South Asian phenomena, wherein whatever partition that may exist between the "immanent-secular" and the "transcendent-sacred" must necessarily be tentative and provisional. We scholars of South Asia run into trouble when bent on binary modes of classification: while it might affront the rational impulse, it is often more useful to adopt the mentality of "both/and" rather than "either/or" while studying social phenomena.

One might soften the mentality of mutual exclusion through use of a multidimensional model. Let us envision that there are forces that are comprehensible, and attributable to perceivable causes, and others which remain unseen and fundamentally subtle in their nature. If the *purohita*, through use of ritual, commands the unseen, and the empirical world is subject to the unseen forces, the *purohita* might be considered more spiritually powerful insofar as he is able to manipulate these subtle forces. However, since all other forces (biological, mechanical, astronomical, political, etc.) are implicated in the unseen play, there can be no "secular" strata fundamentally demarcated from the "sacred" unseen. This distinction, quite simply, does not ultimately apply, and holds only provisional value. "Divine power" from that unseen stratum can be drawn into person and place through means of ritual authority. As such, it stands to reason that the "elements of divinity the king possessed in Vedic times were chiefly connected with his functions as a sacrificer, and were bestowed on him by the sacrificial rituals performed by the priests."[17] The enterprise of sacrifice arbitrates between unseen and seen modes of reality, and while the classical *purohita* commands the former, the king commands the latter.

The king therefore does not necessarily lose hierarchical pre-eminence as such. It is useful to apply a dual-hierarchy model when thinking about the manner in which the priest and the king relate: the king is by definition preeminent in the sociopolitical order, while the priest is necessarily preeminent in the socio-ritual order. While one might be inclined to argue that the king is nevertheless "subordinate" to the priest insofar as the sociopolitical order is dependent upon the socio-ritual order of reality, I would suggest a more nuanced, mutually dependent, configuration between the two. Once consecrated, it is the king, *not* the *purohita*, who possesses the power to influence the very cosmos through his nature, actions, and even absence. He is thus able to manipulate the same level of reality invoked through ritual, and so cannot be considered de facto ritually inferior to the *purohita* proper. Moreover, if it is the king's duty to protect the sacrificer (and thus the sacrifice itself), then the priest can be thought of as subordinate to (i.e., dependent upon) the king. The king guards the physical arena, his priest guards the ritual arena, and these guardians guard each other. Therefore, the priest and king are both preeminent, in their respective orders of reality.

Ritual is necessarily tied to the worldly. Sacrifice is done for the sake of satiating desire, and upholding the cosmos itself. Where there is ritual, there is repetition, for ritual is proper to the maintenance of a universe cyclical in nature. The renouncer proper renounces ritual because he renounces the entire realm of repetition itself, and the need for its maintenance. Ritual, therefore, at its core, is both symbolically and soteriologically antithetical to renunciation. It is perennially an aspect of *pravṛtti* ideology, and antithetical to the aims of *nivṛtti*. Heesterman's perceived problem with the authority of the king mirrors the problem with the temporal world at large: all things are subject to decay with the passage of time, and must be destroyed or renewed. All things manifest must be rejuvenated through sacrifice. If even ethical principles, such as *dharma* itself, are subject to decay with the passage of time, how much more so an earthly institution, however exalted, such as kingship? For this reason, royal consecration cannot induce a permanent state of being. The authority infused into the king through consecration rituals has a lifespan, and requires continual renewal. For Heesterman, the cyclical nature of royal rituals addresses the "open problem"[18] of Indian kingship. But whose "problem" is this? Indeed, for an etic problem, there need be no emic solution. Arguably, the cyclical nature of royal rituals need not indicate a problem regarding the retention of authority, but rather as the natural corollary of a cyclical cosmos, especially given the intimate association between the divine macrocosm and the royal microcosm. The cyclical nature of consecration rituals appears unrelenting to a mentality accustomed to linear temporal processes, whereby once something is "accomplished" there is no "purpose" in repeating that accomplishment. However, the repetitive nature of consecratory ritual befits the backdrop of a universe where *nothing* can be permanently established. Given that cosmic order itself is maintained through ritual repetition, it should come as no surprise that so does royal power.

Ronald Inden's discussion of the oscillating cycles innate to Indian kingship serves as an important corrective to Heesterman's penchant for mutual exclusion. In his discussion of royal ritual and their relationship to the authority of the king in early medieval India (700–1200 CE), Inden wisely cautions:

> At the outset, I should warn the reader that "authority" and "ritual" are categories of analysis defined by scholars of politics and religion and are not coterminous with any indigenous Hindu categories known to me. Royal authority in the Indian context was inextricably bound up with notions of divine power, material prosperity, moral well-being, and cosmic regulation and ritual encompassed many more kinds of activities in the Hindu tradition than in the Christian. Hence, I use these two terms only as convenient points of entry into the question of Hindu kingship.[19]

Inden notes the "hybrid" nature of the Indian king in global context as at odds with both their ancient Egyptian and Japanese counterparts who were wholly transcendent figures of authority, uninvolved in the immanent, mundane aspects of rulership, as well as their ancient Mesopotamian, Persian, and Chinese, as human agents alone. He writes:

> Rather, the Hindu king appears as a contradictory combination of the two, a figure who is expected to transcend the world as a divine, yet humble, almost ascetic worshipper and passive focus of authority on the one hand, and to make himself immanent as a divine warrior and administrator, decisive in the everyday concerns of his realm, on the other.[20]

The "dual" nature of the Indian king pertains to the fact that demarcations between "sacred" and "mundane" are effectively nonexistent in the Indian context. This is unsurprising in a cultural context where even aesthetics and mathematics might be considered branches of "divine" knowledge; where physical oblations are spiritually consumed by the gods, carried to their realm by fire; where the totality of universal consciousness might reside within a single human being.

From the king's capacity to officiate alone, one surmises that he is not necessarily subordinate to his *purohita*, at least by the medieval period. Inden notes, drawing heavily on the *Viṣṇudharmottara Purāṇa*, that eighth to twelfth-century ritual texts called for kings to perform a regimen of auspicious rites, daily, monthly, and annually. For example, kings were required to perform monthly worship of *mūrtis* of the nine planets and twenty-seven lunar asterisms. Additionally, he was to undergo a ritual bath for six months of each year (*puṣyābhiṣeka*), along with an annual ritual bath on the anniversary of his consecration (*rājyābhiṣeka*). Important for our purposes, Inden notes that

> [h]e was also enjoined to perform the honorific worship of Indra's standard, pay homage to a painted image of Durgā, carry out an elaborate Nīrājana ceremony connected with his army, and see to the completion of the most elaborate ceremony performed in his kingdom, the annual procession of the god designated as the "cosmic overlord" in it.[21]

Why is Durgā invoked for royal rituals? While this query warrants a book of its own, the present study demonstrates that the themes of the DM resonate well with its ritual application insofar as both center around sovereignty.

It is also noteworthy that the king performs ritual penance in the forest, away from the settled sphere. In theorizing the forest-kingdom oscillation of the Indian king, Inden proposes that the first half of the ceremony (in the forest) signals the centralization of the sovereign's authority, while the portion of the ceremony occurring upon his return to his kingdom signals the decentralization of his authority. This oscillation rehearses the very process whereby the elements of the world emerged from the body of the Cosmic Man (Puruṣa).[22]

In *purāṇic* accounts of creation, the Cosmic Man emits various items and entities without being depleted in the process: like Durgā of the DM, he retains his power even while that power is harnessed to empower others. As the commingling of what we call "transcendent" and "immanent" aspects of power set the stage for the cosmos itself, it is no wonder that this equally occurs in the body of the king. The king represented the immanent, microcosmic corollary of the transcendent, macrocosmic Puruṣa insofar as just as the body of Puruṣa symbolized order, power, prosperity, and well-being for the cosmos as a whole, so the king symbolized these things for his kingdom.[23] Perhaps the relationship between the universal power of the Cosmic Man and the power localized in the body of the king might be likened to the universal power of a deity, and its localized manifestation in a *mūrti* thereof. The king in the medieval period is therefore the microcosmic corollary of the cosmic supreme, and the *axis mundi* of the kingdom, and, symbolically, of the whole world. It is unsurprising then that medieval Hindu kings referred to themselves as rulers of the entire earth. The king of the DM is in fact described as "a king over the whole earth."[24] The key difference in the DM is that the cosmic masculine is replaced, as it were, by a cosmic feminine; yet the association between earthly sovereignty and supreme cosmic power is indeed underscored throughout the work, discussed below.

The nature of the royal consecration ritual suggests, to Inden, an oscillation between the transcendent function of the Hindu king as ceremonial specialist, and his immanent function as warrior-administrator. That consecration rituals needed to be performed annually indicates the temporary nature of ritual consecration. The authority of the king is much like a battery, which needs to be periodically re-energized. Moreover, for Inden, this oscillation is tied to the cosmic oscillation between dark and light, day and night:

> The oscillation of the day was projected onto the year, said to constitute one day and night of the gods. The cold and hot seasons taken together formed the "day," the rainy season—fullmoon day, Āṣāḍha (June–July) to the same day, Kārtika (October-November)—the "night," darkened by clouds. During this four month period, the gods slept and the king, along with the entire state apparatus, suspended normal administrative and warrior functions. The king retired to a retreat outside his capital and after putting an image of Viṣṇu to sleep, devoted himself to the keeping of a four-month vow (*cāturmāsya*) and the performance of a number of rituals.[25]

This phenomenon perhaps finds corollary in the ritual chanting of the DM at the annual juncture when the gods embark on their seasonal slumber, the first episode of which actually details the slumber of Viṣṇu. In commenting upon the ritual timing of Navarātrī, Fuller mentions that the popular god Viṣṇu (often along with the other gods) goes to sleep around the summer solstice, and hence had been sleeping for four months by the time of the Goddess festival, "thus exacerbating the world's vulnerability at this time [which is consistent with the] notion that Mahiṣāsura and his demon army are able to gather strength and overthrow the gods just before aśvina, approximately one month before Viṣṇu awakens."[26] And it is this vulnerability that necessitates the embellishment of a principle of protection, manifest in both Goddess and king.

The perceived conundrum of the king's authority regarding his position within the world of *brāhmaṇic* sacrifice is nullified in the frame narrative of the DM, wherein the king accesses Durgā's power directly, sans *purohita*, for the purposes of reestablishing his rule. While earlier texts make clear the ruling power's (*kṣatra*'s) dependence upon the priestly power's consecration—e.g., *Bṛhadāraṇyaka Upaniṣad* 1.4.11, which, for Heesterman, renders ever at odds political (temporal) and spiritual power[27]—the DM delegates the role of ritualist to anyone who can invoke Durgā through steadfast and devout recitation of her glories, especially the king. It allows for a king to generate divine energy by performing his own rituals, and by undertaking his own austerities, in order to harness that energy for the sake of sovereignty. Here he assumes the garb of both *purohita* and ascetic; yet the DM necessarily pays homage to *brāhmaṇic* ideology furnishing the frame with a wise *brāhmaṇa* who provides requisite instruction to ritually invoke the Goddess. Nevertheless, in personifying power itself, and making that power available to all who invoke it through glorious praise, the tension between political and ritual power as manifest in the relationship between the king and the *brāhmaṇa purohita* is assuaged. The priest's potential monopoly on the manipulation of spiritual power (e.g., through rituals of royal consecration) is compromised by the king's capacity to directly access that realm of power personified by Durgā. It is she, and not the *brāhmaṇa*, who serves as the womb of royal power.

The Indian king: divine protector

Despite arguments against the divine character of the Indian king, it appears obvious that at least by the time of the epics, the godlike stature of the Indian king was taken for granted. Richards therefore notes:

> Most Indian rulers, Hindu, Jain, or even Buddhist, were accessible and visible to all groups within their kingdoms ... Every action, gesture, and speech of the ruler was an expression of ritual and symbolic significance, to be carefully observed and reported for its iconic reassurance of stability ... The question of divinity, or semi-divinity, or lack thereof, does not seem to have been as meaningful as long-drawn out historical debates imply, for all kings on the subcontinent possessed a numinous or sacral quality, however defined. The seasonal rains, fertility, prosperity, peace, and above all, the proper rank order of society could only be sustained in the presence of a king duly installed, and actively and wisely ruling.[28]

This might take on different hues, of course; for example, the King of Kāśī has been traditionally cast as the *regent* of Śiva. Yet, as J.C. Fuller notes, the (ultimately tentative) distinction between the king as a god and the king as a regent of god takes one only so far in the Indian contexts where the lines between human and divine are ultimately blurred, and the Mahārājā of Kāśī, in many contexts, is treated as Śiva himself. Insofar as power itself inspires awe, it might be considered innately "divine." Therefore the tendency to disambiguate between "secular" and "sacred" power need not apply. Also, the necessity of protection readily likens the function of supreme power on both the level of cosmos and society. If the kingdom is conceptualized as a microcosm of the universe, then he who holds power over the workings of that universe can be no less than godlike. Gonda remarks, for example, that "it is worth noticing that the term *prāsāda*—which has the widest application to denote the temple as the seat and dwelling of divine power, is also used in the sense of residence of a king."[29] Yet the "divinity" of the king need not remotely suggest monopoly, for the king of his neighboring kingdom, along with the holy men stationed within his kingdom, might all be considered equally divine.

It seems likely that the power accompanying the *office* of the king alone would warrant reverence of the one holding that power. Yet Sheldon Pollock cautions:

> the dichotomy between king and kingship finds little support in Indian epic texts. The notion itself is a juristic concept belonging primarily to the European medieval period, which we have little warrant to transpose to South Asia in the first millennium before the common era.[30]

His point regarding the projection of alien conceptualization is well taken; yet perhaps one can arrive at the same destination through means of different cultural routes. Correlate concepts might exist cross-culturally, expressed in different manners; and so the notion that sovereignty itself is a divine office may well resonate in the Indian context, though through use of an alternate conceptual lexicon. While at face value the absence of a dichotomy between king and kingship might be said to apply to *itihāsa* literature in general, one might argue that the personification of the feminine power all too necessary for the functioning of the king (as an embodiment of *śakti* in the abstract) might correlate to the de facto power assumed by him, which transcends the duration of his specific reign: upon his demise, that Śakti of kingship shall accompany another king. Perhaps the most common such faces of royal power itself take form in the goddess Lakṣmī. Similarly, that Śakti simultaneously accompanies multiple kings. It represents the state of power-holding which we might readily correlate to sovereignty itself. The DM presents us with an emphatic articulation of sovereignty-securing feminine power. Regarding the *Vālmīki Rāmāyaṇa* in particular (to which Pollock confined his comment), Phyllis Herman argues for the prevalence of feminine power as key to ideal kingship running through the mythologies of Rāma, Pṛthu, and Indra.[31]

The divinity of the king is clear in *itihāsa* literature insofar as he is said to be composed of the energies of various gods: for example, he is made up of Indra, Vāyu, Yama, Āditya, Agni, Varuṇa, Soma, and Kubera according to Manu (7.4–7) and Agni, Āditya, Mṛtyu, Vaiśravaṇa, and Yama according to the MBh (12.68.41). MkP chapter 27 contains discourse on kingship, placed in the mouth of Queen Madālasā who schools her fourth child (and heir to the throne, since the first three have renounced), Alarka. The section is discussed by Jagdish Lal Shastri, Beni Prasad, and U.N. Ghoshal who outlines that, according to these teachings, the king was to emulate five (of the eight) deities, namely Indra, Sun, Yama, Moon, and Wind. Ghoshal also notes the king's penchant for protection, and principles of government which commence with self-restraint. Furthermore, when the puzzled Yudhiṣṭhira asked how it could be that one mortal man may hold authority over others, the wise Bhīṣma answered that there is only one reason for this: his divinity (MBh 12.59.131). His necessity to the cosmic welfare is a paramount aspect of his function. Take, for example, the account of the legendary king Vena who, though unrighteous (banning sacrifice and thus disrupting the cosmic order), was nevertheless cast as essential to his abode, which was reduced to waste and ruin once he was put to death by holy men.[32]

Despite the absence of consensus on the nature of Indian kingship, the sources *unanimously* agree that kings are necessary for "the protection of the people through the maintenance of moral order."[33] This component of Indian kingship has endured across a vast span of time and cultural transformations, and rightfully so: protection is a human need, not a cultural construct. Given that the *Ṛg Veda* was produced by a nomadic culture, it stands to reason that the king was conceived at this early stage as a protector of people (*nṛ-pati*), rather than a protector of the land (*bhū-pati*). Regardless of whether one places ultimate authority with *brāhmaṇa* or ascetics, they are both dependent upon the king for protection. Pollock writes: "But what is the core of rajadharma? 'The age-old dharma of kings consists of protection, and it is this that maintains the world itself' (57.4278; cf. 32.2). The king provides security, to brahmans and ascetics in particular."[34] Protection is bar none the most crucial, and most pervasive, aspect of Indian kingship. The MBh, for example, states that "a priest without knowledge and a king without protecting power are but wooden elephants,"[35] and furthermore that

> [t]here is no need for such a man on the throne; he is like a eunuch or a barren field, or like a cloud that does not pour rain. But the person who always protects the good and checks the wicked deserves to become a king and to govern the world. For if the king does not observe the duty of protection, ruin would befall everything, no property would be safe, unrighteousness would prevail, everything would be destroyed untimely, the Vedas and morality would disappear, sacrifices would no longer be celebrated, in short society itself would cease to exist.[36]

If we understand the protective aspect of the king itself to be godlike, insofar as gods are invoked for the sake of protection, then we must submit that the conception of rulership in the Indian context is necessarily implicated in Indian conceptions of divinity. Sheldon Pollock, for example, writes: "The king is functionally a god because like a god he saves and protects; he is existentially, ontologically a god because he incorporates the divine essence."[37] The king's godlike power to protect is implicated in his ontological derivation, said to be from the essence of the gods in Manu. Gonda therefore takes Manu's account as representative of the divinity of the Indian king in general, according to which the king was created from "eternal and essential particles of those eight *devas* who are grouped as 'guardians of the world' (*loka-pāla*), and as such are—in post-Vedic times, it is true—believed to protect the eight main points of the universe."[38] The general significance of this origin lies in the indelible association of the office of the Indian king with the protection of the people. As Gonda notes:

> The ideal Indian ruler indeed was always considered a protector, a herdsman of the people, a *nṛpa*, *bhūpa-*, *bhūpāla-*, a *gopā-janasya*. Protecting the people, i.e. meeting external aggression, administering justice, and saving the country from calamities, is the very reason of the king's existence. The better the king, the greater his power to protect. It is in harmony with his important function that he is depicted as physically strong.[39]

He also writes:

> It is of course no matter of indifference that is these main gods, protectors par excellence, whose essence constitutes his majesty (*pratāpa-*). These divinities very significantly represent those functions and activities which are

> the essential characteristics of kingship. Manu himself already observed that the king like the sun, burns (*tapati*) eyes and hearts, "nor," he adds, "can anybody on earth even gaze on him": the Sun indeed shines, dispels the darkness and its beings; he is the "lord of eyes," all seeing and the spy (or witness) of the whole world. Like a man of the military class the Sun slays. The earthly ruler has several qualifications and epithets in common with the great luminary: *pratāpa*—is, in the king, his majesty, brilliance or energy, in the sun, the glowing heat or brilliance; the adjective *pratāpin*—means "burning, scorching" as well as "glowing, shining; splendid, powerful, majestic."[40]

There is also rich symbolic import to be derived from the specific functions of these eight world-protectors, namely Sun, Moon, Fire, Wind, Yama, Kubera, Varuṇa, and Indra. The Sun represents the innate majesty and might of the king. Note that the solar energy, while impressive to be sure, is not necessarily pleasant. It is a burning energy, which cannot be gazed at directly. The same can be said of his association with Fire, who burns and purifies all, itself an emblem of divine purity. Indeed, "... like the sun among the gods in the celestial regions which destroys darkness by its *tejas* (brilliance-and-energy), the king (among men) eradicates sin from the earth."[41] The symbolism of the sun is unsurprisingly as rich as it is prominent in the king's divine portfolio. Gonda writes,

> [l]ike the sun the king dispels the beings of darkness, and slays enemies. He outshines all rivals in wealth and splendor. Like the sun he possesses *pratāpa*—and *tejas*, the supranormal principle of might, which enables him to perform great exploits.[42]

Gonda further notes, "Famous kings are described as exceeding all beings in strength, outshining all the lustre (*tejas*), transcending all in majesty."[43] Scharfe similarly writes:

> When an Indian writer spoke of the "splendour" of his king, it was more than a figure of speech. Kings—just like the gods—were supposed to shine with an inner brilliance powered by their nature of light. The Indian king's brilliance is likened to that of the sun, (Footnote: Arjuna is as hard to look at in battle as the sun (Mbh I 1,83); similar Bhīmasena (MBh VI 19,33) and Kṛṣṇa (MBh VI 78,11).) and in classical poetry, the sharp light (*tejas*) indicates the decisiveness of the king's mind and of his actions. "The strength of the nobility is *tejas*" says MBh I 165,28. (Footnote: This decisiveness is incompatible with fury (*krodha*) which only clouds the mind and leads to disaster: MBh III 30, 16–21.) Indecisiveness and slothfulness are incompatible with being a good king.[44]

The association between *tejas* and sovereignty is harnessed in both the DM when Durgā emerges from the *tejas* of the gods in Episode II. This theme will be examined in greater detail in Chapter 4.

The king's lunar aspect, on the other hand, is mild (*saumya*), gentle, and fortuitous, responsible for plenty (especially vegetation), and it is ever-pleasing.[45] Both solar and lunar aspects are commingled in Indra, who represents raw vitality, and fertility-engendering rainfall all the while. Also, as Inden notes,

> If the king had a special connection with the earth, he also had a special connection with the sun or moon. These two, the "maker of the day" (*divākara*) and the "maker of the night" (*niśākara*), were considered powerful deities transcending the earth but having strong influences on it, especially in regard to the day, month, and the seasons. The *Purāṇas* in their accounts of the past classify India's kings as descended either from the sun or moon and most of the important dynasties of medieval India likewise claim solar or lunar origin. To have the substances of the sun and moon in the bodies meant that kings too were powerful deities transcending the earth and were, like the sun and moon themselves, intimately involved in the regulation of the day, the month, and the year.

The "*Yama*" aspect of the king represents restraint, discipline, and punishment, as does his noose-wielding *Varuṇa* aspect, while *Kubera* signifies riches and material prosperity. The wind signifies the king's freedom to roam about the land, claiming it as his own through conquest. Just as wind fuels fire, so too does this aspect empower the king's intensity. Gonda notes that six of these eight world-protectors (with the exception of the Sun and the Moon) are referred to as kings in their own right. His emergence from their essence, like that of Durgā herself, testifies to the king's prime purpose: protection of the social sphere and the beings enmeshed in it, indeed protection of *pravṛtti dharma* itself.

Royal ideology in the *Devī Māhātmya*

The virtue of violence

The most overt expression of the kingship-asceticism tension revolves around the way in which each station relates to acts of violence. Violence is required of the *kṣatriya*, to whom concerns of governance and defense are entrusted. Ideally, *kṣatriyas* implement force for the protection of their subjects and the punishment of those who transgress the moral order, though of course expansion of territory is a sanctioned royal enterprise. Interestingly, the Indian king is also admonished in some classical texts as the devourer of his people, mentioned alongside calamities such as "floods, fires, and thieves."[46] And this negative portrayal does not necessarily apply only to the unrighteous variety of kings. Heesterman notes that the king's power of punishment is "not a purely secular one,"[47] drawing on the work of Robert Lingat to argue that "the king when inflicting punishment equally fulfills the priestly function of purifying the evil-doer."[48] In addition to being understood as a means of protection for the righteous, the violence of Durgā might also be fruitfully understood as a means of punishing—and indeed purifying—the wicked.

Therefore, as particularly manifest in Episode III, the greater the demons' insistence on *adharma*, the greater the wrath of Durgā. Ariel Glucklich, in analyzing the myth of Daṇḍa, punishment incarnate, as it occurs in the Rāmāyaṇa, notes that

> the key features of Daṇḍa's mythological personality and function seem to crystalize most clearly at their point of intersection with those of the ferocious goddess—Durgā or Kālī. Of the numerous shared characteristics I will discuss only a few prominent ones.[49]

Those include an association with the Vindhyas, and the exhibition of "*non-āryan*" traits such as drinking liquor, repulsive appearance, dark complexion, and red eyes. Irrespective of whether the mythology of Daṇḍa was devised to embellish the mythology of Durgā or vice versa, the association between the two is unmistakable. This bespeaks an understanding of Durgā's wrath as a manifestation of her penchant to punish transgression.

While violence is necessary for protection and punishment, it is forbidden for *brāhmaṇas*, who preserve and propagate the ritual and intellectual spheres of religiosity, often conflated with the figure of the self-composed sage. The symbiosis between these ideals is clear: the ascetic, in pursuit of moral perfection, guards the ethical precept of nonviolence, while the king guards the earth upon which this pursuit necessarily occurs. The *kṣatriya* might be viewed as overall emblematic of political power while the *brāhmaṇa* might be understood to represent spiritual power. One would think that the fact that the supreme spiritual entity of the DM predominantly engages in the bloody business of the *kṣatriya*[50] would trouble the *brāhmaṇa-kṣatriya* caste ranking, yet acts of violence do not so much sully Durgā's hands (rendering her in any way inferior to the nonviolent sage who relays her exploits, for example), but rather serve to elevate the work of warriors to a supreme status. Our text safeguards the enterprise of the king from being subordinated to meeker otherworldly aims, for the DM is compelled to paradoxically embrace both worldly and otherworldly ideals, kingship and asceticism alike. Paradox is, after all, proper to her very nature. As Coburn notes: "The *Devī-māhātmya* is not given to systematic philosophical exposition, so it does not endeavour to resolve this paradox. Rather, it rejoices in it, for paradox is close to the heart of the *Devī-māhātmya's* vision of the Devī."[51]

The DM is extraordinary, not only insofar as it advances a powerful vision of a feminine divine, but particularly also because it synthesizes a vast range of Indic strands, such as motifs and concepts integral to Hindu tradition (e.g., *māyā*, *prakṛti*). I would argue that insofar as Durgā is *śakti*, power itself, nothing is beyond her grasp, and nothing is impossible; she possesses, for example, the *power* to represent both transcendence *and* immanence. As such, Durgā continues to be invoked by both Indian ascetics and Indian rulers for their respective aims, ideologically safeguarding the office of the king from *nivṛttic* ethical hegemony. Indeed, even her chastity—a virtue typically associated with *nivṛtti* religion—might be understood to function within her *pravṛttic* role as protective sovereign.

That the all-protective Durgā is ever chaste conforms with a motif prevailing in the discourse on Indian kings. Chastity is a means for a sovereign to augment his capacity, to provide protection and prosperity for his realm. According to the *Atharvaveda*, the consecrated (*abhiṣikta*) king protects the realm through *brahmacarya* and *tapas* (11.5.17), the ascetic practices proper to the Vedic *dīkṣita*.[52] Ascetic practice in general (and chastity in particular) is thought to benefit not only the king but also the kingdom over which he rules. Gonda therefore writes:

> In a sense a "priestly" or "spiritual" function of the monarch may be attributed to the activity ascribed to the king in the *Atharvaveda* [fn. AV. 11, 5, 17.]), where he is said to defend or protect the kingdom by *brahmacarya-*, i.e. study of the Veda, continence and chastity, and *tapas*, i.e. "asceticism." By the same means, the text continues, the gods warded off death. By *brahmacarya* alone Indra gained heaven for the gods. He who practices *brahmacarya* is Prajāpati, that is the god who "rules widely" (*vi-rāj-*), and the *virāj*—became the controlling Indra. The conclusion might be that the king, when practicing *brahmacarya*, identifies himself with the lord of creation, Prajāpati, bearing rule widely and becoming Indra.[53]

While the tension between the moral necessity for nonviolence and the sociopolitical necessity for violence is stringent and ongoing within the Hindu world, it poses no moral quandary within our text. Exempt from human moral imperatives, Hindu deities need not shirk from martial activity in the interest of retaining their ethical purity.[54] Like most Hindu representations of divinity, Durgā is not intended as a model for human conduct; one is not called to emulate her as one would say, Rāma, who represents ideal human conduct. The status of the Goddess is not one we can aspire after. We mortals are not ultimately comparable to the gods, or they to us.[55] The gods are not bound by the same ethical standards as humans for two reasons: first, evil actions do not incur negative karma for them; and second, they possess the requisite insight into the result of their actions in order to ascertain whether that action—however heinous—can be justified as *ultimately* good. Lacking this knowledge, we might kill one bank robber to save ten hostages (thinking it justifiable), remaining ignorant of the fact that one of those ten hostages will end up taking hundreds of lives. Yet had we possessed the requisite insight into the ultimate fruit of our action, we would have been able to make an informed decision.

In like fashion, sages (and *avatāras*) whose psychologies have been sufficiently extricated from the karmic play might, if inspired, act in a way that would appear wholly unethical to the eyes of the mundane. However, as with any child who has been told by his parent "do as I say and not as I do," while we may temporarily perceive hypocrisy and injustice, in time, with insight, we may ascend to a perspective enabling us to understand. It is noteworthy that deity worship arises from the ethos of *pravṛtti* religiosity and its Vedic antecedents, which know no universal, categorical ethics. Furthermore, keeping in line with the *pravṛttic* model, the gods are not subject to caste, life stage, and gender *dharmas*, hence their freedom to act of their own accord. Although humans, working within a *nivṛttic* model, might need to adhere to the categorical imperative of *ahiṃsā* in order to approach the supreme ontological reality, Durgā, who represents that reality, remains unfettered by human ethical constraints while fulfilling her cosmic purpose: protection of the universe.

Therefore, in the words of David Kinsley, Durgā is

> quite simply, invincibly powerful and accomplished in the martial arts and is clearly at home, perhaps most at home, when pulverizing powerful demons. Time and again it is the physical prowess of the Goddess that is insisted upon in the DM.[56]

It is precisely that prowess which allows her to accomplish the work of the gods, which is the purpose of her manifestation (DM 1.48). We are told that "[t]he queen released weapons and arms at the bodies of the Asuras,"[57] which invokes the necessary association of leadership and martial prowess so celebrated throughout the text.

Pravṛtti *pursuits in the* Devī Māhātmya

While Chapter 2 detailed the extent to which Durgā is seminal in the pursuit of final release from the cycle of rebirth, the DM presents a vision of divinity equally, if not more so, instrumental to the enjoyment of mundane existence. Medhas informs us that she grants prosperity, domestic wellness (DM 12.37), wealth, children, and "an auspicious mind, the pathway to *dharma*."[58] Given the nature of the aforementioned boons, one infers that Durgā paves the way for *pravṛtti dharma*; after all, she constitutes activity itself (DM 5.27), and her activity accounts for the existence of all worlds (DM 4.9b). The field of phenomenal activity, domain of *pravṛtti dharma*, is after all her very nature, and so she unsurprisingly strives to render contented the beings dwelling therein. Her glories in fact constitute the very means of procuring mortal contentedness. Durgā herself declares that from merely hearing her glories, one is endowed, through her grace, with wealth, grain, children (DM 12.11–12), and impeccable health (DM 12.20–21), and that "well-being prevails,/And his family rejoices."[59] The gods, too, sing her *pravṛttic* glories. They inform us that she grants humans repute, wealth, children, partners, servants, and all-round good fortune (DM 4.14); and that she constitutes human virtues such as intelligence, faith, and modesty, manifesting as prosperity within the virtuous (DM 4.4).

Medhas introduces Episode II, the central episode to the text wherein she slays Mahiṣa, by indicating that Durgā emerges from the bodies of the gods "desiring the well-being of the three worlds."[60] She is a bestower of boons upon the triple world;[61] indeed, when she grants the gods a boon at the end of Episode II (DM 4.29) (pleased by their praise when she slew Mahiṣa), the gods express their satisfaction having already had their enemy destroyed, asking only that she return to do so when they are afflicted in future, and further that mortals thus praising her might be granted wealth, wife, success, riches, prosperity, and power (DM 4.30–2). Upon being thus "graciously solicited by the gods both for their own well-being and for that of the world," Durgā consents to the bestowal of those boons.[62] When they again praise her at the end of Episode III, "their faces radiant, their desires made manifest,"[63] they appeal to her as "boon giver to the worlds,"[64] to which she responds by granting a boon, explicitly declaring: "I am indeed a boon giver, O you gods; the boon that you crave with your mind. Choose that: I grant benefaction to the worlds."[65] Durgā's penchant for support of mundane existence is apparent and unparalleled.

In addition to *pravṛttic* worldly enjoyments, Durgā grants the *pravṛttic* enjoyment of heaven. While the association of heaven and pleasure is taken for granted within Sanskrit narrative, the DM explicitly equates the two by having the gods praise Durgā "with heavenly flowers growing in Indra's pleasure garden."[66] The DM indicates at four junctures that Durgā grants heaven,[67] three of which coincide with the junctures wherein she grants *mokṣa*,[68] and therefore the soteriology of *nivṛtti* as endorsed within the text does not compromise the text's overt *pravṛttic* persuasion. The DM goes so far as to indicate that, through her grace, one might even be liberated "right here on earth."[69] While

> *Mokṣa* is unequivocally articulated as the final goal of *nivṛtti dharma*, Dhand notes that the *Mahābhārata*'s views of the content of *mokṣa* are still under construction. Is it achievable while still living? Where does one's body go when one achieves *mokṣa*?[70]

While such considerations continue to plague Hindu philosophers and theologians, it is unsurprising that the DM leaves room for the possibility of attaining liberation while still remaining on earth. Once the acts of the Devī have been relayed, the sage, in appealing to the king to worship Durgā, adds worldly enjoyments (DM 13.4) to the list of benefits, alongside heaven and *mokṣa*. He summarizes: "[p]ropitiated, she grants knowledge; delighted, she bestows prosperity."[71] She gives enjoyment, be it this-worldly, or otherworldly, and so in the end, the king enjoys sovereignty over the world, and then ascends to the cosmic sphere to enjoy sovereignty in his subsequent life as Manu Sāvarṇi.

Durgā does not only grant desires; when angered, she thwarts them (DM 11.28a), manifesting as misfortune for the sake of destruction (DM 12.37). Indeed, when her anger is incurred, she is capable of destroying entire "families in a trice."[72] Yet despite the fact that she is fully capable of manifesting as "great pestilence,"[73] one does not get the sense that this aspect of hers is whimsical, or ultimately cruel. For as she manifests as prosperity for the righteous, we are told that she manifests as misfortune for the wicked (DM 4.4). The DM's references to Durgā as misfortune dim in comparison to a much more prevalent aspect of her relation to her devotees: *pacification* of misfortune. Just as she rescues the gods from the forces of evil (DM 4.22), so too is she a refuge for the whole world (DM 4.6). Indeed, she is the rescuer of the entire triple world (DM 11.17); hence, when granted a boon at the end of Episode III, the gods declare "The pacification of all miseries in the triple world,/Let just that, and the destruction of our enemies, be accomplished by you."[74] She removes all suffering of those who resort to her (DM 11.2). The range of her pacification of misfortune is vast: she destroys all kinds of suffering (DM 4.9), from poverty, to misery, to fear (DM 4.16). She is intent upon rescuing the downtrodden and removing the suffering of all (DM 11.11), capable of pacifying all afflictions (DM 11.34), serving as a refuge to all from mundane calamity such as demons, serpents, enemies, thugs, fire, or flood (DM 11.31). And for this reason, the sage exclaims to the king, once he has relayed her glories, "O king, you should take refuge in her, the supreme queen."[75]

Pacification is bar none the greatest overall benefit of worshipping Durgā and she expresses as much, in her own voice, in the *phalaœruti* chapter. That pacification, of course, takes on many forms. She declares that uttering her glories in the DM yields the destruction of misfortune (DM 12.1), illness-born suffering (DM 12.7a), natural calamities (DM 12.7b), villainous enemies (DM 12.18a), and evil spirits (DM 12.18b). Similarly, from merely *hearing* a recitation of the DM, one receives relief from all affliction (DM 12.11–12): one acquires fearlessness (DM 12.13); one's enemies perish (DM 12.14); calamities and evil omens are destroyed (DM 12.16); one's "[c]hildren who have been seized by evil spirits become calm";[76] one's "broken relationships become mended";[77] and all of one's sins become eradicated (DM 12.21). One who merely *remembers* the acts of Durgā can attain relief from forest fire, ambush, enmity, wild animals (lions, tigers, elephants), unjust punishment (e.g., death sentence from a cruel king), bondage, a capsized boat, and even discharged weapons in the middle of battle. Indeed, one is released from "all terrible afflictions, or tormented with pain" through remembrance of the acts of Durgā.[78] It is clear that Durgā's penchant for pacification is simply unparalleled. Unsurprisingly, one finds echoes of this ability amid the idealized portfolio of the Indian king. Gonda notes:

> Traditions are not wanting in which the people beseech their ruler to rescue them from every grief and misery, from all pains and diseases. To quote a single instance of a successful reign: when Rāma was king, the epic narrates, no widow mourned; neither beasts or prey nor diseases were to be feared; there were no enemies; the younger generation did not die before the older; all men were delighted and observed the dharma; the trees, always flowering, bore fruits without interruptions; it rained when rain was desired; the wind was agreeable to the touch; everybody was content.[79]

As a populace might look to their ruler to pacify misfortune, so too would devotees look to Durgā for the same.

While pacification entails addressing suffering which has *already* begun to ripen, Durgā goes one step further: she benevolently guards against suffering which has yet to arrive. Indeed no accident shall befall one who preemptively resorts to Durgā (DM 11.28b). She declares that those who recite her glories are shielded from misfortune, whether in the form of poverty, separation from loved ones, enemies, villains, the government, weapons, fire, flood, or evil spirits; she safeguards against all types of affliction (DM 12.4–5). Durgā pledges to prevent and address the variegated forms of suffering which plague mortal beings, so that they might thrive *in the world.* Nowhere in the *phalaœruti* does she pledge release from the suffering that is *saṃsāric* existence itself, for doing so would undermine her profound willingness and ability to assist her children in coping with life, however wretched or futile it might be from the perspective of *nivṛtti.* In short, Durgā is protectress without equal.

The protection of dharma, *the* dharma *of protection*

The capacity to protect the righteous in the face of menacing evil is arguably Durgā's prime function. While in the *Brahmā Stuti*, as Brahmā hymns her tripartite nature as universal creator, protector, and destroyer (DM 1.57), the DM places by far the greatest emphasis upon her protective function (DM 1.56). For example, the gods address Durgā in the *Nārāyaṇi Stuti* with the vocative, *œaraṇye* (protectress) (DM 11.9), and also hymn her as protectress of all (DM 11.31–2). Furthermore on four occasions, the gods employ third-person imperative verbal forms to seek protection for the world and for themselves, as follows:

> May she, Caṇḍikā, fix her mind on the protection of the entire world, and on the destruction of the fear of evil.
>
> (DM 4.3b)[80]

> That fearsome trident, terrible with flames, laying waste the Asuras without remainder,
> May that trident protect us from danger; O Bhadrakālī, praise be to you!
>
> (DM 11.25)[81]

> That bell that destroys demonic splendors, having filled the world with its sound,
> May that bell, O Goddess, protect us from evils as if we were children.
>
> (DM 11.26)[82]

> That sword of yours, smeared with mud and the blood and fat of Asuras, gleaming with rays,
> May that sword be for our welfare; O Caṇḍikā, we are bowed down to you!
>
> (DM 11.27)[83]

More directly, they employ second-person imperative singular verbal forms at numerous junctures in order to beseech Durgā's protection as follows:

> Protect the universe, O Goddess!
>
> (DM 4.4)[84]

With (your) spear protect us, O Goddess! And with (your) sword protect (us), O mbikā! Protect us with the sound of (your) bell, and with the twang of your bowstring!

(DM 4.23)[85]

In the east protect (us) and in the west, O Candikā; protect (us) in the south
By the wielding of your spear, likewise in the north, O queen.

(DM 4.24)[86]

Protect us, and also the earth.

(DM 4.25)[87]

And with the weapons, O Ambikā, sword, and spear, and club, and the rest,
Which lie in your sprout-like hands, protect (us) on every side.

(DM 4.26)[88]

Protect us from dangers, O Goddess.

(DM 11.23)[89]

Protect us from all ghosts.

(DM 11.24)[90]

O Goddess, be gracious: protect us always from the fear of enemies, just as you have now promptly saved us from bondage by the Asuras.

(DM 11.33)[91]

Immediately prior to the *phalaœruti* section, Durgā promises to guard the world against future calamity. In addition to slaying another set of demons named Śumbha and Niśumbha and Vaipracitta demons (DM 11.37), she prophesies:

Once again, when there has been no rain, no water, on earth for a hundred years,/Then, remembered by sages, I will come into being without being born from a womb./Since I will look at the sages with a hundred eyes,/ Human beings will then praise me as "Hundred-eyes" *(śatakṣī).*/Then I shall support the entire world with life sustaining vegetables,/Produced from my own body, until the rains come, O gods./In this way, I will attain fame on earth under the name "She-who-supports-with-vegetables" *(śākaṃbharī).*/ There I will slay the great Asura named Durgama./Thus, my name will come to be renowned as "the Goddess Durgā."/And when I have again taken on fearsome form in the Himālayas,/I will destroy demons for the sake of protecting sages./Then all the sages will lower their bodies to me in praise./ My name will become famous as "the fearsome goddess" *(bhīmādevī).*/When a demon named Aruṇa shall do a lot of killing in the three worlds,/Then I, taking on bee-form, consisting of innumerable bees,/Will slay the great demon for the well-being of the triple world./Then people everywhere will

> praise me as "Queen-bee" *(bhrāmarī)*./In this way, whenever there is trouble produced by demons,/Then taking on bodily form, I will bring about the destruction of enemies.[92]

She thus protects from natural disasters, feeding the world with her very body when need be. This again corresponds to what Gonda notes of the Indian king: that "one of his first responsibilities was to see that the people were fed, not by making 'social laws,' but by bringing fertility to the fields."[93] Implicated in protection is the capacity to sustain, to generally support. Durgā is therefore lauded as a source of support throughout the DM. The gods variously praise her as follows: "The incomparable queen of all, supportress of the world, who causes its maintenance and destruction" (DM 1.53a);[94] "by you is everything supported" (DM 1.56);[95] "supportress of the world" (DM 4.27);[96] "To the eternal Gaurī, the supportress, hail!" (DM 5.8);[97] "Hail to the support of the world" (DM 5.11);[98] "You have become the sole support of the world" (DM 11.3);[99] "O queen of all, you protect all; having all for your very soul, you are said to support all" (DM 11.32).[100] Moreover, Medhas reiterates this aspect upon concluding his tripartite account of her acts: "She, the eternal, provides support for what is created" (DM 12.36).[101]

Durgā's manifold blessings can be understood as functions of her protective power: she safeguards well-being itself (DM 12.6). Her capacity to protect is unrivalled. The prevalence of discourse on Durgā's supreme protective capacity is heightened by the manner in which the sage frames her exploits. He begins thus:

> On another occasion she came to be born (from) the body of Gaurī/For the sake of destroying the wicked Daityas Śumbha and Niśumbha,/And *for the sake of protecting the worlds* (as the) benefactress of the gods./Hear this story (now) related by me. I will tell it to you properly.
>
> (DM 4.35–6)[102]

Similarly, at the end of the acts of Durgā proper, Medhas states to the king: "Just in this fashion does the blessed Goddess, even though she is eternal,/*Provide protection for the world*, O king, by coming into being again and again" (DM 12.33).[103] Protection is not only the very purpose of her manifestation, it is the *sine qua non* of the Indian sovereignty, whose function Durgā fulfills on the cosmic level.

Protection is not only the *sine qua non* of Durgā, but also the *sine qua non* of the Indian king, present from the earliest known constructs of Indian kingship. Given that protection is the very purpose for the king on the mundane level, would the protector of the universe not be likened to a universal sovereign? Furthermore, if a king is a king because he protects people, then Durgā is sovereign of kings insofar as she protects *them*. Therefore in the same breath, the gods associate her sovereignty with her capacity to protect: "Be gracious, O queen of all, protect all; you are the queen, O Goddess, of all that does and does not move."[104] As Coburn notes, the DM's second episode "establishes the earthly career of the [Goddess] as the supreme ruler of all creatures, and in order to portray her in this role, the DM draws on the classical Indian model of kingship."[105] She is, without doubt, a queen.

Durgā is undeniably associated with sovereignty: Brahmā lauds her as "the incomparable queen of all, supportress of the world, who causes its maintenance and destruction."[106] Similarly, the gods unambiguously declare to Durgā, "you are the queen" (*īśvarī*).[107] She is referred to as *īśvarī*, "powerful, competent, sovereign, the queen,"[108] on five occasions: once in each of the four hymns, and again while she is combatting Mahiṣa. Medhas introduced her to the king as *sarveśvareśvarī*, "sovereign of all sovereigns."[109] Similarly, Durgā is referred to as Īśā, "the queen, the powerful one, she who rules,"[110] on three occasions in the DM;[111] for example, "queen of all … protect us from dangers, O Goddess; O Goddess Durgā, praise be to you!"[112] She is referred to as "supreme queen" (*parameūvarī*) on four occasions,[113] and "queen of all" (*viūveūvarī*) on three occasions.[114] She is also referred to as Śrī/Lakṣmī,[115] and explicitly referred to as "Lakṣmī of kings."[116] The sage prefaces Episode II by declaring: "Hear again of the majesty [*prabhāva*] of this Goddess."[117] Insofar as she is concerned with the protection of the collective, she is a de facto sovereign, for protection is sovereignty's raison d'être.

The model reader of the DM infers that Suratha is a righteous king based upon the sole description of his capacity to rule provided therein: he was removed from his post "while he was protecting all creatures well, like his own sons."[118] Note the parity between sovereignty and parenthood: protection might also be understood as a *sine qua non* of parenthood, which only serves to enrich the extent to which Queen Durgā is hailed as the "mother of the entire world."[119] The gods in fact explicitly request to be protected, as if they were children (DM 11.26). Just as she protects the cosmic order, and the gods themselves, the king protects the mundane order, and human beings along with it. As with Suratha, there are always others in the vicinity of the forest-exiled king whom he is called to protect. And for this reason, violence is the *justifiable sine qua non* of the Indian king even while in the forest. He proudly wields his weapon there, as paragon of *pravṛtti dharma*, affirming the paramount nature of that *dharma* without which all *dharma*, including *nivṛtti*, would be imperiled.

Violence is a virtue of kingship, and a virtue, too, of the royal Goddess of the DM. It is in light of this association that the gods declare that she is "worthy of praise by all who exercise power [since] those who bow down in devotion to you, they become the refuge of all."[120] This sentiment not only foreshadows the king's worship of her to restore his sovereignty but harkens to the descriptor that piques Suratha's interest in hearing more about her: "she is indeed the queen (governing) all who have power."[121] Those who exercise worldly power should invoke Queen Durgā, for they function as refuge to others on the mundane level, as does she on the cosmic level. The imperiled are at the heart of Indian kings, insofar as they are responsible for safeguarding those in danger. However, what happens when the king or his office is imperiled? Being the refuge of all others, the mundane sovereign, by definition, lacks a refuge of his own; so when imperiled, he may seek refuge in his divine counterpart, that royal Goddess who serves as the refuge of kings: it is she who protects those who protect. The logic behind the creation of such a Goddess is very much ensconced in the need for kings themselves to be protected against greater forces, whether in the form of natural disasters, internal strife, or foreign powers. Queen Durgā, though protectress without equal, does not function as a sovereign with respect to ongoing governance, for she does not occupy a throne, per se; she periodically appears when the throne is imperiled, striving to safeguard it for its rightful occupant, protecting those who protect the welfare of the world. In so doing she *violently* safeguards the very *violence*-dependent ideology of *pravṛtti* from subordination to nonviolent nivṛtti idealism. She thus reorients the *brāhmaṇic* double helix so as to sanction its blood-soaked strand. Hence the DM is not only framed by an encounter between a forest-dwelling ascetic and a deposed king, but culminates in the restoration of that king's power through the blood-soaked grace of the Goddess.

Returning to the overarching methodology of this study, we have now applied our first, ideologically oriented, interpretational tool in grappling with the DM, specifically the thematic double helix at the heart of Hinduism, interlacing royal and ascetic ideologies. In doing so, we have reached a tentative answer as to the rationale behind the work's enframement: Durgā is a royal figure, and in what better manner might the acts of this royal Goddess be framed than by a forest-exiled king whose throne is returned because of her grace? Yet, Queen Durgā's sanctified sanguinary leanings notwithstanding, given that she ultimately grants *two* boons, can we be certain that the DM doesn't *equally* advocate ascetic and royal ideologies? To corroborate our conclusion based on the *content* of the DM, we turn in the following chapter to our second interpretational tool: examination of the work's *form*, specifically of its narrative ring structure.

Notes

1 Heesterman, "The Conundrum of the King's Authority," 13.
2 E.g., Upendra Nath Ghoshal, *A History of Indian Political Ideas: The Ancient Period and the Period of Transition to the Middle Ages* (London: Oxford University Press, 1966); Upendra Nath Ghoshal, "Kingship and Kingly Administration in the Atharva Veda," *Indian Historical Quarterly* 20 (1944): 105–13; Upendra Nath Ghoshal, "Kingship in the Rgveda," *Indian Historical Quarterly* 20 (1944): 36–42; Upendra Nath Ghoshal, "King's Executive Administration in the Dharmasutras," *The Indian Historical Quarterly* 21 (1945): 288–93.
3 Heesterman, "The Conundrum of the King's Authority," 14.
4 Heesterman, 16.
5 J.C. Heesterman, *The Inner Conflict of Tradition: Essays in Indian Ritual, Kingship, and Society* (Chicago, IL: University of Chicago Press, 1985), 12.
6 Heesterman, *The Inner Conflict of Tradition.*
7 Heesterman, 41–2.
8 He writes,

> This does not mean, of course, that the actual *brahmin* is necessarily a renouncer; usually he is not. But it is the ideal image of the *brahmin* that the mainspring of

> *brahmanical* prestige. *Brahminization* (I prefer this term to Sanskritization) is therefore not simply the imitation of the local *brahmin*; it refers to the ideal *brahmin*. The non-*brahmin* is thus enabled to 'out-*brahmin*' the *brahmin*. To a great extent, this may be the ideological background of "anti-*brahminical*" movement past as well as present.
>
> Heesterman, 44

9 Louis Dumont, "Kingship in Ancient India," *Contributions to Indian Sociology* 6 (1962): 48–77. Esp. 52 and 54.
10 Heesterman, *The Inner Conflict of Tradition*, 150.
11 Heesterman, 150.
12 Heesterman, 150.
13 Johannes Cornelis Heesterman, *The Ancient Indian Royal Consecration: The Rājasūya Described According to the Yajus Texts and Annotated* ('s-Gravenhage: Mouton, 1957).
14 Heesterman, *The Inner Conflict of Tradition*, 44.
15 Heesterman, "The Conundrum of the King's Authority," 33.
16 Ronald Inden, *Imagining India* (Oxford; Cambridge, MA: Basil Blackwell, 1990), 201.
17 Basham International Congress of Human Sciences in Asia and North Africa. A.L. and Colegio de México, eds., *Kingship in Asia and Early America: XXX International Congress of Human Sciences in Asia and North Africa* (México, D.F.: Colegio de México, 1981), 115.
18 Heesterman, "The Conundrum of the King's Authority," 26.
19 Ronald Inden, "Ritual, Authority, and Cyclic Time in Hindu Kingship," in *Kingship and Authority in South Asia*, ed. John F. Richards (Delhi; New York: Oxford University Press, 1998).
20 Inden.
21 Ronald Inden, "Kings and Omens," in *Purity and Auspiciousness in Indian Society*, ed. John Braisted Carman and Frédérique Apffel-Marglin (Leiden: E.J. Brill, 1985), 31.
22 Inden, "Ritual, Authority, and Cyclic Time in Hindu Kingship," 42–3.
23 Inden, 46–7.
24 DM 1.3: *suratho nāma rājābhūt samaste kṣitimaṇḍale* ||.
25 Inden, "Ritual, Authority, and Cyclic Time in Hindu Kingship," 81–2.
26 Christopher John Fuller, ed., *The Camphor Flame: Popular Hinduism and Society in India* (Princeton, NJ: Princeton University Press, 2004), 110.
27 Heesterman, *The Inner Conflict of Tradition*, 141.
28 John F. Richards, ed., "Introduction," in *Kingship and Authority in South Asia* (Delhi; New York: Oxford University Press, 1998), 2.
29 Jan Gonda, *Ancient Indian Kingship from the Religious Point of View* (Leiden: Brill, 1969), 54.
30 Sheldon Pollock, "The Divine King in the Indian Epic," *Journal of the American Oriental Society* 104, no. 3 (July 1, 1984): 524.
31 Phyllis Kaplan Herman, "Ideal Kingship and the Feminine Power: A Study of the Depiction of Rāmarājya in the Vālmīki Ramāyana," 1979, 210–11.
32 Viṣṇu Purāṇa 1.3.16–18, cited in: Heesterman, "The Conundrum of the King's Authority," 15.
33 Heesterman, 14.
34 Pollock, "The Divine King in the Indian Epic," 525.
35 MBh 12.78.41. Gonda, *Ancient Indian Kingship from the Religious Point of View*, 3.
36 MBh 12.68.10 Gonda, 3.
37 Pollock, "The Divine King in the Indian Epic," 524.
38 Gonda, *Ancient Indian Kingship from the Religious Point of View*, 172.

39 Gonda, 172.
40 Gonda, 25–6.
41 Gonda, *Ancient Indian Kingship from the Religious Point of View*.
42 Gonda, 26.
43 Gonda, 5.
44 Hartmut Scharfe, *The State in Indian Tradition* (Leiden; New York: E.J. Brill, 1989), 34.
45 Gonda, *Ancient Indian Kingship from the Religious Point of View*, 172–3.
46 Heesterman, "The Conundrum of the King's Authority," 15.
47 R. Lingat, op. cit., 260–2.
48 R. Lingat, op. cit., 260–2.
49 Ariel Glucklich, "The Royal Scepter ('Danda') as Legal Punishment and Sacred Symbol," *History of Religions* 28, no. 2 (1988): 119.
50 As Kinsley remarks, "by far the most dramatic and sustained characteristic of the Goddess as portrayed in the DM is her prowess as a warrior." Kinsley, "The Portrait of the Goddess in the Devī Māhātmya," 492.
51 Coburn, "Consort of None, Śakti of All: The Vision of the Devī-Māhātmya," 155.
52 Heesterman, "The Conundrum of the King's Authority," 15.
53 Gonda, *Ancient Indian Kingship from the Religious Point of View*, 71.
54 Yet not all deities engage in combat. Brahmā is the nonviolent one among the *Trimūrtī*, yet arguably it is Viṣṇu and Śiva who attract followings *because* they are able to defend and protect in times of need. They even protect Brahmā when he is imperiled. It would be scandalous if Brahmā were to take arms. The question becomes whether the *sattva* inherent in their functions renders them "more pure" than deities who shed blood.
55 While one may readily agree with the notion that Hindu gods are "a class of beings by definition totally different from any other; they are symbols in a way that no human being … can ever be" (Doniger, *Hindu Myths*, 19–20), one must qualify that the Hindu gods of course possess qualities and aspects which humans are clearly expected to emulate.
56 Kinsley, "The Portrait of the Goddess in the Devī Māhātmya," 493.
57 Coburn, *Encountering the Goddess*, 43. DM 2.50a: *mumocāsuradeheṣu śastrāṇyastrāṇi ceśvarī* |.
58 DM 12.38. Coburn, 82.
59 DM 12.14. Coburn, 80.
60 DM 4.34. Coburn, 52.
61 In the *Śakrādi Stuti*, the gods address the Goddess thus: "Goddess, who bestow boons even upon the triple world." Coburn, 50. (DM 4.21: *devi varade bhuvanatraye 'pi*.) Similarly, earlier in the hymn, they pose the rhetorical question: "are you not thus the bestower of rewards on the three worlds, O Goddess?" Coburn, 50. (DM 4.15: *lokatraye 'pi phaladā nanu devi tena*.)
62 DM 4.33. "Thus graciously solicited by the gods both for their own well-being and for that of the world,/Having said, 'I consent,' Bhadrakālī disappeared, O king." Coburn, *Encountering the Goddess*, 52.
63 DM 11.1. Coburn, 73.
64 DM 11.34. Coburn, 77.
65 DM 11.35. Coburn, 77.
66 DM 4.27. Coburn, 51.
67 DM 4.15; DM 11.6; DM 11.7; 13.4.
68 The *mokṣa* junctures are DM 11.6, DM 11.7, DM 13.4, and DM 4.8. The sole passage where liberation is mentioned without being directly accompanied by *mokṣa* is DM 4.8, during the *Śakrādi Stuti*. This hymn is treated in "The Measure of Multiplicity: Episodic Expansion in the *Devī Māhātmya*."
69 DM 11.4. Coburn, *Encountering the Goddess*, 74.

70 Dhand, *Woman as Fire, Woman as Sage Sexual Ideology in the Mahābhārata*, 34.
71 DM 12.34. Coburn, *Encountering the Goddess*, 82.
72 DM 4.13. Coburn, 49.
73 DM 12.36. Coburn, 82.
74 DM 11.36. Coburn, 77.
75 DM 13.3b. Coburn, 82.
76 DM 12.17a. Coburn, 80.
77 DM 12.17b. Coburn, 80.
78 DM 12.24b–12.29a. Coburn, 81.
79 Gonda, *Ancient Indian Kingship from the Religious Point of View*, 10–11.
80 Coburn, *Encountering the Goddess*, 48.
81 Coburn, 76.
82 Coburn, 76.
83 Coburn, 76.
84 Coburn, 48.
85 Coburn, 50.
86 Coburn, 51.
87 Coburn, 51.
88 Coburn, 51.
89 Coburn, 76.
90 Coburn, 76.
91 Coburn, 77.
92 Coburn, 78. DM 11.42–51.
93 Gonda, *Ancient Indian Kingship from the Religious Point of View*, 68.
94 Coburn, *Encountering the Goddess*, 36.
95 Coburn, 37.
96 Coburn, 51.
97 Coburn, 53.
98 Coburn, 53.
99 Coburn, 74.
100 Coburn, 77.
101 Coburn, 82.
102 Coburn, 52.
103 Coburn, 82. Emphasis my own.
104 DM 11.2. Coburn, 74.
105 Coburn, "Devi: The Great Goddess," 39.
106 DM 1.53. Coburn, *Encountering the Goddess*, 36.
107 DM 1.60: *tvaṃ śrīs tvam īśvarī tvaṃ hrīs tvaṃ buddhir bodhalakṣaṇā* | *lajjā puṣṭis tathā tuṣṭis tvaṃ śāntiḥ kṣāntir eva ca* || "You are *śrī*, you are the queen, you modesty, you intelligence, characterized by knowing;/Modesty, well-being, contentment, too, tranquillity and forbearance are you." Coburn, 37. Īśvarī is a very significant designation in the DM since it indicates her supreme form on five occasions in the DM. Four of these junctures (1.60, 4,24, 5.35, and 11.22) appear in hymns, while one of them (2.50) appears in the climax of Episode II, in the midst of the battle between the Goddess and Mahiṣa. While Coburn notes that the antecedents of this epithet are modest, he suspects the earliest occurrence of Īśvarī to be in the Śrī Suktam RVK 2.6.9, echoed in TA 10.1: "*īśvarī sarvabhūtānām*," queen of all creatures. See Coburn, *Devī-Māhātmya*, 138–9. Furthermore, "*iśvarī*" is constitutive of the compounds parameśvarī, viśveśvarī, and maheśvarī. While the first two refer to the Goddess in her supreme form, Maheśvarī refers to one of the seven mothers (*saptamātṛkā*), occurring five times in Episode III. See Coburn, 144–5.
108 Coburn, *Devī-Māhātmya: The Crystallization of the Goddess Tradition*, 138.
109 DM 1.44: *sā vidyā paramā mukter hetubhūtā sanātanī* | *saṃsārabandhahetuś ca saiva sarveśvareśvarī* || "She is the supreme, eternal knowledge that becomes the

cause of release/From bondage to mundane life; she is indeed the queen (governing) all who have power." Coburn, *Encountering the Goddess*, 35.

110 Coburn, 176.

111 All three of these occasions occur in the final episode, and during hymns: 5.36, 11.21,22. See Coburn, 176. Its abstract noun counterpart, *īśā*, connotes "capacity, dominion, lordship." Coburn, 176.

112 DM 11.23. Coburn, *Encountering the Goddess*, 76.

113 This epithet occurs once in the Brahmāstuti hymn in Episode I (1.62); once in Episode II during the slaying of Mahiṣa's hordes (3.18); and twice in Episode III: once in combatting Śumbha (10.9), and once when the sage advises the king and merchant to take refuge in her (13.3). See Coburn, 163.

114 This epithet occurs once in Episode I (1.53) and twice in Episode III (11.2, 11.31). Coburn indicates that it emphasizes the Goddess's protective role, e.g., 11.2 indicates that she protects all because she is mother of all (mātṛ jagato 'khilasya) and 11.31 indicates she protects all because she has all for her very soul (viśvātmikā). Coburn notes that "the epithet thus links two rather different notions of protectiveness, the maternal and the mighty" (Coburn, *Devī-Māhātmya*, 198), and I would argue that it is precisely protectiveness which serves as the *sine qua non* of the Goddess, whereby she might be likened to parent and sovereign alike.

115 Śrī occurs once in Episode I and twice in Episode II as follows: DM 1.60, Coburn, *Encountering the Goddess*, 37. DM 4.4 Coburn, 48. DM 4.10: Coburn, 49. Lakṣmī occurs on two: firstly, DM 5.26 Coburn, 54. Secondly, it is compounded in 5.9 to refer to "Lakṣmī of Kings" (see the following note). Coburn, *Devī-Māhātmya*, 157.

116 DM 5.9. Coburn, *Encountering the Goddess*, 53.

117 DM 1.78b. Coburn, 39.

118 DM 1.4a: tasya pālayataḥ samyak prajāḥ putrānivaurasān | "While he was protecting all creatures well, like his own sons," Coburn, 32.

119 DM 11.2. Coburn, 74.

120 DM 11.32. Coburn, 77.

121 DM 1.44. Coburn, 35.

4 Reading the ring

Focusing the frame of the *Devī Māhātmya*

The narrative resolution of the DM is bifurcated so as to address the concerns of both *pravṛtti* and *nivṛtti* religion alike. In the end, the king and the merchant, having been told of the grandeur of the Goddess by sage Medhas, intensely worship her for three whole years. Their devotion earns them a vision of Durgā wherein she offers them each a boon of their choosing. As per their respective propensities, they request divergent boons and Durgā accordingly blesses the king with supreme worldly power and the merchant with supreme otherworldly knowledge, resulting in release from *saṃsāra*. Therefore, though the DM's frame entails the tale of a king regaining his sovereign power through the grace of Durgā, it also chronicles the fate of a merchant who, equally through her grace, attains emancipation from the cycle of rebirth. His liberation serves as the apex of the text's *nivṛttic* themes, as the king's victory bespeaks the text's homage to *pravṛtti*. The DM thus masterfully interweaves both royal and ascetic ideals. It valorizes the violent duty of kings, to be sure, but without forsaking the nonviolent ideals of asceticism. Hence, in order to preserve the *brāhmaṇic* double helix, Durgā must, in the end, bestow two boons: sovereignty to the king, and liberation to his merchant companion, Samādhi.

The parity between Goddess and sovereign in the DM is unmistakable, yet the text celebrates this parity upholding in tandem ascetic ideals. The preservation of this tension should come as no surprise since the religious tradition which has preserved this text for fifteen centuries is one which esteems an ideology of final release from the cycle of rebirth, lauding those brave *nivṛttic* virtuosos who stoically eschew the delights of the world in order to pursue final release from recursive mundane existence. Our initial examination of the primary text (Chapter 2) revealed a marked esteem for *nivṛttic* values, while a reexamination (Chapter 3) revealed the extent to which the work mars ascetic ideals in favor of world enjoyment[1] and world preservation. Yet could the DM not *equally* uphold these vying ideologies? Like its pseudo-ascetic *brāhmaṇa* expositor who privileges neither path, could the text not be said to maintain an ideological ambivalence, despite its equation with Goddess and king? I must answer with a resounding *no*; moreover, my interlocutors Umberto Eco and Mary Douglas would both likewise have to disagree. To remain aloof to the centrality of sovereignty within the DM would be to overlook the profound interpretive cues embedded in the text's narrative ring structure, and to therefore silence its insistence on how it expects to be read.

It is through focusing the frame of the DM that we are able to frame its focus on royal ideology.[2] This chapter argues that valorization of kingship even above and beyond the pursuit of *mokṣa* is fundamental to the rubric of the DM. That *mokṣa* is granted to the merchant does not so much exalt his otherworldly aim over and above the king's worldly variety; it rather subordinates release from this world to an aim supremely glorified throughout the text: world preservation. Therefore, while Doniger asserts "clearly the Vaishya is the man [the DM] greatly prefers,"[3] this discussion demonstrates the exact opposite: it is the bloody business of kings that the DM emphatically extols. By speaking to the greatness of the Goddess, the DM bespeaks to the greatness of kings, whose duty Queen Durgā magnanimously discharges. Despite the overall *nivṛttic* religious practice embraced by the king and merchant at the end of the text, the fact that they make offerings to Durgā sprinkled with "blood of their own limbs"[4] sufficiently sullies the nonviolent paradigm emblematic of *nivṛtti dharma*. Their sanguinary sacrifice constitutes an evocative appeal both to Vedic sacrifice, progenitor of *pravṛtti dharma*, and to the blood-soaked duty of the Indian king, paragon of *pravṛtti dharma*. As demonstrated in the last chapter, the Goddess of our text not only safeguards individual kings, she safeguards their very ideology, exalting it above and beyond the merits of ascetic ideals. What we shall now unpack is the extent to which that exaltation is masterfully encoded within the text through a thematic interplay between its narrative frame and its episodic center: Episode II, the slaying of the demonic despot Mahiṣa.

Focusing the frame of the *Devī Māhātmya*

This discussion draws from the initial enframement of the DM, 1.1–44. For the sake of contextualization, see the essential contours of the DM outlined in Table 4.1 below.

While one might be tempted to dismiss the two-verse sliver frame latching the DM into the *Manvantara* section of the MkP—that which declares the function of the text to be an account of the coming Manu[5]—should we also gloss over, as have our scholarly forebears, the subsequent forty-five verses of narrative detailing the plight of the king and his exchange with a similarly troubled merchant? If, as Pargiter originally supposed, the DM's true narrator is Medhas, *not* Mārkaṇḍeya, then what purpose is served by the events taking place before Medhas is introduced? And what about the exposition on suffering provided by Medhas prior to commencing the glories of the Goddess proper: should we cast this aside too, as superfluous preamble?

Unlike the first two verses, the subsequent initial framing of the DM (1.3–46) is *not* necessary for anchoring the DM into the MkP, and so cannot be dismissed in the name of "interpolation." Were it ancillary to those exploits, it would occur in a chapter of its own, as does, for example, its corollary closing narrative occupying chapter 13. Rather, it functions as a significant narrative component

Table 4.1 The content of the *Devī Māhātmya*

Section	*Ch.*	*#V*	*Main content*
Initial Frame	1.1–44	44	King loses kingdom, enters forest, encounters merchant and sage
Episode I	1.45–77	33	Durgā invoked; aids Viṣṇu to slay Madhu and Kaiṭabha at *pralaya*
Episode II	2	68	Durgā invoked; slays Mahiṣa's army
	3	41	Durgā slays Mahiṣa, restoring Indra's kingship
	4	36	Durgā praised by gods; grants boon
Episode III	5	76	Durgā invoked by gods
	6	20	Durgā slays Dhūmralocana
	7	25	Durgā manifests Kālī, who slays Caṇḍa and Muṇḍa
	8	62	Durgā manifests Saptamātṛkas, Śivadūtī, Kālī, all key in slaying Raktabīja
	9	39	Durgā slays Niśumbha
	10	28	Durgā slays Śumbha, restoring Indra's kingship
	11	51	Durgā praised by gods; grants boon
	12	38	Durgā declares benefits of reciting her glories
Terminal Frame	13	17	King and merchant worship Durgā and receive boons: The king regains kingdom, merchant attains supreme knowledge

implemented in order to thematically contextualize the exploits of Durgā, and structurally uphold the narrative arc of the DM. It is intentionally cast as (formally and thematically) integral to Episode I of Durgā's greatness, for reasons which shall be clarified below. This frame narrative is very much a part of the DM, and as such it accomplishes much; it makes relevant the worship of the Goddess to the world of human beings, and to the social and phenomenal spheres, which require protection for the sake of human welfare. The tale of our fallen king, and his subsequent restoration, is paramount to showcasing the power and the function of the Goddess, insofar as it emphasizes her intimate connection with the safeguard of sovereignty on both mundane and cosmic scales, as articulated throughout the work, evidenced through its narrative structure. Let us examine the tale in detail.

Upon declaring its *manvantaric* function, the DM immediately proceeds to detail the plight of Suratha, king over the whole earth, who, though noble, was defeated by the Kolāvidhvaṃsin kings and left with only his own country to govern.[6] Retreating to his capital city, he faces adversity yet again at the hands of his own nefarious ministers, who seize both his treasury and army (DM 1.6–7). Stripped of his power, he mounts his horse under the pretence of hunting and ventures alone into the forest where he chances upon the hermitage of Medhas, finding temporary respite there (DM 1.8–10). Thus the text immediately presents us with the *primary* problem to be resolved: a virtuous king deprived of his power, and the implicit correlated problem of a realm robbed of proper protection. Order has turned to disorder due to the forces of *adharma*, a scenario that *must* be remedied. The problem centers on power; and only our mother of power may properly tend to it.

A close examination of the DM's enframement structure (as presented in Table 4.2 below) allows one to register the inbuilt textual mechanics adopted to invoke the interplay of *pravṛttic* and *nivṛttic* religious aims. These mechanics are conscious hermeneutic strategies for effecting model readership of the text, and will prove indispensable to the analysis at hand. The DM's layers of enframement follow a chiastic configuration: A-B-C-X-C′-B′-A′.

Prior to unpacking the layers of content, we may note a striking parallel between the DM's enframement structure and that of the BhG as appearing in Table 4.3 below. Since the line of questioning at the heart of this research is synchronic, and not diachronic in nature, I do not look to the Gītā as having influenced the compositional strategy of the DM. Rather, I look to it to further emphasize the presence of conscious compositional strategies at play, rendering textual enframement invaluable to hermeneutic enterprise.

As parallel to the teachings of Kṛṣṇa, the central exposition of the DM occupies the center of gravity for all levels of chiastic enframement. Therefore, it speaks to both *pravṛttic* and *nivṛttic* religious impulses: a work that fails to feature both would not survive in a cultural milieu that continues to value both. The interplay between the two strands of religiosity is moreover maintained via works such as the BhG and the DM; hence, such texts symbiotically owe their longevity to the very ideological double helix they encode. The exploits of Durgā (X) are immediately framed by a mental-emotional impetus (C), harkening to the *nivṛttic* emphasis on the problem of human suffering. As Chakravarti writes:

> the *Devīmāhātmya* begins with an enquiry about the reason why intelligent beings are also found to be victimised by *māyā* or the lack of correct understanding, endowed though they are with the power of discrimination in all matters secular, men cannot rise above their earthly attachments.[7]

But, contrary to what scholars since the time of Pargiter have argued, this is *not* where the DM begins. Else, framed solely by a *nivṛttic* problem, one would infer that it advocates the ideals of *nivṛtti* over those of *pravṛtti*, given that Durgā is, as made explicit by the fate of the merchant, the source of liberation. And this is exactly the interpretation that is favored by scholars such as Wendy Doniger. But ascetic ideology is not the preoccupation of our royal mother of power.

The *nivṛttic* rhetoric of delusion, prompting discussion of Mahāmāyā, is enframed by, and thus subordinate to, the work's primary, *pravṛttic* rhetoric, featuring a physical-social problem requiring a physical-social solution. While the impetus for Suratha's query pertains *prima facie* to appeasement of attachment (C), the impetus for this discourse itself is a prime *pravṛttic* crisis: loss of kingship (B). This sequence of enframement runs *directly* parallel to the enframement we see in the BhG. While Kṛṣṇa's teachings are immediately geared

Table 4.2 The chiastic structure of the *Devī Māhātmya*

Sequence	*Function*	*Dharma*	*Theme*	*Speaker*	*Verse content*
A	Introduces Outer Narrative	*Pravṛtti*	Outer Exposition: How did Sāvarṇi become Manu?	Mārkaṇḍeya	"Sāvarṇi, who is Sūrya's son, is said to be the eight Manu. Hear about his birth from me, speaking at length, How by the power of Mahāmāyā, Sāvarṇi, the illustrious Son of the sun, came to be overlord of a Manu interval" (1.1–2)
B	Introduces Problem I	*Pravṛtti*	Physical-Social Problem: Deposition of King	Mārkaṇḍeya	Loss of Sovereignty (1.3–10)
C	Introduces Problem II	*Nivṛtti*	Mental-Emotional Problem: Delusion	King/Sage	King's Lament (1.11–28) King's Suffering Prompt (1.29–33) Sage's Suffering Exposition (1.34–44)
X	Introduces Content	BOTH	Metaphysical Problem Introduced	King	"O reverend one, who is this Goddess whom you call Mahāmāyā? How was she born? What is her work, O twice-born one? This Goddess, her nature, her own form (svarūpa), her origin, All this I wish to know from you, O best of Brahma-knowers" (1.45–6)
	Core Narrative	BOTH	Exploits of Durgā	King/Sage	EXPLOITS OF DURGĀ (1.47–12.38)
	Concludes Content	BOTH	Metaphysical Problem Addressed	Sage	"Thus have I related to you, O king, the supreme Devī Māhātmya. She is the goddess, with this sort of power, by whom the universe is supported. Just in this way is knowledge fashioned by her who is the illusory power of blessed Viṣṇu" (13.1–2)
C′	Concludes Problem II	*Nivṛtti*	Mental-Emotional Problem Addressed: Delusion Dispelled	Sage	"By her are you, and this Vaiśya, and other men of discrimination deluded; So were others in the past, and will still others be deluded in the future" (13.3)
B′	Concludes Problem I	*Pravṛtti*	Physical-Social Problem Addressed: Despondency Dispelled	Goddess	"In just a few days, O king, you will regain your own kingdom, having slain your enemies; it will then be yours permanently. Upon death, receiving another birth from the god Vivasvan, you will be the Manu named Sāvarṇi here on earth" (13.13–15)
A′	Concludes Outer Narrative	*Pravṛtti*	Outer Expositional Prompt Addressed	Mārkaṇḍeya	"Thus having received a boon from the Goddess, Suratha, the best of rulers, Upon receiving a birth from Sūrya, will become the Manu known as Sāvarṇi, will become the Many known as Sāvarṇi" (13.17)

Table 4.3 The chiastic structure of the *Bhagavad Gītā*

Sequence	*Function*	*Dharma*	*Theme*	*Speaker*	*Verse content*
A	Introduces Outer Narrative	*Pravṛtti*	Outer Expositional Prompt: What happened on the *kurukṣetra*?	Dhṛtarāṣṭra	"In the Field of Law, the Kurus' Field, when my men and the Pandava men had come together so eager to fight, what did they do, Sañjaya?" (1.1)
B	Introduces Problem I	*Pravṛtti*	Physical/Social Problem: Wartime Despondency	Sañjaya; Arjuna	The forces prepare for battle (1.2–11); Arjuna surveys the enemy's army (1.20–7) and laments (1.28–46), growing troubled, despondent, and unable to fight
C	Introduces Problem II	*Nivṛtti*	Mental-Emotional Problem: Delusion	Multiple	Kṛṣṇa attempts to spur Arjuna out of his despondency (2.1–3), and Arjuna conveys his turmoil, submitting himself to Kṛṣṇa as a pupil for instruction (2.4–8); Kṛṣṇa offers his exposition (2.11–72)
X	Introduces Content	BOTH	Metaphysical/Ethical Problem: How can this be right?	Kṛṣṇa	"Krishna, if it is your belief that the way of intelligence is superior to action, then why do you enjoin me, Keshava, to this terrible undertaking?" (3.1–2)
	Core Narrative	BOTH	Kṛṣṇa's Teachings	Kṛṣṇa/Arjuna	TEACHINGS OF KṚṢṆA (3.3–18.72)
	Concludes Content	BOTH	Metaphysical Problem Addressed	Arjuna	"through your grace, Achyuta, I have remembered myself" (smṛtir labdhā, 18.73a)
C′	Concludes Problem II	*Nivṛtti*	Mental-Emotional Problem Addressed: Delusion Dispelled	Arjuna	"My delusion has been obliterated; my doubt dispelled" (*naṣṭo mohaḥ ... gata-samdehaḥ*, 18.73b)
B′	Concludes Problem I	*Pravṛtti*	Physical/Social Problem Addressed: Despondency Dispelled	Arjuna	"I stand [and] shall act in accordance to your counsel" (*sthito 'asmi ... kariṣye vacanam tava*, 18.73c)
A′	Concludes Outer Narrative	*Pravṛtti*	Outer Expositional Prompt Addressed	Sañjaya	Saṃjaya extols the dialogue between Kṛṣṇa and Arjuna, along with their combined prowess (18.74–8)

toward addressing Arjuna's delusion (C), this is merely an intermediary (*nivṛttic*) maneuver toward Kṛṣṇa's primary (*pravṛttic*) goal: empowering Arjuna to stand and fight, in the interest of restoring righteous rulership to the Pāṇḍava faction (B). Finally, while the outermost level of exposition within the BhG (A) consists simply of explaining what went on at the Kurukṣetra, the outermost level of exposition in the DM succeeds in underscoring its emphasis on sovereignty, endeavoring to account for the installment of the Manu Sāvarṇi (A), itself an invocation to the succession of rulership which falls squarely on the shoulders of *pravṛtti dharma*. Therefore, the layers of enframement at play leading up to the exploits of Durgā constitute a text that addresses the concerns of *pravṛtti*, most notably rightful rulership on both earthly and cosmic planes.

Let us more closely examine the dimensions of the *nivṛttic* component of the DM's enframement (C), which after all serves to introduce our Goddess through the lens of ascetic ideology, qua Mahāmāyā. As with the BhG, the primary *pravṛttic* impetus in the DM (loss of kingship) concludes with a lament, serving as precursor to the secondary problem: the suffering of the protagonist. The lament (DM 1.11–28) leading up to the Mahāmāyā discourse is quite clever indeed. Once the king finds himself alone, having retreated to the forest, his thoughts overtake him. He commences worrying after his kingdom (DM 11–15). Note that he is concerned with *protection*: first of his city, then of his elephant, then of his wealth. He essentially expresses concern for his *pravṛttic dharma*, lamenting the compromised protection of his city, rather than his enjoyment of ruling over it. Similarly, he wonders after the *treatment* of his prize elephant, rather than his enjoyment of it; indeed he wonders if his royal pet is being properly protected. Again, when his mind moves to wealth, he is concerned at the *preservation* of a royal treasury which was laboriously amassed by his ancestors, rather than the extent to which he is being deprived of that wealth. He is preoccupied with his royal duty to protect his citizens, animals, and wealth.

The king's internal monologue possesses a reflective "stream of consciousness" quality, perhaps mimicking the fluctuations of *māyā* itself, which will soon enough explicitly enter the discourse once he asks after the nature of his suffering. Like the phenomenal waking dreamscape which is *māyā*, wherein we are but reflections of each other, as soon as the displaced king begins reflecting upon his wealth, a displaced merchant appears, as if projected from his own mental patterning. The merchant conveys that he, too, is displaced and grieving the loss of his social function and afflicted with attachments, particularly to his family (DM 1.18–21). Therefore when the king presses the merchant about being so irrationally attached (DM 1.22), one wonders at the extent to which the king's "dialogue" might serve as an externalized "monologue," whereby the reflecting king reflects alongside the reflecting merchant, who is little more than a reflection of his suffering self: behold the matrix of Mahāmāyā at play. We may note that while the merchant is external to him in the literal narrative, the entire exchange takes place in the covert subconscious terrain, which the forest might be said to represent.

The hermitage represents a liminal space; the king, and the merchant in particular, have no business in the wilderness. Their physical displacement mimics their social and existential displacement. We are told that the king is robbed of his dominion. Is a king a king if he has no power? Likewise, we are told that the merchant is robbed of his wealth. Is a merchant a merchant if he has no wealth? It is noteworthy that the king's inward reflection turns from the preservation of *dharma* (his kingdom), to the preservation of *kāma* (his pastime elephant), to the preservation of *artha* (his treasury). That the merchant enters at this point in his process, at face value, harkens to the king's concern with *artha*,[8] but given the fate of the merchant—and his very name, Samādhi, which would strike anyone receiving the text as an overt cue to the aims of *nivṛtti*—he represents the aim of life with which the king qua king must remain aloof: *mokṣa*.

When the king asks the merchant the cause of his grief, the merchant tells a tale not dissimilar from his own, especially with respect to its function as occasioning existential upheaval. The merchant represents an externalized personification of the king's own inner lament, that aspect of him which ultimately aspires after liberation from the pitfalls of worldly life; yet this impulse must not be ultimately externalized by the king. For he would see, as does Samādhi, that all is suffering, and would opt to renounce the world, remaining in the wilderness indefinitely. And what of the world, then? Who would govern it? The wilderness can only constitute an elaborate pit stop on the king's royal journey, whereby he might become empowered to return to society and justly rule. While Samādhi, our meditative merchant, must sit still, Suratha, our noble chariot-rider, must journey on. The former must acquiesce to *nivṛtti*, while the latter must propel *pravṛtti*. As paragon of *pravṛtti*, the king, in order to be celebrated, must fulfill his duty and protect *pravṛttic* aims: *dharma*, *kāma*, and *artha*. Nevertheless, the collective reflections of Suratha and Samādhi (as if one person) represent pursuit of all four aims of human striving, encompassing the inner and the outer, the goals of *pravṛtti* and *nivṛtti*, alike: *dharma*, *kāma*, *artha*, and *mokṣa*.

In keeping with the tendency of *māyā* to multiply, just as the one became two in the dreamscape of the king, the two become three as they together approach the sage. While the tripartite convergence of *brāhmaṇa*, *kṣatriya*, and *vaiœya* might, at face value, signal a counsel of twice-borns,[9] the juxtaposition of these characters does not primarily represent caste distinction, but is rather emblematic of divergent religious ideologies, broadly indicative of what Heesterman calls "king, *brāhmaṇa*, and renouncer." The king represents the preservation of *pravṛtti dharma*. The merchant, however, does not represent anything particularly *pravṛttic*, despite his caste designation. Bearing the name Samādhi, he represents liberation, and the pursuit of *mokṣa*, requiring one to altogether abandon *pravṛtti dharma* for the sake of final release from society, and from the sacrificial sphere. Standing in for the renouncer, he unassumingly interjects within the text the ascetic ethos, allowing both *kṣatriya* and *brāhmaṇa* to ultimately represent *pravṛttic* life aims.

The sage, Medhas, is the glorified *brāhmaṇa*, representing knowledge of both *pravṛtti* and *nivṛtti dharma* alike. He therefore exists in a liminal pseudo-renounced forest-dwelling state where he is impervious to both the seduction of worldly life and the pitfall of escapism. Equally expert in the ways of the world *and* the way out of the world, he is able to speak to whomever should chance down the narrative rabbit hole, finding themselves in the liminal space of his hermitage. Yet he exhibits no personal interest in *mokṣa*; Agrawala, for example, understands the seer as one who "has knowledge of both Brahman and the world. He does not renounce either one for the sake of the other."[10] He represents *brāhmaṇic* ritual authority, as demonstrated by his name itself, Medhas, meaning sacrifice, specifically evocative of blood sacrifice,[11] which perhaps harkens to the aspirants' own sanguinary offering. Their offering nevertheless constitutes a clever hybrid of the two paradigms: as bloodshed, one associates it with *pravṛtti dharma*, yet as entirely self-directed, one associates it with *nivṛttic* self-castigation. In *brāhmaṇic* ideology, sacrifice can serve as the means for either path; hence, Medhas' instruction ultimately yields sovereignty and liberation alike.

The names of king, merchant, and sage (Suratha, Samādhi, and Medhas) do not function to denote specific personal *identities*. They are as if afterthoughts: the seer of our text is referred to on a total of thirty-five occasions,[12] and yet only once (on the first of these occasions) do we hear the named Medhas (DM 1.9). Similarly, when Samādhi speaks, the text says, "the merchant said" (*vaiūya uvāca*) without making reference to his name. Likewise, when Suratha speaks, the text simply indicates, "the king said" (*rājā uvāca*). That these three figures are archetypal in nature, deployed primarily as symbols, is corroborated not only by their lack of distinctive characteristics throughout the DM, but that *none* of them have existing careers outside of the frame of the DM. Most notable is the absence of a career for our illustrious sage.[13] The seer who serves as the expositor of the DM functions as a symbolic mouthpiece, for nothing else is known of this sage Medhas. Therefore, as per the internal mechanics of the text, it cannot be such that the DM is a "a pure interpolation, in which the real speaker is a *ṛṣi* named Medhas, and which is only repeated by Mārkaṇḍeya."[14] The crucial exchange between the king and merchant detailed above occurs before Medhas is introduced, and is relayed *by Mārkaṇḍeya*. It is *Mārkaṇḍeya*'s voice which authorizes the DM, as he interweaves Medhas, Suratha, and Samādhi as ideological archetypes in his brilliant introduction to the Goddess as Mahāmāyā.

The name Medhas as a proper noun is obscure; to my knowledge there is no mention of it throughout the *Purāṇas*, or the MBh. Similarly, there is mention neither of a merchant named Samādhi nor *any* character named Samādhi that I have come across.[15] We have the opposite (though corresponding) scenario with our noble king. In terms of the name Suratha, it is so ubiquitous that Vettam lists twelve different kings named Suratha. It is the "John Doe" of names one can give to *purāṇic* kings, it seems. However, none of the entries given correspond to the king of the DM.[16] Furthermore, despite the overwhelming popularity of the DM, its king remains obscure: the only detail we catch about Suratha (other than his enmity with the Kolāvidhvaṃsin kings) is that he is from the time of the second Manu, Svārociṣa. The assemblers of the DM could have chosen from a multitude of kings or sages to color or to exalt the DM, yet they specifically opted to paint the frame of the Goddess with an archetypal brush. Throughout the central exposition of the DM, Suratha remains "the king," Medhas remains "the seer," and Samādhi—namesake of the most spiritually lofty human endeavor—remains ignored.

That the merchant enters the scene in the midst of the king's stream of consciousness and his discourse dovetails into that stream of consciousness is not the sole manner in which the merchant functions as merely an externalized aspect of the king. The exposition between sage and sovereign launching the glories of the Goddess serves as a means of educating the king, and apparently, *only* the king. Aside from the sage's exposition, we hear occasional interjections *only* from the king. Yet, Durgā addresses *both* the king and the merchant in the terminal frame of the text. Likewise we are told in the initial frame that, "together they approached the sage [and] having displayed etiquette that was proper and worthy of him, the *vaiœya* and the king sat down and told him their tales."[17] However, the ensuing twelve chapters (comprising the primary exposition of the DM) appear to be a conversation *exclusively* between the king and the sage. The exchange begins with the king speaking on the merchant's behalf, saying, "thus, both he and I are utterly miserable ... how does it happen ... that this delusion has (come upon us, who are) blind to discrimination?"[18] In an effort to instruct the distraught duo, the sage proceeds to narrate the exploits of Durgā. While doing so, he employs the Sanskrit word, *te* (the enclitic dative of the second-person singular personal pronoun), on two occasions.[19] The dual counterpart of this pronoun, *vau*, happens to also be a *guru*, or heavy metrical syllable, and would easily satisfy the prosodic requirements of the verse in both instances. However, it is clear that the sage has no intention of including the merchant in his address.

The fact that the sage employs masculine vocative singular nouns throughout to address the king, and the king alone—calling him, for example, *bhūpa*, "protector of the earth," and *nṛpa*, "protector of men"—further emphasizes the exclusion of the merchant.[20] Upon completion of his narration of the acts of Durgā, Sage Medhas declares: "thus I have related *to you, O king*, the supreme Devī Māhātmya."[21] The sage never once addresses the merchant who is also present for the entire narration. Similarly, during the third episode, the king interjects to address only the sage, speaking in the first-person *singular*, likewise excluding the merchant, saying "it is simply wonderful that you, O blessed one, have told *me* this *mahātmya* of the Goddess ... I want to hear more!"[22] It is noteworthy here that the king refers to himself as the sole audience of the transmission. The exploits of Durgā are relayed by a sage to a king with absolutely no mention of the merchant. Upon conclusion of the narration proper, the sage does make reference to the merchant but does so while addressing only the king (DM 13.2–3). Although he urges only the king to take refuge in Durgā, the merchant not only accompanies the king in propitiation of Durgā, but succeeds in attaining insight into the nature of ultimate reality and subsequently achieves release from the cycle of mundane existence. The fact that the *nivṛttic* ideal of *mokṣa* is represented here by a lowly merchant who is entirely ignored throughout the narration of the glories of the Goddess serves to subordinate that ideal to the overarching thrust of the DM: the significance of sovereignty to the maintenance and preservation of *this* world. Thus, while the text at face value pays homage to the ascetic ideal of *mokṣa*, it cleverly renders that ideal subordinate to the prime *pravṛttic* duty of kingship. Why then is Durgā first introduced as Mahāmāyā?

In examining the sage's response to the king's suffering-born query, we note that he introduces the Goddess as Mahāmāyā, keeping in line with the ideological attitudes of *nivṛtti* which construe the phenomenal world as illusory.[23] The first act of Durgā, which the sage relays in this inaugural episode, likewise features the disruptive quality of Mahāmāyā's occlusive aspect. Upon dissolution of the universe into the primordial waters at the end of the age, Viṣṇu sprawls out upon his serpent couch Śeṣa, and enters his yogic slumber. The demons Madhu and Kaiṭabha emerge from his ears, with the intention of slaying Brahmā, situated in Viṣṇu's navel, about to create the universe anew (DM 1.49–53). Brahmā proceeds to praise the Goddess Yoganidrā, who was resting upon the eyes of Viṣṇu (DM 1.54–67). Viṣṇu, released from her grasp, proceeds to battle the demons for 5000 years (DM 1.69–72). Intoxicated with delusion, the demons offer Viṣṇu a boon; he accepts, and asks to be able to slay them. They (deluded) tell him to slay them where there is no water. Viṣṇu hoists them upon his lap (above the primordial waters) and decapitates them with his discus (DM 1.73–7).

While this relatively brief exchange might itself be considered "Episode I" of the DM (given that it details the first of Durgā's three exploits), the text insists it not be received as such. It is presented as an important extension of the Sage's discourse on delusion. He in fact introduces the delusive aspect of Durgā (as Mahāmāyā) during his exposition on the instinctual compulsions of the creatures of the earth, adding:

> Just in this fashion do they fall into the pit of delusion, the maelstrom of egoism./Giving (apparent) solidity to life in this world through the power of Mahāmāyā./There should be no surprise in this, (for) the Yoganidrā (yogic sleep) of the lord of the worlds,/Hari (i.e., Viṣṇu), is (this same) Mahāmāyā, and through her is this world being deluded.[24]

The chapter functions *as a whole*, episodic frame and all, in accentuating Durgā's dark aspect: her ability to occlude consciousness, bewitching it into individual egoism, as exemplified with Suratha and Samādhi as much as with Viṣṇu.

Moreover, the form of the episode, while admittedly disorderly at face value, purposefully befits the content it conveys. Unlike the two subsequent exploits of Durgā, which are each given multiple chapters, this first exploit is not even given its own chapter. That there is no clear demarcation between the end of the opening frame narrative and the beginning of the exploit proper does not evidence clumsiness or lack of care; rather it evidences a powerful interplay between content and form, one which pervades the work as a whole. Mahāmāyā is intentionally portrayed as elusive. Therefore, formally speaking, does the discourse of "Mahāmāyā" begin when the king asks after her greatness, launching her first exploit (DM 1.45)? Or, prior to this, when the sage first names her (DM 1.42)? Or prior to this when he first starts talking about her bewitching nature (DM 1.34)? How about prior to this when the merchant begins his lament born of her influence (DM 1.19)? Or perhaps prior to this when the king begins *his* lament born of her illusion at (DM 1.10)? Perhaps she is present from the very inception of the text as we hear of the fall of Suratha at the hands of his enemy, "though they were inferior (to him)"[25] (DM 1.5)? The absence of a chapter break serves to unite the plight of the king, the merchant, their interaction with Medhas, and the role of Durgā at the end of the age as *collectively* indicative of the universal dreamscape of Mahāmāyā, where the boundaries between individuals, events, and eons are provisional at best.

Hence, Renate Söhnen-Thieme notes the thematic continuity between the initial enframement and the first exploit of Durgā as follows:

> When the king of the frame story asks for the ultimate cause of his unhappiness, he is told that this is the work of Mahāmāyā, the great illusion, who, when properly worshipped can also bestow freedom from that illusion. This is, to some degree, illustrated by this first myth, when Yoganidrā, praised by Brahmā, leaves Viṣṇu, he is able to wake up and slay the two demons Madhu and Kaṭabhu who had threatened Brahmā.[26]

But, as we know, the king does not desire freedom from that illusion; he desires sovereignty over it. Hence, neither this exploit, nor the face of Durgā presented within it, is central to the DM.

This brings us to the second, more striking, formal reason for compressing the events of the frame and Exploit I into a single Episode. As the first of three episodes, it paves the way for the middle episode to serve as the centerpiece of the work. Mary Douglas, using the language of ring theory, refers to this as the mid-turn, indicating its significance as keystone to the work: "a ring composition condenses the whole burden of its message into the mid-turn. What has been seen through straight linear reading has to be read again with a fresh eye for the message that is in the mid-turn."[27] The generic structure of a ring composition is mapped below in Table 4.4, based on an example work with five episodic units, numbered 1 through 5.

In addition to the centrality of the mid-turn (segment 3 above), the ring structure designates episodic parallelisms. For example, were this structure to apply to an actual composition, we would note thematic parallels between segments 1

Table 4.4 General narrative ring structure

	(3) **Segment C** (mid-turn)	
(2) **Segment B**	← parallelism II →	(4) **Segment B′**
(1) **Segment A**	← parallelism I →	(5) **Segment A′**

and 5 (parallelism I, comprising the A-A′ episodic axis), and likewise between episodes 2 and 4 (parallelism II, comprising the B-B′ episodic axis). Let us now map this configuration on to the actual episodic components of the DM; see Table 4.5 below.

As is typical of narrative ring structure, thematic patterns emerge through the specific orchestration of parallelisms, and particularly through the architectural allocation of the episodic keystone, which highlights the themes central to the work as a whole. The content of these episodes and the themes they relay shall be more closely examined in the following section. For now, Table 4.6 below maps the extent to which the DM's narrative ring structure interweaves the constituent strands of the *brāhmaṇic* double helix, referred to therein as royal versus ascetic ideology.

The DM's movement from Episode I to Episode II then sets the stage for an important ideological turn from Durgā as Mahāmāyā (harkening to ascetic ideology), to Durgā as universal protectress, triumphing over the buffalo-demon Mahiṣa (harkening to royal ideology). There can be little doubt of the significance of the episode as evidenced both by its themes and its central position within the architecture of the text. Söhnen-Thieme therefore notes:

> In the Devīmāhātmya … the Mahiṣāsuramardinī myth occupies the central position, and perhaps it was the one to which the epithet Devīmāhātmya was originally attached, as one may conclude form the first verse of ch. 94 in the MkP, after the DM: sāvarṇika, idam samyak proktaṃ manvantaram tava | Tathaiva devīmāhātmyam mahiṣāsurghātanam ||, "I have duly declared unto thee this account of the Sāvarṇika Manvantara, and also the Devī-māhātmya which tells of the slaughter of the Asura Mahiṣa."
>
> (Trans. Pargiter)[28]

Table 4.5 The *Devī Māhātmya*'s narrative ring structure

Episode I **Initial Frame**	**Episode II** ← parallelism II → ← parallelism I →	**Episode III** **Terminal Frame**

Table 4.6 Royal-ascetic ideological allocation within the *Devī Māhātmya*

Section	*Ch*	*Sequence*	*Ring function*	*Ideology featured*
Initial Frame	1.1–44	A	Mirrors A′ (interplays with C)	Royal-Ascetic Synthesis
Exploit I	1.45–77	B	Mirrors B′	Royal-Ascetic Synthesis
Exploit II	**2–4**	**C**	**Keystone (interplays with A-A′)**	**Royal Ideology ONLY**
Exploit III	5–12	B′	Mirrors B (and C secondarily)	Royal-Ascetic Synthesis
Terminal Frame	13	A′	Mirrors A (interplays with C)	Royal-Ascetic Synthesis

Not only does the MkP know the DM is centered upon the slaughter of Mahiṣa, but the DM anticipates this in Suratha's initial questioning in Episode I; indeed, "the second carita complies more openly with the king's questions ('Who is she? How did she originate? What are her actions?')."[29] The DM compresses its discussion of Durgā's *nivṛttic* aspect as Mahāmāyā into a portion of a single chapter in order to pave the way for its celebration of her *pravṛttic* glory in the remainder of the work's twelve chapters, particularly in the work's high point, her glorious triumph over Mahiṣa having emerged from the combined luster of the gods.

Hence the initial framing of the DM is not given a separate chapter (unlike the terminal frame, which is) because it is an inextricable component of the DM's exposition of the Goddess as Mahāmāyā: she who bewitches the merchant and the king just as she bewitches Viṣṇu. Yet despite the *nivṛttic* nature of his counsel to the king, in the very last line of his speech, he refers to the Goddess, rather unexpectedly, as sovereign (*īśvarī*). And this rather incongruent appellation in the finale of the sage's exposition on the Goddess as the source of attachment in fact serves as the impetus for the king's interest in knowing more about her. Medhas' discourse is thoroughly world-denying except for its very last vestige: "She is the supreme, eternal knowledge that becomes the cause of release from bondage to mundane life; she is indeed the queen (governing) all who have power."[30] It is *governance* that concerns the king and, arguably, his interest would not be so nearly piqued had the sage not slipped in this reference to her power-portfolio at the very end of his suffering sermon. The king offers two discursive prompts, in accordance to the two levels of discourse: firstly, he asks after suffering, and secondly, he asks after the source of all power. Episode I can be easily read as an homage to ascetic ideology given its prejudicial rendering of the Goddess as Mahāmāyā. This clears the way for the royal core of the text, showcased in Episode II, and further embellished in Episode III.

The introduction of the merchant counterpart into the stream of consciousness of the king is nevertheless crucial to allow for the bifurcated paths that we must all somehow straddle: the inner and the outer. Once Medhas addresses the problem of the king's suffering, the king asks after the grandeur of the Goddess. Thus ends his liminal lamentation framing the acts of the Goddess: enticed by the suggestion of the Goddess's colossal power, he loses interest in the ascetic mechanics of suffering and stoic relief, and his thoughts again alight to the summit of royal power. Ironically, he no longer requires that interest since learning about the restoration of power shall prove efficacious in remedying his ultimate dilemma: loss of royal power. Once one's desires are sated, the suffering spawned by their deprivation is automatically appeased. So, our king is of course mesmerized by the very mention of an all-powerful Goddess, who serves as sovereign of kings. The sage then turns to answering the heart of Suratha's royal questioning, fittingly occupying the regal heart of the text.

Reading the ring of power

The centrality of sovereignty

Why *does* Medhas describe Durgā as sovereign of all sovereigns? It is noteworthy that in two of the three episodes of the DM, Durgā manifests for the very purpose of restoring sovereignty to the king of heaven, Indra, whose throne has been usurped by demonic forces. These episodes (II and III) will therefore be referred to herein as "throne episodes."[31] Episode III, though the longest, is in many ways an elaborate refrain of Episode II. This is unsurprising, since Episode II is the chiasmic keystone of the work as a whole. Episode II makes a sharp departure from Episode I, introducing the aspect of Durgā that prevails for the ensuing twelve of the DM's thirteen chapters. It is where we see the Goddess in her full force, functioning as protectress of the universe through means of her colossal martial power. This episode is "central" to the text insofar as it is the "middle episode," located at the heart of the text. Hence, the three episodes of the DM are not numbered per se: rather than being referred to as first, second, and third (*prathamaḥ*, *dvitiyaḥ*, and *tritiyaḥ*) as are the chapters, the episodes are strategically labeled first, middle, and last (*prathamaḥ*, *madhyamaḥ*, and *uttamaḥ*). This nomenclature accentuates Episode II as central, its physical centrality pointing to its thematic centrality.

What Dorsey says about symmetric structure is particularly relevant for the DM. He writes:

> in a symmetric (chiastic) arrangement the central unit generally functions as the turning point or climax or highlight of the piece … therefore is a composition is found to have a symmetric configuration, the central unit's key role in the book should be considered.[32]

Therefore, as Douglas concludes, "in a ring composition the meaning is located in the middle. A reader who reads a ring as if it were a straight linear composition will miss the meaning."[33] As the structural and thematic focal point of the work, we ought to look to Episode II to interpret the work as a whole. It should come as no surprise that this episode showcases probably the most celebrated mythic moment of Durgā's career, as evidenced by Indian artistic outpourings through the centuries: her triumph over Mahiṣa.

The centrality of Episode II perseveres even within the DM's ritual context wherein the text circulates with six standard ritual appendages (*aṅgas*), three before, and three after, maintaining the proportion required to render Episode II as formally central.[34] The three preceding appendages are "praises" (*stotra*) known as *Kavaca*, *Argalā*, and *Kīlaka*,[35] while the antecedent three appendages are "secrets" (*rahasya*), known as *Prādhānika*, *Vaikṛtika*, and *Mūrti*,[36] further adding to the architectural balancing act. As an aside, it is noteworthy that Mārkaṇḍeya figures in each of the antecedent ritual appendages. The ritual appendages do not merely render Episode II as central by virtue of their distribution: they outright tell us so. The *Vaikṛtika Rahasya* (itself the middle of the three secrets) stipulates that a wise man should praise Durgā either with all three episodes, "or with the middle one alone, but not with either of the other two episodes by itself."[37] That the middle episode is ascribed as the most ritually powerful of Durgā's exploits is unsurprising given the current demonstration of its thematic power within the narrative whole. Furthermore, the secrets are revealed by the seer to the king—presumably Medhas and Suratha, though, like in the core narrative itself, they are not named—continuing a conversation which, like Episode II, features the loss and return of sovereignty by the grace of the Goddess.

Moreover, the chiastic trajectory persists even *within* the episode itself: it consists of three chapters, an initial chapter which presents the problem (the gods' loss of power and the emergence of Durgā for the purposes of restoring that power), a terminal chapter wherein the gods praise Durgā for her colossal feat, and a middle chapter which presents the magnanimous slaying of Mahiṣa itself. Indeed, the text revolves around this crucial feat.

Now that we have established the formal centrality of Episode II, we need to elucidate its thematic centrality. While the previous episode emphasizes the Goddess as *māyā*, this one most certainly showcases the extent to which she represents *śakti*, power in its various manifestations, most notably royal power.[38] The frame narrative (Parallelism I) presents and resolves two problems, one *pravṛttic* and the other *nivṛttic*: loss of sovereignty, and loss of awareness (i.e., delusion). These two themes, indicative of the dual strands of the *dharmic* double helix, prevail throughout the work, orchestrated in accordance to its ring structure. In seeking to learn which of these the text prioritizes, we are wise to take counsel from its narrative ring. See Table 4.7 below for a summary.

While the problem in Episode I is Viṣṇu's loss of awareness (and only subsequently his loss of power), the DM's central episode unambiguously advances as

Table 4.7 Thematic allocation within the *Devī Māhātmya*

Section	*Chapter*	*Ring sequence*	*Primary episodic theme*	*Secondary episodic theme*
Initial Frame	1.1–44	A	Loss of Sovereignty (King)	Loss of Awareness (King and Merchant)
Exploit I	1.45–77	B	Loss/Return of Awareness (Viṣṇu/ demons)	Imperilment/Safeguard of Sovereignty
Exploit II	**2–4**	**C**	**Loss/Return of Sovereignty (Indra/gods)**	**N/A**
Exploit III	5–12	B′	Loss/Return of Sovereignty (Indra/ gods)	Loss of Awareness (demons)
Terminal Frame	13	A′	Return of Sovereignty (King)	Return of Awareness (Merchant)

its problem the loss of sovereignty. This central episode therefore works in tandem with the DM's narrative enframement to underscore Durgā's rectification of tyrannical, *adharmic* kingship. While she does so in the heavenly sphere by restoring sovereignty to Indra in Episode II, she does so in the human sphere by restoring Suratha's sovereignty in the concluding frame narrative. The restoration of awareness is an ancillary theme.

The middle episode is steeped in the themes of sovereignty. Medhas prefaces it thus: "Hear again of the *majesty* of this Goddess. I will tell you,"[39] given that Queen Durgā makes her regal appearance in this episode. While the dominant mode (*guṇa*) of the last episode is *tamas* (darkness, occlusion), Episode II most emphatically celebrates the mode of *rajas*, passion. As universal sovereign, she protects the throne of heaven ruled by Indra. The demonic despot Mahiṣa usurps the throne of heaven, having won a hundred-year-long battle with the gods of the Vedic pantheon. The throne of Indra is a most prevalent symbol of the proper flow of divine power, without which order would decay. Indra is a key symbol representing sovereignty and the political order, along with order in the sacrificial sphere. Not only is he king of the gods; he is the only common deity between the world-protectors and deities contributing to the band of mothers arising in Episode III. The text indicates that "Mahiṣa became Indra,"[40] as in he becomes "like Indra," in that he controls the cosmic order through occupation of the office of Indra. Also worth noting is that the previous episode features two demons, as does the following episode, yet Episode II features a single demonic force. This demon is nevertheless shifty: being a shape-shifter, Mahiṣa takes on various forms during combat, and his duplicity is ultimately revealed in the moment of his destruction where he assumes a hybrid asura-buffalo form. Conversely, Durgā retains her supreme personality throughout this episode, whereas she is an ethereal presence in the previous episode, presented as the yogic slumber of Viṣṇu (Yoganidrā), and she emits various subsequent personalities in the following episode. Yet in this episodic central column of the DM, the Goddess remains fixed in form, firmly battling Mahiṣa as *he* shifts from shape to shape during combat with each of her assaults, moving from buffalo to lion, to man, to elephant, back to buffalo, until he is slain in half anthropomorphic-demon form and buffalo-demon form (DM 3.28–39). What the demon's buffalo form actually represents is a mystery, but he is presented as a stubborn bull-headed tyrant in the episode to be sure, one who wreaks cosmic havoc, and needs to be subdued for order to resume.

A key element of this episode is the specific manner in which Durgā emerges. While she is invoked through praise in the first and final episode, in this one she emerges spontaneously from the collective wrath of the outraged gods, for the sake of protecting heaven's throne. The gods are cast out of heaven to wander the earth as mere mortals. Indra, refuge of the gods, is now powerless and this constitutes a cosmic crisis. So the Vedic pantheon then approach Śiva and Viṣṇu as *their* refuge, complaining that Mahiṣa "now wields sovereignty over Sūrya, Indra, Agni, Vāyu, Candra, Yama, And over Varuṇa and the others,"[41] a list of seven which coincides with the list of eight world protectors[42] (only Kubera is missing), and declaring: "we have told you what the enemy of the gods has done, And we have taken refuge (in you). Please put your mind on doing away with him!"[43] Viṣṇu and Śiva then scowl at the audacity of Mahiṣa, outwardly projecting their wrath into converging beams of energy. The other gods follow suit and Durgā manifests from the collective energy (lit. *tejas*, which Coburn translates both as "fiery splendour"[44] and "luminous brilliance"[45]) of all of the tormented gods who, individually, are unable to defeat the menacing buffalo-demon, Mahiṣa. The text reads:

> Having heard these words of the gods, the slayer of Madhu (Viṣṇu)/Became angry, and Śiva too, with furrowed brows and twisted faces./Then from Viṣṇu's face, which was filled with rage./Came forth a great fiery splendor *(tejas)*, (and also from the faces) of Brahmā and Śiva./And from the bodies of the other gods, Indra and the others,/Came forth a great fiery splendor, and it became unified in one place./An exceedingly fiery mass like a flaming mountain/Did the gods see there, filling the firmament with flames./That peerless splendor, born from the bodies of all the gods./Unified and pervading the triple world with its lustre, became a woman.[46]

The energy (*tejas*) of their individual wrath coalesces into Durgā, each of whom contribute to a different part of her body. The text specifically lists twelve contributors included Brahmā, Prajāpati, Viṣṇu, and Śiva, and the eight world guardians.[47] The DM proceeds to detail the manner in which the gods supply Durgā with weaponry and adornments, whereby she is gifted with weapons by nine deities, seven of whom are world-protectors.[48] That the eight world-protectors are implicated in the constitutive function of both Goddess *and* king is unsurprising given that they are all united in their penchant for world preservation.[49]

Coburn calls to our attention the striking similarity between the emergence of Durgā in Episode II of the DM and the account of the creation of the king in the *Laws of Manu* (7.3–10) as follows:

> When these creatures, being without a king through fear dispersed in all directions, the Lord created a king for the protection of this whole (creation), taking (for that purpose) eternal particles of Indra, of the Wind, of Yama, of the Sun, of Fire, of Varuṇa, of the Moon, and of the Lord of Wealth (Kubera). Because a king has been formed of the particles of those lords of the gods, he therefore surpasses all created being in luster [*tejas*.]; And, like the sun, he burns eyes and hearts; nor can anyone on earth even gaze on him. Through his (supernatural) power he is Fire and Wind, the Sun and Moon, he the Lord of Justice (Yama), he Kubera, he Varuṇa, he great Indra … Having fully considered the purpose, (his) power, and the place and rime, he assumes by turns many (different) shapes for the complete attainment of justice. He, in whose favour resides Padmā, the goddess of fortune, in whose valour dwells victory, in whose anger abides death, is formed of the lustre of all (gods).[50]

This motif stems from the earliest Indian accounts of the emergence of a king.[51] Through cataclysmic combat, Durgā finally succeeds in defeating Mahiṣāsura (for which she is known as one of her most famous and most pervasive epithets, *Mahiṣāsuramardinī*, "Slayer of the Demon Mahiṣa"), fulfilling her sovereign duty to protect the cosmic order, the same duty ascribed to the king. According to Coburn this episode functions to

> move from the cosmic-transcendent orientation of the first *carita* to the exuberant exemplification of her mundane activity in the third. Its task is to demonstrate not only that the Goddess has an earthly career, but that of earthly creatures, she us supreme ruler. Put more pointedly, when we ignore the eternal and focus on the temporal, ignore power as a religious phenomenon and focus on it as a secular one, the Goddess has to be shown to be the ultimate agent. What our text has done in its portrayal of the Goddess in this role is to draw on the model which, in Indian culture, most nearly fits those requirements, viz., the model of the king.[52]

He writes:

> that this model of secular power underlies the DM's vision of the Goddess's earthly origin is obvious enough. That its appropriateness is utter is equally obvious, for only one who is of peerless power on the world's own terms can cope with that great disturber Mahiṣa.[53]

He further remarks, "what has thus previously been affirmed of the king on a mundane scale is now in the *Devī Māhātmya* affirmed to be true of the Goddess on a cosmic scale."[54] Coburn goes so far as to assert that the interrelationship of kings and the Goddess is a theme as old as the Indus Valley Civilization. Regardless of the veracity of so ancient an origin as this interrelation, Richard Gombrich notes that:

> Images of [Durgā] start to show in many royal insignia from about 500 AD on … The form in which She slays the buffalo demon, Mahīsāmardinī, was particularly associated with royalty and victory in battle, and from early times Durgā in this form is often shown with a lion, emblem of royalty. A king's throne is a "lion throne" (simhāsana).[55]

Kinsley similarly remarks, "images of the Goddess slaying Mahiṣa are known and fairly common prior to and during the Gupta age, that is, at a time most likely prior to the compilation of the DM."[56] That Durgā appears in the text, more often than not, accompanied by her ferocious lion-mount bespeaks her status as an emblem of royal power. What other animal would better serve as the mount for the universal sovereign?

The association between the Indian king and the acts of Durgā (especially her triumph over Mahiṣa) has endured to much more recent times. J.C. Fuller notes that among the various rituals and festivals significant for Hindu kingship, Navarātrī "eclipsed any other single event as the most prominent ritual of kingship across India."[57] He further notes that: "The goddess' slaying of the buffalo-demon signals the end of demonic supremacy. In this glorious victory and its aftermath, the recreation of a kingly order, Hindu monarchs participate by celebrating royal Navaratri."[58] McDermott notes that Durgā Pūjā has "long been associated with sovereignty, useful in the context of eighteenth century Bengal for bolstering the rajas' claims to identity and power,"[59] and notes further that sovereignty was "clearly the central purport of the Navarātra celebrations for the rulers of the last great Hindu empire, which flourished from the fourteenth to the seventeenth centuries at Vijayanagara in South India."[60]

The festival occurring on *Vijayadaūamī* (*Dasara*) in Mysore has most probably been maintained since the decline of the Vijayanagara empire, five centuries ago. In his analysis, Fuller notes that "the festivals reiterated the durable relationship between the goddesses and their principal worshippers, the respective kings who presided over the rituals."[61] He writes:

> In several ways, Navaratri identified the kings of Mewar and Mysore with the goddess and made them participants in her victory over Mahishasura. But in the myth, as we know, Durga's triumph allows the gods to regain their kingdom, reinstall their own king on his throne, and reestablish the proper order of the universe. The rituals bear a parallel message and Navaratri also showed the Mewar and Mysore kings as restorers, alongside the goddess, of the rightful order that is predicated on the royal authority of the gods. Furthermore, the festivals commemorated the reestablishment of a divine sovereignty in which the human kings themselves respectively shared as regents … In brief, through the victory enacted at Navaratri, the order of Mewar and Mysore kingdoms was recreated in the likeness of the order of the universe.[62]

Mysore's tutelary deity is Cāmuṇḍeśvarī (a form of Durgā), whose shrine is in the royal palace itself. There is a public temple nearby on Cāmuṇḍī Hill, to the Goddess in the form Cāmuṇḍī, a derivative of Cāmuṇḍā. However, despite the fact that *Dasara* in Mysore focused on the worship of Cāmuṇḍeśvarī, the slayer of Mahiṣāsura, the festival did not incorporate the chanting of the DM.[63]

In the DM, Cāmuṇḍā is the epithet given to Kālī for slaying Caṇḍa and Muṇḍa. Coburn's comprehensive analysis of the epithets of the Goddess of the DM corroborates Pargiter's assertion that the name Cāmuṇḍā enters the Sanskrit world for the first time in the DM.[64] He writes: "In the case of Cāmuṇḍa, we seem to have the explicit assimilation of a non-Sanskritic goddess to the Goddess, for our investigation has not uncovered a single instance of this epithet in the Vedic or epic literature."[65] The soil of Mysore is perhaps the soil of her non-Sanskritic veneration. The absence of an association with the DM proper at Mysore might even suggest that both the myths of Durgā slaying the buffalo-demon and their use for the ritual consecration of the king were established at a time before the composition of the DM. The city's name itself is an Anglicization of Mahiṣāsura, who presumably played an important role in the mythic heritage of that locality.

The kings at Mysore (and probably elsewhere) would consecrate their very sovereignty through the ritual invocation of the myths of the DM. During this festival, the emperors identified themselves with Durgā and with the divine king Rāma of the epic *Rāmāyaṇa*, and would consecrate their thrones, along with all weapons and military apparatus, during the ritual worship of Durgā. It is significant that the seat of royal power itself was consecrated as an aspect of Durgā, independent of the king proper. According to Biardeau's firsthand account of the Navarātrī proceedings at the court of Mysore, the first important event at the start of the Navarātrī festival was in fact the ritual consecration and veneration of the throne in the Durbar Hall, *even before the worship of Durgā herself.* Fuller notes: "At the same time, however, the Mysore royal regalia were associated with Indra as well as Cāmuṇḍeśvarī. The king's throne contained the Goddess' power, but when worshipped it was also referred to as Indra's throne."[66] Here we find evidence of an understanding of sovereignty as different than, but interrelated with, sovereign. Given that she never herself occupies Indra's throne—or *any* throne, for that matter—the Goddess may be understood as emblematic of sovereignty itself, that power whereby governance occurs, that wellspring from which all sovereigns must draw. Durgā not only functions as an Indian king, insofar as she competently protects her subjects (indeed all beings), but she also, through her monumental martial prowess, restores and defends the throne of heaven. That the centrality of the Durgā's conquest over Mahiṣa within rituals of kingship should correspond so well to the physical centrality of this episode suggests a system of sophisticated architecture at work within the DM that we are perhaps only beginning to uncover. Let us now examine Episode III's role in the DM's narrative ring.

The ambivalence of Episode III

Episode III comprises an intricate embellishment of the themes of kingship established in Episode II wherein demon hordes, this time headed by Śumbha, again succeed in usurping the throne of Indra, and again, through a series of violent encounters, Durgā succeeds in destroying the enemy of the gods. While invoking her, the gods explicitly invoke Durgā in her capacity as their sovereign, whom they beseech for protection as follows:

> Praised of yore by the gods because refuge was desired, similarly praised by the lord of gods day after day, may she, the *queen*, the cause of what is bright, accomplish for us bright things, auspicious things: may she destroy misfortunes. She, the *ruler*, is now reverenced by us, the gods, who are tormented by haughty demons. And at this very moment, she who has been called to mind by us, whose bodies are prostrated in devotion, destroys all misfortunes.
>
> (DM 5.35–6)[67]

Furthermore, not only is the motif of demons usurping Indra's throne repeated in this episode, we also learn that Śumbha and Niśumbha specifically usurp the power of the eight world-protectors: they "[t]ook away Indra's three worlds and shares in the sacrifice./Similarly they took away the powers of the sun, the moon,/Kubera, Yama, and Varuṇa./The two of them took over Vāyu's authority and Agni's proper action."[68] The passage then follows with: "[t]hen the gods, fallen from their kingdoms, were scattered about and defeated. All the gods, bereft of authority and conquered by those two Great Asuras, remembered the invincible Goddess."[69] The association between sovereignty and sacrifice is supported by the fact that the word for authority used here (*adhikāra*) carries within its semantic range both "royalty, rule, administration, rank, office" as well as "privilege, claim, claim, right, especially to perform sacrifices with benefit." Sovereignty and sacrifice are intertwined in this episode.

Episode III is framed through the lens of sacrifice,[70] since the crisis commencing the episode is Śumbha and Niśumbha usurping the gods' sacrificial shares, which is tantamount to usurping their sovereignty (DM 5.1–3). Hence, it asserts a fundamental cosmic interconnectedness between the mechanisms of rulership and sacrifice. It is Indra who holds sovereignty but all the gods lose their sacrifices when he loses sovereignty. Sovereignty is geared toward collective welfare and order. Therefore it is not whimsical that the gods should have sovereignty and not the demons; it is necessary for cosmic equilibrium to be preserved. Following sacrificial suit, Durgā dispatches an ultimatum to Śumbha-Niśumbha in the middle of the episode, ordering them to restore the gods' share of the sacrifice, or else face annihilation (DM 8.25–6). The battle for the sacrificial order of the world is itself an act of sacrifice: Kālī, for example, presents the lopped-off heads of Caṇḍa and Muṇḍa to Caṇḍikā as slain in the sacrifice of battle (DM 7.23). After her cosmic duel with the formidable Śumbha himself, Durgā reigns victorious, restoring the throne to Indra, and subsequently restoring order to the cosmos. At the conclusion of this cataclysmic duel between Durgā and the demon Śumbha, we are told that:

> When that wicked one was dead, the whole universe became soothed, regaining its natural condition once more, and the sky became spotless. The flaming clouds of portent that formerly had gathered became tranquil, and rivers once again flowed within their banks.
>
> (DM 10.23–8a)[71]

Once Śumbha is finally slain, order is restored, order which coincides with, and depends upon, the restoration of the sacrificial fires. The text cleverly attunes us to the significance of this by having Agni lead the ensuing thanksgiving praise (DM 11.1), while Indra leads the parallel thanksgiving praise at the end of the previous episode. We are told that since their enemies are now slain, the gods might enjoy both sovereignty and their shares in the sacrifice (DM 12.29a–32). The safeguard of sovereignty amounts not only to the restoration of the throne but also the safeguard of the interrelated allotment of sacrificial shares.

Sacrifice must exist for one to feed oneself and for one to feed even the gods. The very material universe is predicated upon sacrifice. That Durgā is construed as the guardian of sacrifice, the domain of the *brāhmaṇa*, likens her function to that of the earthly *kṣatriya*, in general, and king, in particular. While the (post-*upaniṣadic*) *brāhmaṇa* resorts to non-animal sacrifice for Vedic ritual and non-animal sacrifice regarding consumption, the king's duty to guard the *brahmaṇical* sacrificer ironically necessitates the sacrifice of blood. It is telling that the destruction of the demon Śumbha coincides not only with the restoration of Indra's rule, but also with cosmic order as a whole. For this is the very purpose of Durgā's manifestation: the restoration of cosmic balance through means of violent force.

Though the portrayal of the Goddess in the DM is extraordinarily complex—she after all represents the one and the many, the divine and the demonic, the immanent and the transcendent, knowledge and ignorance—her basic function, especially in the throne episodes, mirrors the function of the Indian king. Kinsley notes that Durgā

> is not just a powerful transcendent force whose sole concern is maintaining the cosmic rhythms, who is moved to action only when the world itself is threatened. She is attentive to the needs of her devotees and intervenes on their behalf if asked to do so. She is a personal savior as well as a battle queen who fights to defeat the enemies of the gods.[72]

However, these two functions are vitally linked: in safeguarding sovereignty on cosmic and mundane levels, Durgā indirectly safeguards the welfare of her non-sovereign devotees. Like the king (and unlike the ascetic), she does not have the luxury to dispense with violent means.

Given the extent to which themes of kingship are ensconced in Episode III, we must entertain the following challenge: if, as we suppose, the DM does in fact cohere to a structural parallelism taking Episode II as a midpoint, should Episode III not parallel Episode I? We should not be too hasty to abandon our thesis just yet; as Douglas wisely cautions: "When the reader finds two pages set in parallel that seem quite disparate, the challenge is to ask what they may have in common, not to surmise that the editor got muddled."[73] A closer examination of Episode III (through the lens of Episode I) reveals very clever craftsmanship: it reflects the *pravṛttic* themes featured in Episode II, while in tandem harkening to the *nivṛttic* ones established in Episode I.

Episode III again brings to the fore Durgā's delusive potency. Like in Episode I, the demons fall prey to her *māyā*. Once Durgā appears, in her enchanting splendor, Caṇḍa and Muṇḍa (servants of Śumbha and Niśumbha) behold her in her supreme mind-boggling form, and report her exceptional magnificence to Śumbha, impelling him to seize her. They argue that since she is a bedazzling jewel among women, Śumbha should possess her alongside the jewels he usurped from the gods. When they present her with Śumbha's marriage offer, she mischievously replies that she can only marry he who can conquer her in battle, which, of course, is an impossibility. This spawns a serious of encounters between the demon forces and Durgā, and with her various wrathful emanations, most notable Kālī, Śivadūtī, and the *Saptamātṛkas*.

Episode III accentuates her delusive nature during its martial climax, when Durgā engages Śumbha and he accuses her of relying on the strength of others, bewitched by her *māyā*. In response, she declares: "When I was established here in many forms, it was by means of my extraordinary power. That has now been withdrawn by me. I stand utterly alone. May you be resolute in combat!"[74] While Episode I presents delusion as a detriment to be overcome *viz.* Viṣṇu needing to be awakened so as to combat the demons, no such negative spin is placed on the Goddess's delusion in Episode III. Like Episode I, Episode III details the annihilation of demons who are deluded by Durgā's *māyā* until their bitter ends. Episode III therefore evokes the loss of awareness we see in the frame narrative, but given that it is the demons who Durgā bewitches, we are very content that they remain deluded. In fact, while her delusive potency is presented in ascetic ideology as detrimental, and she therefore mercifully releases Viṣṇu from his yogic slumber upon Brahmā's supplication in Episode I, her delusive potency is appropriated for royal ideology in Episodes I and III, whereby it afflicts the demonic forces, occasioning their destruction and the subsequent restoration of royal power. See Table 4.8 below.

This maneuver serves to further subordinate the ascetic theme of loss and restoration of awareness to the royal theme of loss and restoration of power within the work as a whole. While she is Mahāmāyā in Episode I and she is Viṣṇumāyā in Episode III, make no doubt she is Īśvarī in Episode II, the centerpiece of the

Table 4.8 Royal-ascetic thematic allocation within the *Devī Māhātmya*

Section	*Ch*	*Ring sequence*	*Royal ideology*	*Ascetic ideology*
Initial Frame	1.1–44	A	Loss of Sovereignty (King)	Loss of Awareness (King and Merchant)
Exploit I	1.45–77	B	Imperilment/ Safeguard of Sovereignty Loss of Awareness (demons)	Loss/Return of Awareness (Viṣṇu only)
Exploit II	**2–4**	**C**	**Loss/Return of Sovereignty (Indra/gods)**	
Exploit III	5–12	B′	Loss/Return of Sovereignty (Indra/gods) Loss of Awareness (demons)	
Terminal Frame	13	A′	Return of Sovereignty (King)	Return of Awareness (Merchant)

text, which serves to amplify the significance of her royal boon over its ascetic counterpart in the work's terminal frame. It is worth noting that we come to appreciate these thematic parallels thanks in no small part to *the text itself*, complete with its sophisticated ring structure and the structural parallels it produces. We have therefore capitalized upon the second interpretational tool expected of us by the text, as presented in Chapter 1: knowledge of the DM's intricate structure and its ramifications on model readership. Such a one would most probably conclude, in combining this tool with the ideological orientation afforded by the previous two chapters, that while the Goddess encapsulates the hybrid double-helical ideology represented by the *brāhmaṇa* sage, her penchant for royal ideology (represented by the king) outshines her penchant for ascetic ideology (represented by the merchant). Therefore, the work's advancement of Goddess as supreme knowledge is subordinated by its celebration of Goddess as sovereign power.

Episodic expansion

One more potential challenge to our structural parallelism argument needs to be addressed. Given that Episode III occupies the *overwhelming* bulk of the narrative (chapters 5–13), does this not compromise the structural "centrality" of Episode II (chapters 2–4) argued for above? Can we really ignore so great an asymmetry in the two arms of the text's parallelism? Though occurring in our text on a much grander scale, what Douglas says of the two arms of the parallelism in Genesis 22 holds true to the DM: we can indeed "ignore the asymmetry of bulk."[75] And we do so with good cause: rather than undermine the textual architecture argument outline above, this seemingly contradictory observation ironically upholds it, further embellishing our evidence for a highly conscious narrative structure at play in the DM. Mirroring the contradictory nature of Durgā it details, the DM embodies two opposing structural tropes working in tandem: the first is based on symmetry (outlined above), and the second is based on expansion.

The episodes of the DM successively portray the expansion of the Goddess from "the one" to "the many." That "the first episode [of the DM] is told succinctly, with almost telegraphic brevity,"[76] is to be starkly contrasted with the final episode, told in great detail. The work thereby functions to simulate the expansive quality of the Goddess, as she emanates herself from cosmic to earthly spheres. The DM's form mirrors this element of its content; hence each successive episode contains three times the chapters as the one before: Episode I comprises one chapter, while Episode II comprises three times that. Furthermore, Episode III contains three times the chapters in Episode II. The distribution of chapters over episodes therefore results in a 1–3–9 configuration. The effect of cosmic expansion is given not only by the number of chapters, but by the density of those chapters.

One way to roughly gauge that density is through registering the number of proper nouns used, since *māyā*, after all, is implicated in the names and forms it generates. The number of nouns associated with demons grows from a mere two occurrences in Episode I, occurring at eight textual junctures,[77] to twenty-three in Episode II, occurring at forty-four junctures,[78] to twenty-two in Episode III, occurring at a whopping 112 junctures.[79] The same trend is all the more prevalent with the proper nouns associated with the Goddess herself, *tripling* with each episode. The number of nouns associated with the Goddess moves from five in Episode I, occurring at eleven textual junctures,[80] to ten in Episode II, occurring at twenty-seven junctures,[81] to thirty-five in Episode III, occurring at a whopping 149 junctures.[82] The same overall trend can be somewhat observed by the proper nouns associated with the gods as well: while there is relative paucity in Episode I, the tallies for Episodes II and III are more or less interchangeable. This makes sense since the gods of heaven are consistent between Episode II and III. The number of nouns associated with gods moves from seven in Episode I, occurring at twenty-four textual junctures,[83] to twenty in Episode II, occurring at fifty-one junctures,[84] to fourteen in Episode III, occurring at forty-one junctures.[85] Table 4.9 below summarizes these findings.

Over the course of the three episodes, we move from the cosmic sphere, to the heavenly sphere, to the earthly sphere. While she protects in all three episodes, she engages in personal combat only in the "throne" episodes: Episodes II and III. She fights primarily with her delusive power in Episode I, and with her power to multiply in Episode III (though she also draws upon her delusive power to engage the demons). Episode I, by far the briefest, is the most resonant with the themes of *nivṛtti*, occasioning the awakening of Viṣṇu so that he may confront the demons of his unconscious. However, the throne episodes, as one might expect, resonate most with the ethos of *pravṛtti*, celebrating themes of protection, sacrifice, and multiplicity. The gestalt of the DM is its Goddess's expansion from Mahāmāyā—the one invisible, dark, occlusive presence—to Viṣṇumāyā—the manifestation of a myriad of perceivable forms, in celebration of her power to multiply. And, harkening to the paradox of the Goddess, the expansiveness formally encoded in the text by virtue of its expanding number of chapters is tempered by its episodic centrality, which focuses on a single moment of conquest emblematic of the centrality of the Goddess's universal power.

The text's symmetry and asymmetry exist in tandem. The DM serves as a brilliant encapsulation of two formal motifs, indicative of the tensions innate to the Goddess it portrays: it contains the irregular multiplicity of the Goddess's goriest exploits, within a controlled narrative ring which makes evident the text's central turning point, featuring the Goddess as singular apex of martial, social, and cosmic power. The scholarship on the Goddess of the DM tends to focus on

Table 4.9 Proper nouns in the *Devī Māhātmya* (by episode)

	Deity	*Junctures*	*Demon*	*Junctures*	*Goddess*	*Junctures*
Episode I	7	24	2	8	5	11
Episode II	20	51	23	44	10	27
Episode III	14	41	22	112	35	149

the latter of these themes, while this work, as shall be discussed in the following chapter, is useful for shedding light on the former. The narrative ring of the DM is primarily a ring of power, specifically royal power.

Framing finale

Mary Douglas notes that in the case of ring composition, narrative endings are predestined by virtue of how they began. She lists three observations about the function of such endings: (1) they necessarily evoke the beginning, closing off the ring by revisiting and reestablishing the themes established therein; (2) they necessarily evoke the mid-turn which itself derives its thematic centrality from the opening and closing of the work; and (3) there is oftentimes a double closuring, the first of which seals off the narrative proper, and the second of which latches the text as a whole to a larger narrative context.[86] That each of her three observations directly apply to the conclusion of the DM adds credence both to her theory of the nature of ring composition, and to the proposition that the DM exemplifies such a composition.

Regarding the first of Douglas' observations, in turning to the final chapter of the text (its terminal frame), we note that sage Medhas systematically closes off the various levels of textual enframement at play (see Table 4.1 provided at the outset of this chapter): he provides a summation for central exposition on the acts of Durgā (DM 13.1), moving next to the work's *nivṛttic* impetus (DM 13.2–3), before calling the king and merchant to worship Durgā (DM 13.4). That the sage addresses the king's delusion (born of his attachment to kingship) is a *prima facie* appeasement of the concerns of *nivṛtti* religiosity, for even upon engaging in ascetic practice for three years, he still longs for kingship. And this desire is entirely validated by the sage's central exposition on she who is sovereign of all sovereigns. Nor does that universal sovereign's ability to grant *mokṣa* serve as an affront to the *dharma* of the Indian king. As Gonda notes, the Indian "… ruler was to help men of all the classes in realizing their earthly and spiritual aims."[87] Pollock similarly notes that by the medieval period, the king functioned as "spiritual redemptor, [n]ot as an intercessor with the gods but directly is the king said to secure the spiritual welfare of his people."[88] In support of his position, he quotes MBh XII.68.59, "[p]utting their reliance in their king, people win this world and the world to come."[89] Despite the sage's expositions on the pitfalls of attachment at the outset, the DM does not chastise Suratha for his attachment. Rather Suratha's attachment is rewarded on the *pravṛttic* basis that it is a necessary, and noble one; called to kingly *dharma*, Suratha desires to serve and protect the workings of the collective and especially the human beings implicated in those workings.

The central exposition of the DM, like that of the BhG, concerns the restoration of kingship. The secondary theme of suffering plays an important role in both texts, to be sure; it is mental anguish which compels Arjuna to seek Kṛṣṇa's counsel and likewise compels Suratha and Samādhi to seek Medhas' insight.[90] Insofar as the king-merchant duo operate as if a single protagonist, we may liken

Samādhi to Suratha's externalized higher self, silently witnessing as the intellect (Medhas) counsels the mind (Suratha), who ends up free of suffering, detached from the affairs of the world. In the absence of the merchant, there is no mention of liberation in the text, save for hymned laudations of Durgā as the cause of liberation. The text is about worldly accomplishment, kingship; what makes it a tale of two *siddhis* (kingship *and* liberation) is the presence of the merchant, probably introduced for that very purpose. Like the BhG, the DM sheds light not only on the nature of suffering but the imperative of action in the midst of that suffering. This discourse, however, is not of use to the bent of the merchant who is unconcerned with power and disenfranchised with possessions and toxic social relations. Unlike Samādhi, Suratha does not have the luxury of renouncing,[91] and neither does Arjuna. Kṛṣṇa eventually succeeds in *mobilizing* the disheartened Arjuna, whose despondency compromises the Pāṇḍavas ability to restore righteous rule. Arjuna has grace on his side, but needs to regain his will to fight. Suratha has the will to fight, but needs to procure the grace: Suratha, "[d]espondent because of his excessive concern for himself,/And because his kingdom had been taken away,"[92] is moved to practice austerities. While Arjuna is conflicted because he doesn't want the kingship badly enough, Suratha is conflicted because kingship is all he really wants.

Coburn notes that while "elements of supplication and requests for beneficence are as old as the hymns of the *Rg Veda*,"[93] the DM entails "the more specific kind of protection that is provided when the world order is about to crumble, on either a grand or a minor scale."[94] He looks to the BhG as the major antecedent of this vision of protection, specifically invoking Viṣṇu's *avatāric* promise to personally manifest amid mortals, for the protection of the righteous and the destruction of the wicked, whenever *dharma* is endangered.[95] The DM and BhG therefore share an interplay surrounding this theme of "regally protecting the world."[96] In addition to the more commonly known "intimate historical connection between the cowherd Krishna (Krishna Gopāla) and the worship of Durgā in north India during the early centuries of the Christian era,"[97] Coburn calls to our attention an element of this interplay most crucial for the work at hand: the assemblers of the MBh include, within the epic folds, two hymns to Durgā, the first of these occurring immediately prior to the BhG.[98]

Kṛṣṇa asks Arjuna to recite the *Durgā Stotra* for the sake of conquering his enemies,[99] which he does, "after which the Goddess appears to him, assures him of victory, and then vanishes."[100] Tradition lays stake at this precise juncture so as to capitalize on prime hermeneutic textual real estate which serves to thematically focus what follows. That Durgā's myths revolve around the reinstatement of usurped sovereignty corroborates why Arjuna would be wise to invoke her at that point. In making sense of this textual fluidity, Coburn concludes that "[t]he conception of deity as periodically incarnate for the sake of redeeming the world has been employed in the service of both Krishna and the Goddess."[101] However, more immediately, on the mundane scale, that process of "redeeming the world" is dependent upon the restoration of sovereignty.

This falls in line with the interrelation between kings and the Goddess which Coburn perceives: while one might doubt that "seems as old as the Indus Valley civilization,"[102] one might readily assent that it pervades the literary sources occurring prior to the DM, is central to the DM itself, and constitutes "an important dimension of contemporary celebration of Durgā Pūjā."[103]

The extent to which the king's desire (for sovereignty) is privileged over the merchant's desire (for liberation) is made apparent in the closing verses of the DM, despite the appearance that she favors both equally. In light of this appearance, Brubaker notes that while the DM presents the world as both "sacred and ultimately imprisoning" and "seduces us into delusion, craving, and bondage … for the sake of the world, that it may thrive and be perpetuated," the world is "none other than the realm of *saṃsāra*, from whose fertile yet fatal embrace she would also release us."[104] He quotes sage Medhas' delusion discourse—"[h]uman beings have a craving for offspring,/Out of greed expecting them to reciprocate"[105]—to conclude that "even the dharmic duties to produce children and to perform *śrāddha* rites for parents are revealed to be rooted in egoism and to bear the fruit of bondage."[106] He notes that the reciprocity between the world-denying and world-affirming visions is "delicately balanced, for it lies in the two hands of the One Devī. Her left hand continually takes away what her right hands puts in place and her right hand continually replaces what her left hand removes."[107] However, to draw an analogy from her iconography, Durgā possesses multiple hands, the majority of which are geared to guarding this world.

When Durgā appears and offers them each a boon, "the king chose a kingdom that would not perish even in another lifetime, *and* his own kingdom now, with the power of his enemies forcibly overthrown."[108] The king actually requests *two* boons while the merchant chooses one: "And the wise *vaiśya*, his mind despairing of things of this world, chose knowledge/Which destroys attachment to the notions of 'I' and 'mine.' "[109] That the king chooses two boons might represent that he opts for the duality of phenomenal existence over the oneness of liberation. It also signals a dual emphasis on his leanings, over Samādhi's.

Just as the text systematically interweaves the aims of *pravṛtti* and *nivṛtti*, moving from the king's request to that of the merchant, it continues the pattern with Durgā's response. Durgā expresses no qualms about the dual weight of the king's request and furthermore, she *rewards* him for his request, granting him "more than he asked for."[110] She declares not only that he will slay his enemies and regain his kingdom in a few days' time, and that it will permanently be his (DM 13.13–14), but further that upon his death, he will be reborn as the son of the sun-god Vivasvan whereby he "will be the Manu named Sāvarṇi here on earth."[111] Note that she blesses the king with the *martial power* to overthrow his enemies himself; she does not overthrow them for him. While she would possess the power to accomplish this task for him, she empowers him to do it himself and her empowerment is an emphatic endorsement of his blood-soaked duty as an earthly king.

Regarding Douglas' second rule about ring closures, the restoration of Suratha's sovereignty directly harkens to the mid-turn of the text, Episode II, where Indra's sovereignty is lost (as with Suratha's in the opening of the ring) and then restored by the grace of the Goddess (as with Suratha's in the closing of the ring). Moreover, the hero of our text not only refrains from ending his cycle of rebirth, but succeeds in securing an exalted future birth; hence the *nivṛttic* insight into the suffering of cyclical existence is muted by the suggestion of contented *saṃsāric* existence. Not only is she unstained by bloodshed because of her supreme stature, but so, too, is the king, by virtue of the stature of his office and the supremacy of the world-affirming ideology it upholds. She then proceeds to bless the merchant, granting him his noble *nivṛttic* desire: "knowledge that is conducive to perfection."[112] The text proceeds to indicate that immediately after granting their boons, Durgā vanishes, while merchant and king devoutly praise her.

Were the text to conclude here, the DM's terminal frame would emphasize Samādhi's spiritual attainment, since it would be the final sentiment sealing off the work and closing its narrating ring. But this cannot be the case. Therefore, harkening to the *pravṛttic* thrust central to the work of the Goddess, and the work of the DM in thematically and structurally representing that Goddess, Mārkaṇḍeya is certain to seal off the DM's narrative ring with a fundamentally *pravṛttic* closure as follows:

> Thus having received a boon from the Goddess, Suratha, the best of rulers,
> Upon receiving another birth from Sūrya,
> will become the Manu known as Sāvarṇi,
> will become the Manu known as Sāvarṇi.
>
> (DM 13.17)[113]

Douglas notes that ring closures often evoke their beginnings "using some of the same words."[114] Hence, its closing reads "Upon receiving another birth from Sūrya, [Suratha] will become the Manu known as Sāvarṇi,"[115] repeating the proper nouns Manu, Sūrya, and Sāvarṇi as occurring in the opening lines of the DM: "Sāvarṇi, who is Sūrya's son, is said to be the eighth Manu."[116] The repetition of this last line not only doubly signals that our narrative ring has come full circle, but underscores Douglas' third observation that ring closures often serve to latch "the text as a whole in a larger context, less parochial, more humanist, or even metaphysical";[117] in this case, the *manvantara* section of the MkP. In appointing Suratha as the overlord of a future eon, the DM's ring of sovereign power comes full circle. The work finds its resolution in issuing two sovereignty-oriented boons to its noble king, the second of which is doubly voiced, echoing the work's overarching emphasis upon the *pravṛttic* work of kings, and the work of a grand Goddess sworn to safeguard them, all the while enacting the world-affirming ideology for which they stand.

Notes

1 This theme befits the text's religious application, largely adopted in pursuit of worldly blessings, rather than liberation. For example, in the final verse (39) of the *Vaikṛtika Rahasya* (one of the six traditionally appendages to the DM), Medhas declares to Suratha: "Therefore, O king, worship the great queen of all the worlds, Caṇḍikā, in the way that has been prescribed: you will attain (every) happiness." Coburn, *Encountering the Goddess*, 191.

2 For a streamlined articulation of this argument, see Raj Balkaran, "The Safeguard of Sovereignty: Focusing the Frame of the Devī Māhātmya," in *Proceedings of the 16th World Sanskrit Conference (Bangkok, 2015)* (Delhi: Motilal Banarsidass Publishers, 2018).

3 Wendy Doniger, *The Hindus: An Alternative History* (New York: Penguin Press, 2009), 389.

4 DM 13.9. The merchant and king "gave her offerings sprinkled with blood from their own limbs." Coburn, *Encountering the Goddess*, 83. For related discussion on the role of blood sacrifice in modern tantric ritual dedicated to Durgā, see Hillary Peter Rodrigues, "Fluid Control: Orchestrating Blood Flow in the Durgā Pūjā," *Studies in Religion/Sciences religieuses* 32, no. 8 (2009).

5 DM 1.1–2: "Mārkaṇḍeya said: Sāvarṇi, who is Sūrya's son, is said to be the eighth Manu./Hear about his birth from me, speaking at length,/How by the power of Mahāmāyā, Sāvarṇi, the illustrious/Son of the sun, came to be the overlord of a Manu-interval." Coburn, 32.

6 DM 1.3–5. Coburn, 32.

7 Prabhat Chandra Chakravarti, *Doctrine of Sakti in Indian Literature* (Patna: Eastern Book House, 1986), 80.

8 To characterize the Merchant's qualms as solely pertaining to *artha* would be inapt; he also expresses the concern as to whether his children were behaving in accordance with *dharma*.

9 As Dhand notes, "In *pravṛtti dharma*, asceticism, and the *āśrama* scheme into which it is interjected, are both explicitly limited to males of the three upper castes." Dhand, *Woman as Fire, Woman as Sage Sexual Ideology in the Mahābhārata*, 73.

10 Coburn, *Encountering the Goddess*, 159.

11 cf. *medhā*, "intelligence, knowledge, understanding." Monier-Williams et al., "Sanskrit-English Dictionary."

12 The phrase "*ṛṣir uvāca*" ("the seer said") occurs at twenty-seven places within the text, ten of which are to commence separate chapters. Similarly, the sage is referred to at five junctures by an honorific: DM 1.29: *bhagavat*, "venerable sir," Coburn, *Encountering the Goddess*, 34; DM 1.33: *mahābhāga*, "O illustrious one," Coburn, 34; DM 1.45: *bhagavat*, "O illustrious one," Coburn, 36; DM 9.1: *bhagavat*, "O blessed one," Coburn, 68; DM 13.5 *mahābhāga*, "illustrious seer," Coburn, 83. Furthermore, he is referred to as *muni* on two occasions: DM 1.10: *muniṇā tena satkṛaḥ*, "honored by the sage," Coburn, 32; DM 1.27: *tam muniṃ samupasthitau*, "then together they approached the sage," Coburn, 34.

13 One wonders whether the "*śākta* interpolators" would bother to "Trojan horse" the DM into the MkP, only to accord it to an obscure sage (Medhas) rather than the illustrious Mārkaṇḍeya himself.

14 Pargiter, *Mārkaṇḍeya Purāṇa*, iv.

15 Mani Vettam, e.g., makes no reference to either character in his cataloguing of such figures; see Vettam Mani, *Purāṇic Encyclopaedia: A Comprehensive Dictionary with Special Reference to the Epic and Purāṇic Literature* (Delhi: Motilal Banarsidass, 1975).

16 Mani, 768–9.

17 DM 1.27–9. Coburn, *Encountering the Goddess*, 34.

18 DM 1.32–3. Coburn, 34.
19 E.g., DM 1.78b. Coburn, 52.
20 DM 4.34: bhūpa; DM 8.51: mahīpāla; DM 8.51: nṛpa; DM 12.34: bhūpa; DM 13.1: bhūpa.
21 DM 13.1: etat te kathitaṃ bhūpa devīmāhātmyam uttamam | "Thus have I related to you, O king, the supreme *Devī-Māhātmya.*" Coburn, *Encountering the Goddess*, 81. Emphasis my own.
22 DM 9.1. Coburn, 68. Emphasis my own.
23 I overheard someone say the other day, "if you can't measure it, it doesn't exist." It occurred to me that, etymologically, the opposite is true of the Sanskrit term "*māyā*": stemming from the root "mā" (to measure), it implies that if you *can* measure it, then it does not exist. Another way of putting this is that ultimate truth is literally immeasurable.
24 DM 1.40–1.41. Coburn, *Encountering the Goddess*, 35.
25 Coburn, 32.
26 Renate Söhnen-Thieme, "Goddess, Gods, Demons in the Devī Māhātmya," in *Stages and Transitions: Temporal and Historical Frameworks in Epic and Purāṇic Literature: Proceedings of the Second Dubrovnik International Conference on the Sanskrit Epics and Purāṇas, August 1999*, ed. Brockington Dubrovnik International Conference on the Sanskrit Epics and Purāṇas Mary, Radoslav Katičić, and Hrvatska akademija znanosti i umjetnosti (Zagreb: Academia Scientiarum et Artium Croatica, 2002), 244–5.
27 Douglas, *Thinking in Circles: An Essay on Ring Composition*, 58.
28 Söhnen-Thieme, "Goddess, Gods, Demons in the Devī Māhātmya," 242.
29 Söhnen-Thieme, 246.
30 DM 1.44. Coburn, *Encountering the Goddess*, 35.
31 While one might argue that Episode I details the Goddess's role in restoring Viṣṇu's "sovereignty" in a broad sense, returning control of the cosmos to him, her action in this episode is of a very different texture than in the throne episodes. Hence the text makes an important "turn" from the Goddess as Mahāmāyā, to the Goddess as sovereign of all lords.
32 Dorsey, *The Literary Structure of the Old Testament*, 17–18.
33 Douglas, *Thinking in Circles: An Essay on Ring Composition*, x.
34 See Coburn, *Encountering the Goddess*, 99–117.
35 See Coburn, 104–8.
36 See Coburn, 109–17.
37 Vaikṛtika Rahasya, 31–2. Coburn, 190.
38 This is not to say that these are mutually exclusive. DM 4.6, for example, reads:

> (You are) the cause of all the worlds; although possessed of the three qualities *(guṇas)*, by faults you are not known; (you are) unfathomable even by Hari, Hara, and the other gods./(You are) the resort of all, (you are) this entire world that is composed of parts, for you are the supreme, original, untransformed Prakṛti.
>
> Coburn, 48

39 DM 1.78. Coburn, 39. Italics my own.
40 DM 2.2. Coburn, 39.
41 DM 2.5: *sūryendragnyanilendūnāṃ yamasya varuṇasya ca* | *anyeṣāṃ cādhikārān sa svayam evādhitiṣṭhati* || "He himself now wields sovereignty over Sūrya, Indra, Agni, Vāyu, Candra, Yama,/And over Varuṇa and the others." Coburn, 39.
42 The Goddess's manifestation is repeatedly harkened to the eight world-protectors. These are: Indra, Sūrya, Candra, Kubera, Yama, Varuṇa, Vāyu, and Agni. I suspect that there are gaps in our knowledge regarding the symbolism of the number eight as it pertains to Durgā. For her function is not only representative of the eight

world-protectors but the DM itself accounts for the installation of the eighth Manu. One can surmise that the number continued to be auspicious to Durgā, given that she is most often ichnographically represented in eight-armed form, and that the most auspicious *tithi* for her worship is *aṣṭhamī*, the day of the lunar calendar.

43 DM 2.7. Coburn, *Encountering the Goddess*, 40.

44 Coburn, *Devī-Māhātmya: The Crystallization of the Goddess Tradition.*

45 Coburn, "Consort of None, Śakti of All: The Vision of the Devī-Māhātmya."

46 DM II.8–12. Coburn, *Encountering the Goddess*, 40.

47 DM 2.13–18. Coburn, 40–1. Note that the contributors include the eight world guardians (in addition to Brahmā, Prajāpati, Viṣṇu, and Śiva).

48 DM 2.19–2.30a. Coburn, 41. Note that the weapons were contributed by seven of the eight world-protectors (except for the moon), in addition to Kāla and Viśvakarman.

49 Ron Inden writes:

> Bursting with the radiant energy of the gods, the king was to reintegrate or recentralize the units of his kingdom on a periodic, continuing basis by exercising royal power (daṇḍa), clearly seen as an earthly, immanent form of divine, radiant energy (tejas).
>
> Inden, "Ritual, Authority, and Cyclic Time in Hindu Kingship," 49

50 Coburn, *Devī-Māhātmya: The Crystallization of the Goddess Tradition*, 26; Coburn, *Devī-Māhātmya*, 229–30. He uses Buhler's translation; see fn. 65.

51 Arthur Llewellyn Basham, *The Wonder That Was India: A Survey of the Culture of the Indian Sub-Continent Before the Coming of the Muslims* (New York: Taplinger Publ. Co., 1968), 82.

52 Basham, 19.

53 Coburn, *Devī-Māhātmya*, 230.

54 Coburn, *Encountering the Goddess: A Translation of the Devī Māhātmya and a Study of Its Interpretation*, 26.

55 Richard Gombrich, "Kings, Power and the Goddess," *South Asian Research* 6, no. 2 (1986). Yokochi calls into question the compatibility between the literary description of the Goddess's killing of Mahiṣa in the DM and the iconographical depictions thereof in the Gupta period, arguing that the DM's description conforms more so to the iconographical depictions from the early medieval period, eighth to ninth century. See Yokochi, "The Rise of the Warrior Goddess in Ancient India."

56 Kinsley, "The Portrait of the Goddess in the Devī Māhātmya," 493.

57 Fuller, *The Camphor Flame*, 108.

58 Fuller, 111.

59 Hillary Rodrigues, *Ritual Worship of the Great Goddess: The Liturgy of the Durgā Pūjā with Interpretations* (Albany, NY: State University of New York Press, 2003), 293.

60 Rodrigues, 290.

61 Fuller, *The Camphor Flame*, 118.

62 Fuller, 118–19.

63

> Nevertheless, the texts in praise of the goddess recited during the Mysore festival do not appear to have included the Devīmāhātmya (Biardeau 1989b: 303), the most famous classical myth of Durgā's victory. Biardeau's research shows that it would be wrong to take the Devīmāhātmya (or other comparable texts) as a kind of script for royal Navarātrī celebrations. Rather, there is a common core of symbolic themes, particularly focused on the Goddess and her sacrifices, which are developed at both ritual and mythical levels, but not by any predetermined connection between them.
>
> Fuller, 117

64 Coburn, *Devī-Māhātmya*, 134–6.

65 Coburn, 135.
66 Fuller, *The Camphor Flame*, 115.
67 Coburn, *Encountering the Goddess*, 55.
68 DM 5.1–3. Coburn, 52. This motif is later echoed when we learn that Śumbha has usurped treasures from five of the world-protectors: Indra's elephant (Airāvata), his Pārijāta tree, and his horse (Uccaiḥśravas); Kubera's "Great Lotus" treasure; Varuṇa's royal umbrella, showering gold; Yama's spear; Varuṇa's noose; and garments from Agni.
69 DM 5.4. Coburn, 52.
70 Cf. Episode II where, apart from the *Śakradi Stuti* (which, as with all of the hymns, showcases many of the facets of the Goddess), there is no mention of sacrifice.
71 Coburn, *Encountering the Goddess*, 73.
72 Kinsley, *Hindu Goddesses: Vision of the Feminine in the Hindu Religious Tradition*, 103–4.
73 Douglas, *Thinking in Circles: An Essay on Ring Composition*, 36.
74 DM 10.5. Coburn, *Encountering the Goddess*, 71.
75 Douglas, *Thinking in Circles: An Essay on Ring Composition*, 22.
76 Thomas B. Coburn, "The Threefold Vision of the Devī Māhātmya," in *The Great Goddess*, ed. Dehejia, Vidya (New York: Arthur M. Sackler Gallery, 1999), 50.
77 Madhu (1.50, 1.66, 1.68, 1.71); Kaiṭabha (1.50, 1.66, 1.68, 1.71).
78 Mahiṣa (2.1, 2.2, 2.6, 2.18, 3.10, 4.1, 4.11, 4.12, 4.13) and Mahiṣāsura (2.4, 2.35, 2.39, 2.46, 3.20, 4.30); Madhu (2.8); Cikṣura (2.39, 3.1); Cāmara (2.40, 3.10, 3.12, 3.13, 3.15); Udagra (2.40, 3.16); Mahāhanu (2.41, 3.18); Asiloman (2.41); Bāṣkala (2.42, 3.17); Parivārita (2.42); Viḍāla (2.43); Karāla (3.16); Uddhata (3.17); Tāmra (3.17); Andhaka (3.17); Ugrāsya (3.18); Ugravīrya (3.18); Biḍāla (3.19); Durdhara (3.19); Durmukha (3.19); Kaiṭabha (4.10); Śumbha (4.35); Niśumbha (4.35).
79 Śumbha (5.1, 5.39, 5.42, 5.43, 5.54, 5.57, 5.67, 5.70, 5.71, 5.73, 5.74, 5.75, 6.6, 6.17, 7.23, 8.2, 8.6, 8.23, 9.2, 9.3, 9.6, 9.7, 9.15, 9.21, 9.23, 9.24, 9.25, 10.1, 10.6, 11.37, 12.2, 12.31); Niśumbha (5.1, 5.39, 5.42, 5.52, 5.64, 5.67, 5.70, 5.71, 5.74, 5.75, 6.6, 7.23, 8.23, 9.2, 9.3, 9.4, 9.7, 9.9, 9.10, 9.12, 9.15, 9.27, 9.30, 9.32, 11.37, 12.2, 12.32); Caṇḍa (5.42, 5.54, 6.17, 6.18, 7.1, 7.15, 7.19, 7.20, 7.21, 7.22, 7.23, 7.25, 8.1); Muṇḍa (5.42, 5.54, 6.17, 6.18, 7.1, 7.16, 7.20, 7.21, 7.22, 7.23, 7.25, 8.1, 11.20); Sugrīva (5.54); Dhumralocana (6.2, 6.5); Udayudha demons (8.3); Kambu (8.3); Koṭivīrya demons (8.4); Dhūmra demons (8.4); Kālaka demons (8.5); Daurhṛda demons (8.5); Maurya demons (8.5); Kālakeya demons (8.5); Raktabīja (8.39, 8.41, 8.48, 8.49, 8.56, 8.60, 9.1, 9.2, 9.3); Diti (9.28); Vṛtra (11.18); Durgama (11.45); Aruṇa (11.48); Madhu (12.2); Kaiṭabha (12.2); Mahiṣa (12.2).
80 Mahāmāyā (1.2, 1.40, 1.41, 1.42, 1.45, 1.73); Yoganidrā (1.49, 1.52); Svāhā (1.54); Svadhā (1.54); Sāvitrī (1.55).
81 Caṇḍika (2.48, 3.27, 3.33, 3.34, 4.3, 4.24); Ambikā (2.51, 2.66, 3.1, 3.11, 3.23, 4.2, 4.23, 4.26, 4.32); Bhadrakālī (3.8, 4.33); Śri (4.4, 4.10); Alakṣmī (4.4); Prakṛti (4.6); Svāhā (4.7); Svadhā (4.7); Durgā (4.10, 4.16); Gaurī (4.10, 4.35).
82 Prakṛti (5.7); Gaurī (5.8, 11.9); Kūrmī (5.9); Nairṛti (5.9); Lakṣmi (5.9, 11.21); Śarvāṇī (5.9); Durgā (5.10, 5.66, 9.29, 10.2, 11.23, 11.46); Pārvatī (5.37, 5.40, 5.41); Ambikā (5.40, 5.42, 6.9, 6.20, 7.4, 8.8, 8.16, 9.15, 9.22, 10.4, 10.8, 10.14, 10.20, 11.29); Kauśikī (5.40); Kālikā (5.41); Kālī (7.5, 7.15, 7.18, 7.22, 7.24, 8.9, 8.10, 8.31, 8.52, 8.56, 9.20, 9.27, 9.35, 9.39); Caṇḍikā (7.22, 7.24, 8.7, 8.12, 8.21, 8.22, 8.52, 8.56, 9.6, 9.8, 9.13, 9.26, 9.28, 9.30, 9.31, 9.32, 10.13, 10.18, 10.21, 11.27, 12.29, 13.10); Cāmuṇḍā (7.25, 8.52, 8.58, 8.59, 11.20); Brahmāṇī (8.14, 8.32, 9.36, 10.4, 11.12); Māheśvarī (8.15, 8.33, 8.48, 9.37, 11.13); Guha (8.16); Kaumārī (8.16, 8.33, 8.48, 9.36, 11.14); Vaiṣṇavī (8.17, 8.33, 8.46, 8.47, 9.38, 11.15); Nārasiṃhī (8.19, 8.36); Aindrī (8.20, 8.34, 8.41, 8.46, 9.38, 11.18); Śivadūti (8.27, 8.37, 9.21, 9.35, 9.39, 11.19); Kātyāyanī (8.28, 11.1, 11.24); Vārāhī (8.35, 8.48, 9.37); Nārāyaṇī (11.7, 11.8, 11.9, 11.10, 11.11, 11.12, 11.13, 11.14, 11.15, 11.16, 11.17, 11.18,

11.19, 11.20, 11.21, 11.22); Svadhā (11.21); Sarasvatī (11.22); Bābhravī (11.22); Bhadrakālī (11.25); Raktadantikā (11.41); Śākaṃbharī (11.45); Bhīmādevī (11.48); Bhrāmarī (11.50); Mahākālī (12.35).

83 Sāvarṇi (1.1, 1.2); Sūrya (1.1); Hari (1.41); Viṣṇu (1.41, 1.49, 1.50, 1.51, 1.52, 1.53, 1.64, 1.65, 1.68, 1.70, 1.72, 1.73, 1.75); Brahmā (1.50, 1.51, 1.69, 1.71, 1.78); Prajāpati (1.51); Śiva (1.65).

84 Indra (2.1, 2.2, 2.5, 2.14, 2.21, 4.1, 4.27); Prajāpati (2.3, 2.16, 2.22); Śiva (2.3, 2.8, 2.9, 2.13, 2.19, 4.3, 4.10); Viṣṇu (2.3, 2.8, 2.9, 2.13, 4.3, 4.10); Sūrya (2.5); Agni (2.5, 2.16, 2.20); Vāyu (2.5, 2.20); Candra (2.5); Yama (2.5, 2.13, 2.22); Varuṇa (2.5, 2.22, 2.14, 2.20); Brahmā (2.9, 2.15, 2.22, 4.3); Soma (2.14); Vasus (2.15); Kubera (2.15, 2.29); Kṛṣṇa (2.19); Kāla (2.23); Viśvakarman (2.26); Śeṣa (2.29); Hari (4.6); Hara (4.6).

85 Indra (5.1, 5.47, 5.73, 8.12, 8.20, 8.25, 8.41, 11.1); Kubera (5.2, 5.49); Yama (5.2); Varuṇa (5.2, 5.50, 5.51); Vāyu (5.3); Agni (5.3, 5.52, 11.1); Viṣṇu (5.6, 5.12, 8.12, 11.4, 13.2); Brahmā (5.48, 8.12, 8.14, 12.23, 12.24, 12.35); Prājapatī (5.50); Śiva (8.12, 8.21, 8.23, 8.27, 8.28, 8.31); Skanda (8.12, 8.16); Hari (8.18); Vivasvān (13.14); Sūrya (13.17).

86 Douglas, *Thinking in Circles: An Essay on Ring Composition*, 126.

87 Gonda, *Ancient Indian Kingship from the Religious Point of View*, 4.

88 Pollock, "The Divine King in the Indian Epic," 526.

89 Pollock, 523.

90 It is noteworthy that the Gītā's expositor (Kṛṣṇa) is physically present from the outset; yet he operates as a dialogical speaker and only assumes his expositional stance in response to Arjuna's lament, when he is "approached" as a teacher.

91 Coburn writes,

> The first half of the frame story recounts how a king and a merchant are beset by mundane adversity, the king betrayed by his ministers, the merchant robbed of his wealth by wife and sons. And so they renounce the world and retire to the forest, a venerable option in India for the past 2500 years.
>
> Coburn, *The Conceptualization of Religious Change*, 11

However, let us recall that the king does not actually renounce the world, nor does he retire to the forest for more than a temporary respite. He is there under the pretence of hunting, which signals his intent to return.

92 DM 13.5. "Having paid homage to the illustrious seer who practiced severe austerities,/Despondent because of his excessive concern for himself, and because his kingdom had been taken away," Coburn, *Encountering the Goddess*, 83.

93 Coburn, 25.

94 Coburn, 25.

95 Coburn's translation reads:

> Although being unborn (and) having an eternal soul *(ātman)*, (and) even though I am Lord of creatures, Having resorted to my own material nature *(prakṛti)*, I come into being by means of my own magic power (māyā), For whenever the proper state of affairs (dharma) declines, O Son of Bharata, Whenever disorder is on the rise, then do I send myself forth. For protection of the good, and for destruction of evildoers, To make a firm foundation for *dharma*, I come into being in age after age.
>
> Coburn, 25

96 Coburn, 25.

97 Coburn, 26.

98 Coburn writes,

> In the critical edition of the *Mahābhārata*, the *Bhagavad Gita* begins in chapter 23 of book 6 (the Bhīṣma Parvan). At the very end of chapter 22, a number of

manuscripts insert what has become known as the *Durgā Stotra.* The context, of course, is exactly the same as that of the *Bhagavad Gitā*, with Arjuna and Krishna surveying the battle lines for the impending combat.

Coburn, 26

99 Coburn, 27.
100 Coburn, 27. Coburn notes that the Durgā Stotra "concludes with a *phala-sruti* or statement of the results for one who, like Arjuna, recites the *Durga Stotra:* 'He never knows any fear … and has no enemies—In controversy he obtains victory he inevitably crosses over difficulty …; he is always victorious in battle.' "
101 Coburn, 27.
102 Coburn, 172.
103 Coburn, 172.
104 Richard L. Brubaker, "Comments: The Goddess and the Polarity of the Sacred," in *The Divine Consort: Radha and the Goddesses of India*, ed. John Stratton Hawley (Delhi: Motilal Banarsidass, 1984), 205–6.
105 *Devī-māhātmya*, line 39, trans. Thomas Coburn.
106 Brubaker, "Comments: The Goddess and the Polarity of the Sacred," 205–6.
107 Brubaker, 205–6.
108 DM 13.11b–12a. Coburn, *Encountering the Goddess*, 84.
109 DM 13.12b–13a. Coburn, 84.
110 Coburn, 162.
111 DM 13.13b–15a. Coburn, 84.
112 DM13.15b–16a. Coburn, 84.
113 Coburn, 84.
114 Douglas, *Thinking in Circles: An Essay on Ring Composition*, 126.
115 DM 13.17b: *sūryāj janma samāsādya sāvarṇir bhavitā manuḥ* || *sāvarṇir bhavitā manuḥ* || Coburn, *Encountering the Goddess*, 84.
116 DM 1.1a: *sāvarṇiḥ sūryatanayo yo manuḥ kathyate 'ṣṭamaḥ* | Coburn, 32.
117 Douglas, *Thinking in Circles: An Essay on Ring Composition*, 126.

5 Mother of power

Focusing the Goddess of the *Devī Māhātmya*

How should we characterize Durgā of the DM? Is she an angry entity, eager to receive the blood of sacrifice? Is she a compassionate mother? Does she delight in destruction, or is she contented by caring for her children, all beings within creation? While either of these divergent descriptions might be apt in any given *juncture* of the text, what do we see when we examine the vision of the feminine divine in the DM *as a whole*? All too often the Goddess's dark, wrathful aspect is overemphasized, decontextualized from its function as a response to a virulent foe. Durgā of the DM is a principle of power, and, harnessing that power for the sake of world welfare, she serves, by extension, as a principle of protection. Functioning as a royal figure, she is undoubtedly an agent of order.

Building on the findings of this work thus far, this chapter reevaluates prevalent characterizations of the Goddess of the DM within Hindu Studies, demonstrating the perils of refracting her image through the lenses of ritual, devotion, and tantric traditions. It sets aside what we know of historical and contemporary appropriations of the text in order to isolate the visage of the Goddess dwelling in the chambers of the DM. It demonstrates the extent to which characterizations of the Goddess in the DM are all too often projected from outside of the DM, through various historical and literary depictions of Durgā, and of Kālī. Scholarly encounters with Durgā have been ironically obscured by encounters with her *māhātmya*. This discussion deconstructs the breast–tooth typology commonly imposed on the Goddess of our text, demonstrating the ineptitude of that binary in capturing her complexity. It then looks to the presence of a second, subordinate narrative ring within the text, which serves to subsume her wrathful "tooth" aspect by her compassionate "breast" aspect. The final section of this chapter reflects upon the vision of divine power artfully personified within the DM.

Breaking through the breast–tooth binary

Much scholarship on the DM falls prey to the binary trope of Hindu female deities existing as either beneficent "goddesses of the breast" versus maleficent "goddesses of the tooth." Wendy Doniger famously sums up the dichotomy in question as follows:

> Indian goddesses can be divided into two distinct categories. The first group are goddesses of the tooth (or of the genitals—the concepts being linked in the motif of the vagina dentata); they are worshipped in times of crisis, such as epidemics, and are ambivalent, dangerous, and erotic figures. The second group are the goddesses of the breast, endemic and auspicious, bountiful and fertile, linked to the life-cycle.[1]

While this typology can be useful in grappling with Hindu goddesses at large, it greatly curtails the complexity of the Goddess of the DM, which, contrary to prevalent scholarly assertions, squarely bucks the breast–tooth binary. Doniger credits A.K. Ramanujan for this "useful terminology,"[2] and again reiterates her gratitude to him in 1993 in her introduction to the volume of Ramanujan's collected essays.[3] In tracing the origin of the breast–tooth bifurcation, we note Ramanujan's assertion that "consort Goddesses are benevolent Breast Mothers; Kālī and her various allomorphs are Tooth Mothers."[4] He first fleshes out his typology of goddesses of the breast and tooth in his 1986 article, *Two Realms of Kannada Folklore*, in a table entitled, "Two Types of Indian Goddesses."[5] It is duplicated in Table 5.1 below.

Table 5.1 Ramanujan's breast–tooth typology (bolded elements apply to the Goddess of the DM)

Breast Mothers (Consort Goddesses)	*Tooth Mothers (Virgin Goddesses, Amman)*
Married; subordinate to the male consort.	**Basically independent**; if married, insubordinate or fatal to consort; male could be consort, brother, servant, or guardian.
Related to auspicious, life-cycle rituals; weddings, good fortune.	**Crisis-deities**, invoked when life-cycles are disrupted; seen as inflicting as well as removing epidemics, famine, etc.; leaving one alone is part of their grace.
Household deities; temples within village.	Temples often outside village boundaries; goddess brought into village only on special occasions.
Well-sculpted faces and images.	Rough-hewn, often faceless images; often objects other than icons, like pots.
Not born of the earth.	Of the earth, earthy, often literally.
Pure, chaste.	Seen often as lustful, **angry**, coquettish.
Claims to universality.	Associated, most often, only with a village after which she is named.
Benevolent, unless offended. Lakṣmī intercedes for mortals with the great god in *Vaisnava bhakti*; Parvatī, in folk-tales.	Ambivalent; dread an intimate part of the devotion. Possession a part of the ritual.
Vegetarian.	**Blood sacrifices (or substitutes) demanded, offered**.
***Brahman* or *brahmanised* priests**.	Mostly non-*brahman*, often untouchable.

Insofar as meeting the criteria he lists for "goddesses of the tooth," the Goddess of the DM is indeed independent, and invoked in times of crisis. However, counter to his other criteria for goddesses of the tooth, she is *not* worshipped away from the domestic sphere, she is *not* portrayed as a faceless icon, *nor* is she of the earth, *nor* is she primarily invoked by non-*brāhmaṇa* officiants. Furthermore, Durgā's anger is episodic, while her chastity, on the other hand, is a permanent state. Conversely, with respect to his criteria of "consort goddesses," while the Goddess is most certainly unmarried, she, in many ways, supports his characterization of breast mothers. Not only does she possess a well-sculpted face, and is worshipped in the domestic sphere by *brāhmaṇa* priests, but she, like breast mothers, is not born of the earth, is chaste, and possesses claims to universality.

Upon examining the Goddess of the DM within its own textual parameters, we see that its representation of the feminine divine actually fits more with Ramanujan's characterization of breast Goddesses, though the typology ultimately loses traction. While Ramanujan admits that "there are minor exceptions to these contrasts, and in particular cults some features may cross over from one side to another, in myth, name, degree of benevolence, or ambivalence,"[6] one can hardly call probably the most popular pan-Indic goddess a minor exception. One suspects Ramanujan refers primarily (if not exclusively) to village culture and not necessarily to the Goddess of the DM.[7] Yet nevertheless his typology was harnessed to grapple with the Goddess of the DM, most prominently by Wendy Doniger, who problematically refers to her as the "paradigmatic tooth goddess in India."[8] According to Ramanujan's original typology, Durgā of the DM might be described as an independent breast goddess who bares her teeth in times of need.

The DM presents a Goddess of order, not disorder, contrary to the portrait painted by David Kinsley,[9] who overstates the extent to which the Goddess of the DM represents anti-structure and taboo. In his article, "The Portrait of the Goddess in the Devī Māhātmya," Kinsley draws on material that lays well beyond the pages of the DM, while failing to register crucial aspects of the Goddess which occur in the text itself. Following suit with how Purāṇic narratives have been studied in the west, he dissects the text in order to delimit the various goddess traditions of which he finds traces within the text.[10] His article is insightful indeed; however, into what does it offer insight—the world *within* the DM, or the one *behind* it? One can certainly not arrive at a portrait of the Goddess of the text through sectarian dismemberment. His article is therefore poorly named; perhaps "The Historically Derived Composite Portrait of the Goddess in the *Devī Māhātmya*" would be more descriptive of its aims. He writes:

> In the *Devī Māhātmya*, Durgā is also described as quaffing wine before her battle with Mahiṣa (3.33) and as laughing and glaring with reddened eyes under its influence. In the concluding scene of the Devī Māhātmya, her devotees are instructed to propitiate her with offerings of their own flesh and blood (13.8). Durgā's preference for inaccessible dwelling places, her

> worship by tribal peoples, her taste for intoxicating drink, meat, and blood, her ferocious behaviour in battle, and the preference for the flesh and blood of her devotees portray a goddess who stands outside the civilized order, whose presence is to be found only after stepping out of the orderly world into the liminal space of mountainous regions where she dwells.[11]

Much of the above passage is predicated on reading into the DM various ancillary historical and literary depictions of Durgā, and especially of Kālī. In the DM, not only does the Goddess not "stand outside the civilized order,"[12] she consecrates and defends the civilized order as represented by the throne of the Vedic god Indra. She likewise safeguards earthly order through reinstatement of Suratha, and extends her safeguard of sovereignty to the cosmic sphere by appointing the next Manu. She is a cosmic queen.

Durgā is indeed described as red-eyed and intoxicated by an energy-granting elixir, which enables her to combat the demon Mahiṣa. However, regarding his observation that "her devotees are instructed to propitiate her with offerings of their own flesh and blood (DM 13.8),"[13] there is certainly no such instruction to be found in the DM. We are told in the closing frame narrative that the merchant and the king, having taken leave of the *brāhmaṇa* from whom they hear the glories of the Goddess, settled down on the banks of a river to practice austerities and recite the hymns of the Goddess in order to obtain a vision of her. We are further told that they worshipped her "with flowers, incense, fire and water,/Sometimes fasting entirely, sometimes restricting their diet, with their minds on her, composed in thought."[14] The DM then tells us that they offered her "blood of their own limbs."[15] This is a choice they make in order to express their devotion, austerity, and steadfastness: neither the *brāhmaṇa*, who instructs them in the ways of the Goddess, nor the gods, who invoke and praise her throughout the text, make any blood offerings, or mention thereof. This is a far cry from a Goddess who has a "preference for the flesh and blood of her devotees."[16]

Kinsley appears to draw on representations of Kālī (in the DM and elsewhere) and conflate those with the Goddess of the DM as a whole. For example, with respect to the Goddess being bloodthirsty, it is crucial to contextualize that it is Kālī (Durgā's projection) who laps up blood in the DM, and only because it is the only method whereby to defeat the demon Raktabīja, who was able to duplicate himself whenever his blood hit the earth. The Goddess's dark side in the DM is construed as a necessary measure while dealing with demons. While Kālī is a deity stigmatized throughout the majority of the modern Hindu world outside of the Indian state of Bengal, Durgā most certainly is not. While Kālī is construed as inauspicious overall, Durgā, despite her at times taboo associations, is an auspicious deity, worshipped throughout temples and homes at her nine-day autumnal festival, and by many Hindus throughout the year. Hence the ineptitude of binary assessments such as "consort Goddesses are benevolent Breast Mothers; Kālī and her various allomorphs are Tooth Mothers."[17] Should we consider Durgā (the benevolent progenitor of Kālī) as a "variant" of Kālī?

In his discussion of Kālī, Kinsley includes the famous episodes of the DM where

> Durgā [taunted by the demons Caṇḍa and Muṇḍa] loses her composure, grows furious, and from her darkened brow springs Kālī [who then] howls loudly, wades into the demon army crushing and eating her enemies, and finally decapitates Caṇḍa and Muṇḍa.[18]

However, it is for the purpose of depicting Durgā as a principle of cosmic and social order that this more disruptive aspect of life is called forth in the form of an alter-ego (Kālī) which, however unruly, is *always* folded back into the face of compassion which comprises the Goddess of the DM. Kālī represents disruption while Durgā represents the disruption of disruption; that is, the reinstatement of harmony. Kālī is the fire that Durgā projects when she is confronted with fire. Kinsley therefore misrepresents and distorts the nuances of the Goddess of the DM by painting her as possessing "taste for intoxicating drink, meat, and blood,"[19] whereas Durgā consumes neither blood nor meat in the DM, and imbibes an intoxicating elixir once, in the context of battle. Kinsley dwells on aspects of Kālī, Durgā's projected wrath, which, as the DM insists, must always be reabsorbed into the beneficent goddess for the sake of the maintenance of cosmic order. This conflation is curious considering the fact that Kinsley appears to be fully cognizant of the fact that Kālī serves as one of the Goddess's episodic moods, elsewhere describing her as "Durgā's personified wrath, her embodied fury."[20] Yet in the discussion above he uses Kālī's characteristics to describe the Goddess as a whole.

C. Mackenzie Brown, on the other hand, offers a sensible counterpoint in noting that in the DM

> Kālī is not yet the supreme creator and controller of the universe; she is clearly subordinate to [Durgā] and that in the ancient account of her exploits, Kālī lacks any maternal role, and it is one of the intriguing questions of Hinduism as to how she came to eventually be regarded as the mother of the universe. Yet even in the early literature, Kālī is not merely horrific and destructive. After all, her essential purpose in these stories is to serve and protect the interests of the gods and goddesses against the malicious and arrogant demons.[21]

It is misleading to conflate the Goddess's "tough love" persona with her compassionate essential nature, and a scholar such as Brown, who has spent sufficient time with the text as a whole, is able to recognize this. However, even Brown overemphasizes the wrathful aspect of the Goddess of the DM in an essay comparing the creation accounts of the Goddess in the DM to that in the *Devī Gītā*[22] (circa 1500 CE). Writing of the Goddess in the *Devī Gītā*, Brown states that "her truest, most sublime nature, is not the implacable and blood-thirsty warrior of the *Devī Māhātmya*, born of the anger of the gods. Rather she is the benevolent

World-Mother."[23] Can we consider the supreme form of the Goddess in the DM as "blood-thirsty"? Also, do the gods not specifically address the Goddess as a gracious "mother of the entire world"?[24] And yet this occurs in tandem with her demon-crushing wrath.

The wrath of the Goddess is celebrated as wholesome in the text, because it is subsumed by the Goddess's motherly compassion: it is only the demons who incur her wrath. Take, for example, the artful pair of verses (both rhetorical questions) from the *Śakrādi Stuti* whereby Indra and the entourage of gods praise the Goddess for defeating the demon Mahiṣa:

> Gently smiling, your shining face resembles the full moon's orb and is as pleasing as the luster of the finest gold. Beholding it, how could Mahiṣāsura, even though enraged, be moved to strike it?
>
> Still stranger was it, O Devī, that Mahiṣa did not perish the instant he beheld your wrathful face, reddened like the rising moon and scowling frightfully. For who can behold the enraged face of death and still live?[25]

If one were to isolate and focus on only the second verse, one would see only a dark and wrathful face, indeed the "enraged face of death." However, if one contextualizes the verse, one would realize it is part of a pair of rhetorical questions, both drawing on lunar imagery, and that the second is to be framed by the first. The face of death then becomes an episodic break from the full moon's orb, one as pleasing as the lustre of the finest gold.

This bifurcated sentiment is vital: it occurs in the center of the *Śakrādi Stuti*, occurring at the episodic center of the work as a whole, the significance of which is laid out in the previous chapter. The hymn goes on to inform us that the world is made happy by the Goddess's conquest of these demons, and that her doing so sends them to heaven, despite their deserving hell (DM 4.17). It proceeds to indicate that she purifies them with her weapons (DM 4.18), calming the activity of such perpetrators, showing compassion to her enemies (DM 4.20), that indeed she is a being in whom coincides "compassion in mind and severity in battle"[26] (DM 4.21). But this rich paradox too often gets lost in the shuffle: in dissecting narratives such as the DM, we tend to polarize the tensions they masterfully interweave. Owing to a legacy of reading Purāṇic texts as fragments and not as wholes, the unfortunate scholarly trend is therefore prone to dwelling on the darkened and frightful face of the Goddess, rather than viewing it in accordance with its portrayal as merely the waning aspect of an oscillating and ultimately resplendent full moon.

The Goddess of the DM is bent on bloodshed, to be sure. So, let us consider: outside of tantric traditions, why would Durgā's bloodshed be celebrated en masse within a cultural context that esteems *ahiṃsā*? Based on his ethnographic findings, J.C. Fuller writes:

> In Bengal, Durgā is widely worshipped too, especially at her annual Durgā Puja, and although Durgā's character is less extreme than Kālī's, the two

> goddesses share a lot. Durgā is also portrayed as a ferocious murderess, slayer of the buffalo-demon, and is offered animal sacrifices; indeed, Kālī is often considered to be a specifically violent form of Durgā.[27]

It is perilous to grapple with the wrath of Durgā in the absence of proper contextualization. The mythologies articulating the necessity of her cosmic purpose are well known within the Hindu tradition, and serve as an implicit backdrop within cultural imagination to even her most grotesque and gory depictions. In the language of Indian human archetypes, she is the protective king, not the destructive hunter; hence her bloodshed is celebrated.

Yoko Yokochi's thesis is centered upon what she conceives as a "pan-Indian martial Goddess" whom she dubs in her work "The Warrior Goddess,"[28] and particularly the contribution of Vindhyavāsinī to the construction of this goddess. The martial agency of such pan-Indian divine personas is typically couched in a protective presence. They combat to protect. While Yokochi notes "the Warrior Goddess of the Devīmāhātmya, who slays demons and preserves order in the world, may be regarded in essence as a likeness or symbol of a king,"[29] she dissects the royal dimension of the Goddess of the DM from her martial dimension. As evidenced from the DM's frame, the text's "message seems to be clear: by following Suratha's example and taking refuge in the Goddess, terrestrial kings can gain the Goddess's protection, share in her power (*Śakti*), and attain their sovereignty in the coming ages,"[30] a message which "would have been welcome among kings and would-be kings at the time of its composition."[31] But this extends far beyond the DM's time of composition.

The Goddess of the DM is a royal figure insofar as she is a protectress of her realm, which happens to encompass the entire universe. If Durgā of the DM is the face of this pan-Indic Goddess, then who might be said to represent "the Warrior Goddess" outside of a royal context? Therefore, while Yokochi concludes that "in this way the Devīmāhātmya succeeded in establishing the Warrior Goddess as an accessory to the royal power in Sanskrit literature and, simultaneously, in the mainstream of Hinduism,"[32] the text itself knows no such bifurcation between a Warrior Goddess and a Sovereign Goddess: it repeatedly hails its Goddess as universal sovereign *because of*, not ancillary to, her propensity to protect through feats of colossal martial power. Failing to view the destructive propensity of Durgā as a means of preservation, Yokochi writes of the *Taittirīya Āraṇyaka* verse to Durgā[33] that, despite its attestation to Durgā's role in saving people from danger (*durga*), "there is no indication that she was regarded as either the Warrior Goddess or a warrior-type goddess." Yet, in the Indian context, who but warriors protect from danger? And who do so better than sovereigns? The bifurcation between warrior and protector is imposed. Hence, can we really disambiguate this protective royal goddess from a "warrior goddess"? Yokochi likewise separates the Goddess's "Supreme" aspect from her "Warrior" aspect as follows: "In the Devīmāhāmtya, the Warrior Goddess became the Supreme Goddess; nevertheless, she remains the Warrior Goddess in terms of her character and her association with kingship."[34] Again, the text of the DM simply knows no such distinction. Rather, the literary force of the DM lies in its capacity to integrate various strands into the figure of its Goddess; to pull apart that tapestry is to silence the voices that weave it.

The DM extols a Goddess wherein devastating martial prowess coincides with compassionate care. While wrathful violence is quintessential to the Goddess's capacity to safeguard the universe against the most virulent of demons, we must note that it is her heartfelt concern for worldly welfare that ironically occasions that wrath. Our pulverizing Goddess is "always tender-minded."[35] The text does not therefore paint the picture of a Goddess who relishes bloodshed for its own sake. Hers is a violence of necessity, for the destruction of destructive forces, and thus constitutes an aspect of preservation, and not destruction. In this manner, the Goddess invokes the prime *dharma* of the India king: benevolent protection of the collective through means of brutal force.

The ring of wrath

The ferocity of the Goddess might be fruitfully understood as protection through destruction; that is, *desirable* destruction of *undesirable* destruction, in the interest of protection. Thus, Durgā's fierce forms do not exist outside of the context of combat with equally fierce demonic foe. As universal mother and universal sovereign, her fundamental function is doubly one of protection, not destruction; much like the nursing tigress, her teeth are bared only toward those who endanger her cubs, while the cubs themselves may lay at ease in her protective underbelly. In the *Nārāyaṇi Stuti*, the gods hymn: "with your gentle forms that roam about in the triple world, And with the exceedingly terrible ones, protect us, and also the earth."[36] The fiercer the foe, the fiercer the form of the Goddess required to combat that foe. The greater the enemy forces, the more multitudinous her manifestations. The Goddess's unique ability to multiply herself in order to destroy the forces of *adharma* is encapsulated by the following sentiment, uttered by the gods in wonder: "This destruction of great *dharma-hating* Asuras, which you have now accomplished, O Goddess,/Having multiplied your own body into many forms—O Ambikā, what other goddess can do that?"[37] The Goddess is ultimately beyond the fierce faces she manifests for the destruction of destruction: indeed her ferocity is worthy of praise.

For example, having emerged through the amassed *tejas* of the gods in Episode II, Durgā is described as follows:

> She bellowed aloud with laughter again and again. The entire atmosphere was filled with her terrible noise,/And with that measureless, overwhelming (noise) a great echo arose./All the worlds quaked, and the oceans shook./The earth trembled, and mountains tottered./And the gods, delighted, cried, "Victory!" to her whose mount is a lion./And sages praised her, their bodies bowed in devotion./Having seen the triple world trembling, the enemies of the gods,/With all their armies prepared for battle, their weapons upraised, rose up together./Mahiṣāsura, having fumed in anger, "Ah, what is this?!"[38]

The Goddess's vivid wrath—from her maniacal laughter, to the tumult she causes, to her martial barrage, to her unparalleled rage—function within the context of protecting the imperiled gods. Later in the episode, the text explicitly casts the wrathful aspect of the Goddess as a response to the wrath of her enemy, whom she must slay: "Having seen the great onrushing Asura, inflated with anger,/Caṇḍikā got angry in order to slay him."[39] Her ferocity is shown to the enemies of *dharma*,[40] while her pleasant form is shown to the adherents of *dharma*. The Goddess's wrath is a direct response to the belligerent insistence by the demons of retaining power that is not rightfully theirs, oblivious to the disruption caused by their acts. There is a direct correlation between the wrath of the Goddess and the peril presented by the demons.

The demon Raktabīja is a prime example of this principle: for every drop of his blood which hits the earth, a newly cloned Raktabīja would emerge. Much of his blood is spilled while combatting the virulent Band of Mothers, and thus demons emerge by the hundreds (DM 8.49–52). As a direct response to the calamity afoot, Durgā dispatches her most powerful manifestations, Kālī, instructing her to devour the new demons, and lap up every drop of blood so that no more can emerge (DM 8.52–5). Hence, the ensuing gore:

> Having spoken thus, the Goddess then gored him with her spear./With her mouth Kālī seized upon the blood of Raktabīja./The latter then struck Caṇḍikā with his club./But the blow of the club did not cause her even the slightest pain,/While much blood flowed from his body when struck./ Cāmuṇḍā took it all into her mouth, from every direction./And also into her mouth entered the great demons who were born from his blood./Cāmuṇḍā chewed them up, and drank his blood./With spear, thunderbolt, arrows, swords, and lances the Goddess/Wounded Raktabīja, whose blood was being drunk by Cāmuṇḍā./Mortally wounded by that constellation of weapons, the great demon Raktabīja/Fell to the earth bloodless.[41]

This gore is lauded because it responds to the fact that the gods were "utterly terrified"[42] at the sight of the multiple Raktabījas menacingly springing forth from his torrents of spilled blood. This wrath follows Durgā's unheeded ultimatum, and escalates in response to an escalating threat, punishing the demons on account of their belligerence.[43] Relieved by Kālī's gruesome deed, "the gods entered into boundless joy."[44]

Durgā's wrath is a blessing to her devotees, always available to destroy the most destructive forces imperiling them. Therefore, when she prophesizes her future acts of cosmic protection, she indicates that she will descend to earth "with a most dreadful form"[45] to devour the Vaipracitta demons such that her teeth will be red as pomegranate. And this act will incur praise on behalf of gods and mortals, for her bloodstained mouth is understood as a means of protection rather than destruction (DM 11.39–41). She continues to convey she will again assume a "fearsome form"[46] to destroy demons, and thereby protect the sages. And this act of annihilation will earn her the reverence of the sages (DM

11.46–8). She then details another future manifestation where she will assume the form of a swarm of bees, slaying the demon Aruṇa who "shall do a lot of killing in the three worlds."[47] Her wrath warrants reverence, because it quells the destruction of deeply imperiling forces. That she destroys destructive forces for the welfare of the world renders her wrath a function of preservation. Hers is a righteous wrath, stemming from compassionate care. The DM's content corroborates this at every turn; and, in case we weren't paying proper attention, it provides a second narrative ring to help us along. What better way to facilitate model readership centuries down the road?

The DM's secondary narrative ring cleverly takes as its inception the mid-turn of the major narrative ring governing the work as a whole: chapter 3, the slaying of Mahiṣa. It is thus a subring thereof. It terminates in chapter 13, along with the major ring, and therefore takes as its own mid-turn the equidistant chapter 8. That this episode serves as the dramatic turn of the second ring is evidenced not only by virtue of its climactic quality (detailed below), but by the fact that the king interjects so as to prompt the second half of the ring, as follows:

> It is simply wonderful that you, O blessed one, have told me This Māhātmya of the Goddess's activity connected with the slaying of Raktabīja. I want to hear more, about what Śumbha and the outraged Niśumbha did when Raktabīja was killed.[48]
>
> (DM 9.1–2)

Medhas is *in medias res* of transmitting Episode III, having only completed the sub-episode of the slaying of Raktabīja. This is one of a sequence of six such sub-episodes where the king bothers to pipe up. Since there appears to be no indication that Medhas would not have gone on anyhow, I had long puzzled over the presence of the seemingly superfluous interjection, for it could not serve a purpose in advancing the narrative. I now realize it serves as structural punctuation: in interjecting the voice of the king, it reasserts the frame narrative, and its royal themes, to accentuate this second mid-turn. Outside of the frame narrative, it is the only place throughout the *māhātmya* where the king's voice is heard, thereby serving as a minor frame.

This second ring warrants more careful study, but I nevertheless present the essential thematic parallelism it establishes in Table 5.2 below.

Table 5.2 The secondary narrative ring in the *Devī Māhātmya*

Parallelism	*Chapter pairs*		*Theme common to both chapters*
Parallelism 1	Chapter 3	Chapter 13	Bloodshed as Sovereign Sacrifice
Parallelism 2	Chapter 4	Chapter 12	Goddess's Benediction
Parallelism 3	Chapter 5	Chapter 11	Hymn to Goddess
Parallelism 4	Chapter 6	Chapter 10	Goddess Slaying Demon Alone
Parallelism 5	Chapter 7	Chapter 9	Goddess Slaying Demons with Śaktis
Mid-turn	Chapter 8		Bloodshed as Sovereign Sacrifice

Let us set aside the central theme, as implicated by Parallelism 1, for the end of our analysis. Parallelism 2 express the Goddess's pledge to destroy the misfortune of her devotees, particularly those who sing her praises, granting them with worldly prosperity. The third parallelism features the gods hymning the Goddess. The fourth parallelism itself parallels the fifth parallelism. The former of these (occurring in the six to ten-chapter axis) relates the first instance where Devī fights alone to the last time she fights alone: she defeats Dhūmralocana in chapter 6, immediately before she begins emanating her *Śakti*, and defeats Śumbha in chapter 10, immediately after all of her *Śakti* have been reabsorbed into her being. The second of these parallelisms (Parallelism 5 occurring in the seven to nine-chapter axis) relates the first time the Goddess fights using one of her *śaktis* to the final time she does so: she emanates Kālī to defeat Caṇḍa and Muṇḍa in chapter 7, and the entire entourage of her *Śakti* emanations is used to defeat Niśumbha and his forces in chapter 9. This pair of parallels fittingly frames chapter 8, the height of her manifestation of *Śakti*, wherein emerge Śivadūtī and a band of seven gory mothers, the *Saptamātṛkas*. One can therefore easily read these four chapters as a tertiary subring of their own, featuring the expansion and reabsorption of *Śakti* occurring in chapters 6–10. But, as noted above, the parallelism persists in the two to twelve and three to eleven-chapter axes as well. Let us now turn to the prime parallelism governing the mid-turn (chapter 8) and frame (chapters 3 and 13) of this secondary ring composition, for it contextualizes the gore pervading this narrative ring.

While the major ring of the DM is a ring of *power*, culminating in the restoration of kingship in its final frame (Suratha's in chapter 13), and showcasing the same in its mid-turn (Indra's in chapter 3), this subordinate narrative ring is a ring of *blood*. Chapter 8 is literally the most blood-soaked chapter of the work: the text's explicit references to blood are by far concentrated in this chapter.[49] It fittingly features Raktabīja, from whom a clone demon is spawned for every drop of blood which hits the ground. The chapter showcases the climax of the acts of Kālī in the DM, whose maniacal prowess succeeds in devouring Raktabīja's clones faster than they appear, lapping up every drop of blood all the while, leaving the demon bloodless by the end of the encounter (DM 8.61). This secondary ring takes as its starting point Chapter 3, the triumph over Mahiṣa, soaked in the themes of sovereignty. There is nothing particularly sanguinary about chapter 3, but intriguingly, it is one of three junctures where we hear of the Goddess drinking: she becomes flushed in inebriation from consuming a concoction empowering her to defeat Mahiṣa. Likewise, chapter 8's climax details Kālī sucking dry the blood of Raktabīja and his spawns. Occurring in the next line, and ending the chapter, we catch a reference which appears to unite these themes: the mothers dance about, intoxicated by blood.

That the king explicitly refers to Raktabīja in his mid-turn interjection serves to emphasize a crucial dimension of the ring structure: the king's sanguinary offering to the Goddess in chapter 13, and the closing of both this minor ring and the major one dominating the work as a whole. That this ring of blood takes as its genesis the conquest of Mahiṣa, which restores power to Indra and the gods, is crucial: it invites us to receive Suratha's offering as a sovereignty-soaked sacrifice. Because of his blood sacrifice, the Goddess proclaims he will regain his own kingdom, having himself spilled the blood of his enemies (DM 13.13–14). This proclamation causes him to rejoice, praising her with devotion as she vanishes (DM 13.17). In the context of sanctioned battle, for example one safeguarding righteous power or cosmic order, the spillage of blood is cause for jubilation. Therefore, in the opening frame of this ring of blood, the text notes that when the Goddess finally fells Mahiṣa (safeguarding *their* sovereignty) "all the throngs of gods attained the highest bliss. The gods together with the great heavenly seers praised the Goddess. The leaders of the Gandharvas sang, and throngs of Apsarases danced"[50] (DM 3.40–1). Similar to the mid-turn of this ring, the text tells us that when Raktabīja falls to the earth, bloodless, "the gods entered into boundless joy [and] the band of Mothers danced about, intoxicated by his blood"[51] (DM 8.61–2). This bloodshed, like Suratha's, is by virtue of this narrative parallelism construed as a sacrifice which safeguards rightful sovereign power, shed to quell tyrannical oppression: it is a cause for jubilation. The DM thus brilliantly orchestrates a narrative whereby its ring of bloodshed is fittingly subsumed by its ring of royal power, offered in devotion to our mother of kings.

In understanding the Goddess of the DM, then, we must not overlook the overwhelming textual material explicitly depicting her compassionate care, an aspect to which her crushing martial prowess is subordinate. While acts of senseless destruction of life constitute the acts of a murderer, Durgā's violence is celebrated because it is necessary, despite the fact the she relishes her wrathful function. Similarly, while making sense of the extent to which Kṛṣṇa and Arjuna appear to relish the slaughter of the creatures at Khāṇḍava, maniacally laughing throughout the ordeal, Chris Framarin asserts that such colossal destruction invokes the destruction at the end of the age, *pralaya*, of which "the laughter of the god of destruction is itself a standard image."[52] He notes that they laugh "not out of scorn or indifference, but out of amoral necessity,"[53] and further that "this kind of imagery is typical in descriptions and performances of the destruction of the world by Kālī and Durgā as well."[54] Durgā's gruesome martial exploits are not whimsical. Her endangered children, the gods themselves, petition her for their protection. She is invoked for the purposes of preservation and accomplishes what her children require of her. Which mother would not strive to destroy a foe that was bent on imperiling her young? The DM presents the gods as victimized by *adharmic* demons who forge their own paths to self-destruction through belligerent malice. It is misleading then to characterize the Goddess's violence as *adharmic*, likening it to murder, the apex of violent vice. Why, then, do we not characterize Viṣṇu, demon-slayer extraordinaire, as murderous? What about soldiers at large?

Emphasizing the carnage caused by the Goddess without contextualizing that violence is akin to referring to the Allies of WWII as murderers (which, technically, much like Durgā, they of course were), without ever referring to the forces they were up against, or the justification for their cause. Similarly, should we represent the citizens of France as murderous when in 1789 they stormed the

Bastille? The lyrics of the French national anthem to this day call its citizens to water the fields with an impure blood. However, one must contextualize this "war cry" in hopes of understanding the communal sanction behind it. Which culture is not mindful to disambiguate heinous and sanctioned usages of lethal force? The multitudinous contexts which occasion the taking of life carry with them significant ethical nuances: hence we disambiguate between slaughter, extermination, assassination, manslaughter, execution, euthanasia, self-defense, vengeance, etc. These terms exist because of the various psychological and sociological factors vastly nuancing the taking of life. Insofar as one can dare to disambiguate between justified and unjustified losses of life, then one must regard as justified Durgā's gory exploits. Without this insight, one is hard-pressed to account for the en masse veneration of a figure responsible for such colossal devastation.

The legacy of dissecting Purāṇic narratives, which was established by our colonial forefathers, is yet trenchant. It accounts for why scholars such as Doniger, Kinsley, and Yukochi opt to approach the DM (a remarkably stable text) and the Goddess therein piecemeal: the distorted portraits they render result from fragmenting the likeness of the Goddess bequeathed to us (and framed for us) by her ancient authors. This project demonstrates the merits of a sustained analysis of the fabric of the DM itself and the ways in which it presents the Goddess it features. A full portrait of the Goddess of the DM can only be painted with synchronic strokes, drawing from the colors of the text itself, and of its rich framing. Having deconstructed prevalent scholarly caricatures of Durgā of the DM, let us conclude with a reflection upon the figure we see in the text.

Mother of power

Who is Durgā? Let us examine the junctures whereby this particular appellation comes to the fore. You may recall the juncture mentioned at the outset of this study, wherein the Goddess reabsorbs all of her emanated *Śakti* before Śumbha, professing her status as singular font of cosmic power. Putting aside this juncture, the name Durgā is used on seven other occasions in the DM. The Goddess herself puns on this name, declaring that in a future age, having slain the demon Durgama, she will be known as the Goddess Durgā (DM 11.46). More telling is the name's association with impassability. For example, the name Durgā is used in conjunction with hailing the Goddess as an inaccessible further shore (DM 5.10), as well as a vessel upon the ocean of life, which is so difficult to cross (DM 4.10). The most telling occurrence of this connotation occurs when, upon receiving Śumbha-Niśumbha's wedding proposal, we are told that "the blessed and auspicious Goddess Durgā,/By whom this universe is supported, spoke melodiously with a deep inner smile"[55] (DM 5.66), coquettishly passing along a vow she dimwittedly made, as follows: "He who conquers me in battle, he who overcomes my pride,/He whose strength is comparable to mine in the world, just he will be my husband"[56] (DM 5.69). This exchange hails the Goddess's delusive power which she harnesses so as to ensnare the demons into an impossibility:

that she is ever chaste is testament to the simple fact that she is, quite literally, impassable.

Durgā is impassable to the demons, and it is they who suffer her wrath. For example, when Niśumbha, having assumed a 10,000-armed form, hurls 10,000 discuses at the Goddess, we are told that then "the blessed, angry Durgā, who destroys adversity and suffering,/Shattered those discuses and arrows with her own arrows"[57] (DM 9.29). Her anger is sanctified by virtue of its necessity to protect the world. Yet, as argued above, she shows her tenderness to her children. The gods therefore hymn her thus:

> O Durgā, (when) called to mind, you take away fear from every creature; (when) called to mind by the healthy, you bestow an exceedingly pure mind./O you who destroy poverty, misery, and fear, who other than you is always tender-minded, in order to work benefits for all?[58]
>
> (DM 4.16)

She is, after all, the benevolent queen of all creatures, ever ready to launch her wrath in their protection. Hence, the gods hail her: "O you who have the very form of all, queen of all, endowed with the power of all,/Protect us from dangers, O Goddess; O Goddess Durgā, praise be to you!"[59] (DM 11.23). Let us reflect on the royal image of this mother of power and protection we see within the DM.

Among its many accomplishments, the DM advances a consciously allegorical narrative about various types of power, *śakti*. While Durgā is all-powerful, what she ultimately represents is *power itself*. As powerful as any given deity might be, he or she can only ever contain a portion of that totality of cosmic power, which Durgā represents. Rather than consider the Goddess as power, it might be useful to think of power itself as the mother of existence, personified in the figure of Durgā. Power is presumed innate to existence, *a priori*, more primordial than the act of harnessing that power for creation itself. Power is the very energetic matrix of phenomenal reality upon which creation depends.

To invoke classical philosophical concepts, while Durgā can be equated with *prakṛti* as comprising the mechanics of nature, her core manifestation is as *Śakti*, the power propelling *prakṛti* itself, along with all of its constituent processes. Likewise, she can be associated with *māyā*, that evasive transitory phenomenal illusion bewitching us into individual ego consciousness, which guarantees our suffering. In short, she is the power behind the mechanics of *māyā*, as for *prakṛti*. She is also, paradoxically, that power to know what lies beyond the play of *māyā*, bringing to an end the bewitching she incurs. Therefore, she represents the power of knowledge and the power of ignorance alike.

Through her penchant for the paradoxical, she collapses virtually all pairs of conceptual opposites into her matrix of possibilities: she is both beautiful and grotesque, maternal and martial, *mahāvidyā* and *mahāmāyā*, transcendent as well as immanent, indwelling, all-pervading, and embodied, yet also beyond phenomenal reality, transcending space and time. In personifying all available universal power through a sole entity, Durgā must necessarily be even *mahāsurī* as well as *mahādevī*, since power is required for good and evil works alike. She also possesses the power to override the contradiction between the many and the one, and so in the one Goddess we see many forms, and in her story we see many stories, especially those of Viṣṇu, Skanda, and Kṛṣṇa's cowherd aspect.

We may note that she is paradoxical in all senses except for two: firstly, she is forever feminine, and secondly, she is unmistakably omnipotent. She is, by definition, that beyond which no greater power can exist, and so, despite her predilection toward paradox, she presents no paradox when it comes to the strength–weakness polarity. It is her nature as power, *śakti*, which enables her to transcend non-contradiction; in the words of Coburn: "there need be no paradox or contradiction between transcendence and immanence, nor between either of these and internality, because all of these are manifestations of power. The forms of power are many, but the fact of power is one."[60] Therefore, Durgā declares to Śumbha, as she reabsorbs the individual *Śakti* back into her singular manifestation: "When I was established here in many forms, it was by means of my extraordinary power./That has now been withdrawn by me. I stand utterly alone. May you be resolute in combat!"[61] While paradox and power are foremost among Durgā's multiple noteworthy attributes,[62] the latter prevails as her very nature.

As power is inherently feminine (*śakti* being a feminine noun), Durgā does not oscillate between maleness and femaleness. Power is dynamic, and dynamism is feminine, hence Durgā serves as a necessarily feminine personification of the principle of power. We may note that while the feminine noun *devī* might in some circumstances carry the same ambiguity as the masculine term "*deva*" (god) with respect to which deity it refers to, the term *devī* (goddess) can be used in an all-encompassing sense which *deva* cannot. For a masculine correlate, one might perhaps look to the term *īśvara*. There is a sense of the one underlying feminine power even within Śaiva and Vaiṣṇava contexts, hence the relative absence of sectarian clashes with Śāktism as with each other. The implicit understanding is that, power being feminine, the power wielded by Śiva and Viṣṇu alike can be readily represented by a female personification in the form of consort to these male deities. But when these female deities act, they need draw only upon themselves, for they are faces of power itself.

Despite scholarly conceptions to the contrary, while Durgā's form emerges from the gods, the origin of her power pervades the world, and does not originate from the gods. The *Śakrādi Stuti* makes explicit note of the fact that she is "the Goddess by whom this world was spread out *through her own power*, whose body is comprised of the powers of all the hosts of gods."[63] Is it such that Durgā is an emanation of a god, or multiple gods, in the sense of originating from them? As Rodrigues notes, the works of scholars such as Kinsley and Coburn have "exhaustively shown that Durgā is most pervasively seen as the Supreme Power, the *Śakti* of all male deities, and the consort of none."[64] This is also the way the Goddess is understood in modern practice: in the words of Rodrigues' research subject Mr. Lahiri, "Durgā was built with the power to destroy demons. Durgā is Power. Pure Power."[65] Yet Doniger, for example, considers the

Goddess of the DM as one whose power "emanates not from within herself but from the energy (*tejas*) of the male gods."[66] To my mind, the Goddess of the DM is emblematic of the very field of power which constitutes the individual gods and their respective potencies, indwelling in their bodies, and in their weapons. Furthermore, the DM's conception of *śakti* is not only the inherent absolute cosmic power, but equally an earthly expression of that cosmic power, manifesting even in terms of power socially defined.

Just as power itself knows no end, the manifestations of Durgā's power know no end. As power itself, she represents all forms of power, most notably: cosmic power; ritual power; individual spiritual power derived through asceticism; royal power and all types of political power implicated by governance; and martial prowess, including all types of physical strength. *Śakti* in its raw form is universal cosmic power, which can be harnessed and refined in various manners, like an electrical current might energize a multitude of appliances. The merchant and the king amass the same spiritual power for different aims. The one supreme *Śakti* can be said to entail two overall religious applications: one worldly, one otherworldly; one inner, the other outer. The apex of *nivṛtti* expression of power entails power used for inward emotional and mental control. Asceticism may be constructed as that power internalized, for the control of self. It is directed toward the individual alone. The apex of *pravṛttic* expression of power is, on the other hand, communal, entailing control of others. It manifests as physical and social power. Kingship, inversely, might be conceptualized as the harnessing of that power for its utter externalization, specifically for the control of others. Since the sovereign is the apex of power harnessed for the ordering of the mundane collective, then it stands to reason that the highest expression of power harnessed for the ordering of the cosmic collective (the Goddess) is a de facto sovereign. She is the *sovereignty* (supreme power, supreme authority) upon which individual sovereigns depend; Durgā represents the face of sovereign power itself, rather than the face of a particular sovereign.

Royal power in the Indian context is an intriguing hybrid of what we might think of as spiritual power and political power. Yet if power itself is a divine entity, those who possess it, such as rulers, might be considered godlike; hence the porousness between sacred and secular concepts of the Indian king. Political power seems nevertheless dependent upon spiritual power, and hence needs to be recharged constantly, through means of *brāhmaṇic* ritual. The Goddess represents the field of spiritual power from which the *brāhmaṇa* draws by means of ritual sacrifice, and from which the renouncer draws by means of ascetic sacrifice. The power yielded by either of these forms of sacrifice can be harnessed for the support of social (royal) power. When power itself is divinized, and conceived as originating from a singular universal fount, then one can readily link political, personal, social, and spiritual spheres of life. *Śakti* can mean physical power, royal power, ritual power, ascetic power, spiritual power, or any particular ability. Ability itself is an aspect of the Goddess. To "possess" power is to partake in the grace of the Goddess, like a metallic object might "possess" heat, partaking in the power of the sun. Those possessing great power (e.g., the ascetic, the *brāhmaṇa*, the king) necessarily have the Goddess at heart, wittingly or otherwise. It is through her blessing that she lends her essence to both the ruler and the renouncer. That Durgā represents the energy behind worldly and otherworldly aims makes her an apt emblem for the tension between the ascetic and royal ideologies. The question only becomes: how shall one draw from that field of power, and for what purpose shall that power be harnessed?

The merchant may well be the wiser of the two disenfranchised fellows, but his desireless wisdom is not subordinated to the desire of the king. For without the impulse to order and protect, how could universal manifestation itself ever arise? And once existent, how could its rhythms be guarded? The state of peace, once attained, is not innately everlasting: it needs to be guarded with vigilance in order to endure. And this takes striving. A *pravṛttic* dilemma can have no *nivṛttic* solution; one calls for actions, the other for cessation thereof. While the success of the king's efforts may well have been *ordained* by the Goddess, that ordinance cannot replace the effort itself: it is the might of the king which conquers his foes, irrespective of whether that might ultimately belong to the Goddess. And this is her *māyā*: he does nothing more than borrow from her might, but must nevertheless act out his illusory individuality for the sake of fulfilling his purpose. She is the field of power which both comprises and engenders the renewal of the king's power. Her personal installation transcends the need for cyclical regeneration typical of royal consecrations; it grants Suratha not only his kingdom permanently returned, but also lordship over an entire age. Yet despite the fact that these reigns are ultimately impermanent—for the age, too, shall rise and fall, and with it even Manu himself—the Goddess toils to protect them as vital aspects of universal order.

Accessing the supreme field of power, which is one and the same as Durgā, is paradoxical: the practitioner might both be understood to draw power externally, tapping into the Goddess's cosmic presence, *and* internally, tapping into the Goddess's indwelling presence. Hence the DM repeatedly assigns the body as the residence of Durgā, most notably when she emerges through the collective *tejas* of the gods: that neither the gods nor their *tejas* is depleted in this process bespeaks that her essence transcends them, yet dwells within them. Nevertheless, the DM, in the spirit of *bhakti*, depicts a king (and merchant) capable of directly accessing the power of Durgā, without ritual intercessor, albeit only through means of the knowledge imparted by the *brāhmaṇa* sage. The king no longer requires the *purohita*. In the DM, royal power depends upon the Goddess, who can be accessed directly, independent of a ritual intercessor. The king generates his own spiritual power (through *brāhmaṇa* ritual means, and through renouncer ascetic means), and through this spiritual merit, regains his political power through the grace of the Goddess. The frame of the DM might be read as a self-directed royal reconsecration, softening what Heesterman calls the conundrum of the king's authority.[67] In personifying power as an ever-accessible universal mother, the aspirant need not conduct austerity or ritual to access spiritual power. To this end, the gods beseech her to grant whatever mortal who hymns her with the hymns of the DM to grow in worldly attainments "by means of riches, prosperity, and power."[68]

Yet though the king may sanctify his authority without the *brāhmaṇa*, one cannot dispense with the act of sanctification itself. Possessing unsanctioned authority alone is insufficient, for it represents power usurped from another (e.g., demons usurping Indra's throne, or the Kolāvidhvaṃsins usurping Suratha's throne), and must be returned to its rightful wielder: he who possesses the requisite spiritual sanction. The demons suffer colossal misapprehension regarding the mechanics of power, seduced either into claiming universal power as their own (as with the demons Madhu and Kaiṭabha who were drunk with self-importance), or usurping another's power as their own (as with Mahiṣa, Śumbha, and Niśumbha). The universe holds a trump card (in the form of Durgā, who is ultimately inseparable from the universe itself), to ensure victory over the forces of *adharma*. She always protects the rule of the righteous. One who *adharmically* usurps power from another, however, forfeits any claim to appealing to that higher order which is her essential nature.

While Durgā is the power that propels even the demonic, she neither establishes nor defends the rule of the unrighteous. While she is the totality of all things, it is clear that she overall favors order over disorder. And yet, in no Indian myth (not even in these threefold episodes of the triumph of Durgā) do we find a complete annihilation of the forces of evil, for in no conceivable world can light exist without shadow. While Durgā represents the power to order and the power to disrupt, she intervenes to protect the balance between the two when it is sorely disrupted by the dark side. In like fashion, as representing phenomenal existence, she stands for world-affirmation. Thus this supreme power manifests to destroy demons in order to protect the world and the beings in it. In protecting the world, which she comprises, she is also, in a sense, defending herself. She manifests to grant boons of entailing worldly enjoyments, and, like a king, to protect from mundane adversity. Durgā empowers, Durgā protects.

In discussing the theme of communal power, Cynthia Ann Humes argues against the impulse of ascribing masculine ideals of power to the Goddess of the DM (e.g., the quality of *vīrya*, manly strength), and she instead suggests we adopt a superior stance of exalting strength from *within* rather than celebrating power *over*. She writes that,

> power from within is not a power of control, but one which comes from valuing self, community, and experience. It is the power which can heal and renew, a power which—like the Goddess of our text—exemplifies compassion even when violent, and strives to contribute to an ultimately positive outcome for the greater good.[69]

Such power can be readily ascribed to a Goddess who represents that power which is both cosmically supreme, and resident within all beings (DM 5.18). The Goddess of the DM stands not merely for social power itself, then, but for social empowerment. She is that principle from whose field of power all sovereigns borrow, that principle which restores and protects that principle of power. She particularly empowers those charged with preservation: in empowering the gods of heaven and the kings of the earth, the Goddess of our text represents the empowerment of the collective, and the order, stability, and harmony engendered by that empowerment. The king, and not the *mokṣa*-seeking merchant, is the hero of the DM insofar as he represents the function on the earthly level which is occupied by the Goddess on the cosmic level: that office which is charged with communal welfare.

The dynamism innate to the Goddess readily associates her with the locus, fluctuations, and predilection of *pravṛtti* religion. Indeed *prakṛti* itself is predicated upon sacrifice, be it the ecological variety, which propels the food chain, or the ritual variety which supports the cosmic rhythms themselves. It is by means of phenomenal processes that the ardent renouncer arrives at liberation from the phenomenal. Spiritual striving is just as much a part of Durgā's matrix as objects of mundane entanglement. Despite the fact that our Goddess represents the dance of *pravṛtti*, she in tandem readily represents the ideals of *nivṛtti* insofar as she is independent of any of the individual creatures which depend upon her. She acts freely, entirely of her own accord, unfettered by the pressures of karmic interdependence. She incurs neither meritorious nor non-meritorious residue since she is beyond the processes of cyclical existence. She remains unblemished. She is more than a lotus in a swamp; she is the most mysterious type of lotus which both subsumes the swamp within her petals, and yet evades its wetness while standing in the middle of it.

There are two perceptible faces to Durgā, to be sure: the fierce face of the royal warrior, and the gentle face of the contented mother. But one would be mistaken to accord them the same status, for her wrathful aspect remains volatile and unpredictable, while, by contrast, her benevolent face betrays composure and control. For Durgā to be the supreme Goddess, her controlled face must implicitly prevail at all times. Just as she governs her own wrath, she quashes the wrath of her own foe in order to govern the universe. She, like a king, must exert inner and outer control in order to perform her most vital duty. Durgā is the queen of the universe, yet she dwells, like the ascetic, in the periphery, unnoticed until a time of need. The DM therefore alerts kings to the tremendous power awaiting them not only within their core being, but in the periphery of their kingdoms, power which rests in tribal and ascetic manifestations alike.

That Durgā's power is absolute is evident. In ascribing a personage to the principle of power itself, that personage becomes logically impervious to conquest. Hence, Durgā is never defeated. Her very constitution precludes the possibility of defeat. She *is* victory; hence she is intrinsically impassable. While even Śiva and Viṣṇu might at times suffer defeat, there exists, to my knowledge, *no known account where Durgā is defeated*, for she represents the state of invincibility itself. Representing a power greater than which no power can exist, she is de facto invincible. The DM suggests that power's ultimate justification is protection against the unrightfully overpowered. Durgā is power personified in order to represent the principle of cosmic protection. The affirmation of life is implicitly exalted in this fact. Her absolute power is justifiable in that it is ultimately harnessed for preservation, such that there can be no greater power left to be harnessed for destruction: she represents the very life force, which she toils to protect, albeit through destructive means.

The extent to which the DM extols the need to protect this realm is but an aspect to which it adheres to a theme of life-affirmation. It accomplishes this task more directly by emphasizing an embodied state of being throughout. For example, Medhas, just prior to expounding the three glorious manifestations of Durgā, says to the king that she has the world as her form (DM 1.47). It is telling that Durgā emerges from the bodies of other beings in all three episodes of the DM. In the first episode, she emerges from the body of Viṣṇu, "having gone forth from his eyes, nose, arms, heart, and breast"[70] (DM 1.69a), in order to appear before Brahmā. Moreover, just prior to her appearance, Brahmā invokes her in his hymn wherein he declares to the Goddess: "Viṣṇu, Śiva, and I have been made to assume bodily form by you" (DM 165a).[71] In the second episode, she manifests from the energy emitted from the bodies of the various gods: "And from the bodies of the other gods, Indra and the others,/Came forth a great fiery splendor, and it became unified in one place"[72] (DM 2.10). Likewise, in the final episode, she emerges from the body of the goddess Pārvatī (DM 5.38). The text explicitly underscores the significance of this bodily emergence, declaring: "Since Ambikā came forth from the body sheath (kośa) of Pārvatī,/She is sung in all the worlds as Kauśikī"[73] (DM 5.40).

The DM not only celebrates the emergence of the Goddess from the bodies of others; it conversely details the emergence of various personified powers from the body of the Goddess. While these emanations famously include the goddesses Kālī, Śivadūtī, and the *Saptamātṛkas*, who are all features in Episode III, the text is sure to indicate that even the nameless, faceless masses comprising her hordes in Episode II emerge from her very breath: "The breaths that Ambikā released while fighting in battle,/These immediately became her hosts, by the hundred and thousand."[74] This is in fact the only biographical detail we receive about these hordes. While the supreme Goddess certainly possesses the power to manifest "out of thin air," so to speak, the text is sure to appoint as her point of entry into the narrative the bodies of other beings: gods, humans, and animals likewise appoint her own body as the portal through which emerge her own forces. Likewise, all of the other beings she manifests directly emerge from her own body. Durgā may thereby be understood as inextricable to the embodied force of life itself; that is, the energetic principle at play animating embodied beings. This emphasis on embodiment, along with the text's esteem for the function of preservation, imbues it with an indelible ethos of world and life-affirmation. Hence our mother of power has at heart the work of kings, whose function is to preserve this realm, and all embodied beings within it.

Notes

1 Wendy Doniger, *Women, Androgynes, and Other Mythical Beasts* (Chicago, IL: University of Chicago Press, 1980), 90–1.
2 Doniger, 337. See note 7.

3 A.K. Ramanujan, Vinay Dharwadker, and Stuart H. Blackburn, *The Collected Essays of A.K. Ramanujan* (New Delhi; New York: Oxford University Press, 1999).
4 Ramanujan, Dharwadker, and Blackburn, 497.
5 Ramanujan, Dharwadker, and Blackburn, 498; Originally published in: A.K. Ramanujan, "Two Realms of Kannada Folklore," in *Another Harmony: New Essays on the Folklore of India*, ed. Stuart H. Blackburn and A.K. Ramanujan (Berkeley, CA: University of California Press, 1986).
6 Ramanujan, Dharwadker, and Blackburn, *The Collected Essays of A.K. Ramanujan*, 498.
7 Surprisingly, Ramanujan alludes to the DM just once in all of his essays, when he states, "in the mythology of goddesses, the Sanskrit great goddess is created by the gods who pool all their weapons and powers and send her forth to conquer a demon they cannot singly vanish. But in south Indian village myths, the goddess is primal, she gives the great gods their insignia and weapons." Ramanujan, Dharwadker, and Blackburn, 31; Originally published in A.K. Ramanujan, "Where Mirrors Are Windows: Toward an Anthology of Reflections," *History of Religions* 28, no. 3 (February 1, 1989): 187–216. (One readily suspects Ramanujan of referring to the DM in his reference to the mythology of the Sanskrit great goddess.) As discussed, it is not such that the Goddess of the DM is created by the joint efforts of the gods. Ramanujan may be referring to its second episode, which cites an example of her being an earthly manifestation of the wrath of the gods. However, the first episode of the DM (and references made throughout) make it abundantly clear that she is uncreated, and self-existent.
8 Doniger, *The Hindus*, 390.
9 David Kinsley, "The Portrait of the Goddess in the Devī-Māhātmya," *Journal of the American Academy of Religion* 46, no. 4 (December 1, 1978): 489–506.
10 Hillary Rodrigues, "Scrutinizing Devī: Does She Live Up to Her Portraits in Kinsley's Analysis?," *Studies in Religion/Sciences Religieuses* 30, no. 3–4 (September 1, 2001): 489.
11 David Kinsley, "Durgā, Warrior Goddess and Cosmic Queen," in *The Goddesses' Mirror: Visions of the Divine from East and West* (Albany, NY: State University of New York, 1989), 10.
12 Kinsley, 10.
13 David Kinsley, *The Goddesses' Mirror: Visions of the Divine from East and West* (Albany, NY: State University of New York, 1989), 10.
14 DM 13.8. Coburn, *Encountering the Goddess*, 83.
15 DM 13.9. Coburn, 83.
16 Kinsley, "Durgā, Warrior Goddess and Cosmic Queen," 10.
17 Ramanujan, Dharwadker, and Blackburn, *The Collected Essays of A.K. Ramanujan*, 497.
18 David R. Kinsley, "Kālī: Blood and Death Out of Place," in *Devī: Goddesses of India*, ed. John Stratton Hawley and Donna Marie Wulff (Berkeley, CA: University of California Press, 1996), 78.
19 Kinsley, "Durgā, Warrior Goddess and Cosmic Queen," 10.
20 McDermott and Kripal, *Encountering Kālī in the Margins, at the Center, in the West*, 25.
21 Cheever Mackenzie Brown, "Kālī: The Mad Mother," in *The Book of the Goddess, Past and Present: An Introduction to Her Religion*, ed. Carl Olson (Prospect Heights, IL: Waveland Press, 2002), 110–23.
22 For a lovely English translation, see: Cheever Mackenzie Brown, *The Devī Gītā: The Song of the Goddess: A Translation, Annotation, and Commentary* (Delhi: Sri Satguru Publications, 1999).
23 Cheever Mackenzie Brown, "The Tantric and Vedantic Identity of the Great Goddess in the Devī Gītā of the Devī-Bhagavata Purāṇa," in *Seeking Mahādevī: Constructing*

the Identities of the Hindu Great Goddess, ed. Tracy Pintchman (Albany, NY: State University of New York Press, 2001), 34.

24 DM 11.2. "O Goddess, who takes away the sufferings of those who take refuge in you, be gracious; be gracious, O mother of the entire world./Be gracious, O queen of all, protect all; you are the queen, O Goddess, of all that does and does not move." Coburn, *Encountering the Goddess*, 74.

25 DM 4.11–12. Coburn, 49.

26 Coburn, 50.

27 Fuller, *The Camphor Flame*, 86.

28 Yokochi, "The Rise of the Warrior Goddess in Ancient India," 3.

29 Yokochi, "The Warrior Goddess in the Devīmāhātmya," 90.

30 Yokochi, 91.

31 Yokochi, 91.

32 Yokochi, 91.

33 See Chapter 1.

34 Yokochi, "The Rise of the Warrior Goddess in Ancient India," 24.

35 DM 4.16b. "O you who destroy poverty, misery, and fear, who other than you is always tender-minded, in order to work benefits for all?" Coburn, *Encountering the Goddess*, 50.

36 DM 4.25a. Coburn, 51.

37 DM 11.29. Coburn, 76.

38 DM 2.31–5. Coburn, 42.

39 DM 3.27. Coburn, 46.

40 For the message dispatched to the Goddess from Śumbha, wherein he details the extent to which he has usurped the portion of the gods' sacrifice, along with their finest possessions, see DM 5.57–5.65, Coburn, 57.

41 DM 8.55–61. Coburn, 67.

42 DM 8.49–51: "The great demon Raktabīja, filled with rage, struck/Each and every one of the Mothers with his club./From the flow of blood that fell in torrents to the earth/From the one who was wounded by the spear, lance, and so forth, demons were born by the hundreds./By those demons born from the blood of this one demon, the entire world/Was pervaded; then the gods became utterly terrified." Coburn, 66–7.

43 Yet demons cannot be annihilated en masse; only kept in check when they grow unruly. In the words of Biardeau: "The demons are not a portion of the world's inhabitants that must be exterminated to the last. The world cannot live without them even if they stand on the impure side of society. They are needed, just as, for instance, the cesspool cleaner is needed. But they must behave themselves, and respect the world-dharma and their own dharma." Madeleine Biardeau, "Brahmans and Meat-Eating Gods," in *Criminal Gods and Demon Devotees: Essays on the Guardians of Popular Hinduism*, ed. Alf Hiltebeitel (Albany, NY: State University of New York Press, 1989), 30–1.

44 DM 8.61b–2. Coburn, *Encountering the Goddess*, 67.

45 DM 11.39: "On another occasion descending to earth with a most dreadful form,/I will slay the Vaipracitta demons." Coburn, 77.

46 DM 11.46b: "And when I have again taken on fearsome form in the Himālayas." Coburn, 78.

47 DM 11.48–50: "When a demon named Aruṇa shall do a lot of killing in the three worlds,/Then I, taking on bee-form, consisting of innumerable bees,/Will slay the great demon for the well-being of the triple world./Then people everywhere will praise me as 'Queen-bee' *(bhrāmarī).*" Coburn, 78.

48 Coburn, 68.

49 Nineteen of the twenty-six references to blood within the entire gory text occur in this chapter alone. Sixteen of these deal with shedding blood on the battlefield (8.34, 8.40, 8.42, 8.43, 8.44, 8.45, 8.47, 8.50, 8.51, 8.53 (twice), 8.54, 8.56, 8.57, 8.58, 8.59), and

three refer to drinking blood: two refer to Kālī drinking Raktabīja's blood (8.59, 8.60), and another indicates the Mothers were intoxicated by his blood (8.62). Furthermore, there are only three more references to blood in the entire gory episode: the lion drinks blood on the battlefield (6.14), there is a reference to blood in the Nārāyaṇi Stuti (11.27), and the king and merchant offer their blood at the end of the text (13.9). There are only two additional references to blood in the work, occurring on the battlefield in Episode II (2.57, 2.65). These are: the defeat of Dhumralocana (chapter 6), the defeat of Caṇḍa and Muṇḍa (chapter 7), the defeat of Raktabīja (chapter 8), the defeat of Niśumbha (chapter 9), and the defeat of Śumbha (chapter 10).

50 Coburn, *Encountering the Goddess*, 47–8.
51 Coburn, 67.
52 Christopher G. Framarin, "Environmental Ethics and the Mahābhārata: The Case of the Burning of the Khāṇḍava Forest," *Sophia* 52, no. 1 (2013): 25.
53 Framarin, 25. Fn. 61.
54 Framarin, 25. Fn. 61.
55 Coburn, *Encountering the Goddess*, 57.
56 Coburn, 58.
57 Coburn, 70.
58 Coburn, 50.
59 Coburn, 76.
60 Coburn, *Devī-Māhātmya*, 305.
61 DM 10.5: *ahaṃ vibhūtyā bahubhir iha rūpair yadāsthitā | tat saṃhṛtaṃ mayaikaiva tiṣṭhāmy ājau sthiro bhava* || Coburn, *Encountering the Goddess*, 71.
62 Cf. Coburn's final thoughts at Coburn, *Devī-Māhātmya*, 303–5, where he advances eight overall characteristics of the DM's vision of ultimate reality. She is: (1) feminine; (2) transcendent; (3) interior; (4) immanent; (5) powerful; (6) paradoxical; (7) associated with Agni; and (8) one whose confluence of myths implicate those of other deities, particularly Viṣṇu, Skanda, and Kṛṣṇa Gopāla.
63 DM 4.2a. Coburn, *Encountering the Goddess*, 48. Emphasis my own.
64 Rodrigues, "Scrutinizing Devī," 397; For specific works demonstrating this point, see: John Stratton Hawley and Thomas B. Coburn, eds., "Consort of None, Śakti of All: The Vision of the Devī-Māhātmya," in *The Divine Consort: Radha and the Goddesses of India* (Delhi: Motilal Banarsidass, 1984), 153–65; Kinsley, "The Portrait of the Goddess in the Devī-Māhātmya."
65 See chapter 7: "Function of the Durgā Pūjā" in Rodrigues, *Ritual Worship of the Great Goddess*, 288–96.
66 Doniger, *The Hindus*, 390.
67 And if one is intent on maintaining, as Heesterman repeatedly argues, that the conundrum of the king's authority is an insoluble one, then it may find a happy home in narratives such as the DM, furnished with tasteful tensions.
68 DM 4.31–2: "(Let it be that) whenever you are remembered by us, may you destroy (our) greatest misfortunes. [35]/And whatever mortal praises you with these hymns, O one whose face is without blemish,/May you, O Ambikā, who are resorted to by us, the grantress of everything,/Be concerned with his growth through wealth, wife, success, (etc.,) by means of riches, prosperity, and power." Coburn, *Encountering the Goddess*, 51–2.
69 Alf Hiltebeitel and Kathleen M. Erndl, eds., *Is the Goddess a Feminist? The Politics of South Asian Goddesses* (New York: New York University Press, 2000), 48.
70 Coburn, *Devī-Māhātmya*, 38.
71 Coburn, 38.
72 Coburn, 40.
73 Coburn, 57.
74 DM 2.51b–252a. Coburn, *Encountering the Goddess*, 43.

Conclusion

Framing frontier

Closing frames, framing closures

The DM is keen to seal off, in its final chapter, the various layers of enframement it initiates at its outset. It does so, quite sensibly, in reverse order: the discursive frames at the outset of the work exert a centripetal force toward the acts of the Goddess, moving from Manu-making, to Suratha's loss of power, to the problem of suffering, to the acts of the Goddess themselves; the work's concluding frames, on the other hand, exert a corresponding centrifugal force moving from the acts of the Goddess, to the suffering of Samādhi, to the restoration of Suratha's sovereignty, and back again to the making of Manu Sāvarṇi. Such is the nature of narrative rings, and this work has chosen to follow suit, organizing its conclusion through a centrifugal motion inversely addressing the frames centripetally established at its outset.

Frame I: ideology

Given the trajectory established above, we must commence our conclusion with the heart of the matter: the central line of questioning poised at the very outset of this work: why are the monumental exploits of the Goddess of the *Devī Māhātmya* framed by this encounter between a forest-dwelling ascetic and a deposed king? How does this frame serve to ideologically contextualize the exploits of that Goddess? What aspects of the Goddess are accentuated through use of this narrative lens? Narrative description is invariably accompanied by ideological prescription. In telling you what is, a narrative work tells you what should be. Ideology pertains more so to a worldview than to a world in its own right. So, a slightly modified version of our triple-world schema is in order: we are dealing with the *worldview* within the text as it reflects both the *worldview* behind the text and the *worldview* in front of the text. This thematic stream flows across the boundaries of these otherwise disparate worlds.

We conclude that the exploits of the Goddess are framed by a forest-dwelling ascetic and deposed king so as to draw our attention to the world-denying/world-affirming tension that the text engages throughout its exploits, explicitly evidenced by the Goddess's granting of divergent boons in the end. We refer to the

MBh's *pravṛtti-nivṛtti* typology as emblematic of a lasting Hindu tension between the ideology of householding and the ideology of renouncing, which, though opposed, are tacitly synthesized, as expressed through Durgā's divergent boons. We furthermore conclude that the text overall favors the *pravṛttic* side of the ideological coin since it embraces the sovereign penchants for violent protection of the *saṃsāric* sphere, culminating on the earthly sphere as the king, on the heavenly sphere as Indra, and on the cosmic sphere as the Goddess herself. By extension, we conclude that the Goddess's primary function is one of preservation, not destruction, which is further evidenced by the fact that her emanations, however harrowing, are celebrated, and always folded back into her ultimately composed being.

Therefore, this research serves as a small step toward understanding the long-standing Hindu association between the DM and royal power. This study demonstrates the intrinsic centrality of sovereignty as an underlying theme of the DM, showcased through the architecture of the work. Coburn remarks in the introduction to his 1991 translation on the centrality of the relationship between Goddess and king to the DM, along with the importance of that dimension to contemporary Durgā Pūjā:

> I have been reluctant to leap from the relatively narrow focus I have adopted in this book into extended discussion of a subject that is so enormously consequential for the understanding of Indian culture as a whole. Others will surely be less reluctant, and I, for one, will welcome such ventures.[1]

The present study constitutes a step toward addressing this gap in our understanding, insofar as it demonstrates the thematic primacy of kingship in the DM, which the text exalts in tandem with its antithesis: Indian asceticism. The tension to which it speaks bespeaks a religious tension in Indian culture as a whole. Furthermore, the DM provides an ideological platform within the Hindu world upon which an ethos of world-affirmation and social engagement may proudly stand, thereby offsetting narrow yet prevalent caricatures of Hindu religious ideology as ultimately promoting an ethos of world-denial.

The extent to which the Purāṇas were composed with a mind to privilege the dictates of *pravṛtti* is yet to be explored, and we are a very long way from substantiating just about anything made of a Purāṇic corpus as a whole. Yet the fact that they boast the descent of Manus and kings as among their core features holds intrigue. Indeed, all five of their alleged marks pertain to *pravṛtti*. One final note to be made is that for a Purāṇa to be a Purāṇa, it must be understood as ancient: *viz*. that which has *originated a long time ago.* This definition seems to defy, on some level, notions of eternality or self-existence.

Frame II: methodology

Implicit in asking *what* the frame of the DM tells is the supposition *that* the frame narrative tells us anything at all. This research conveys not only the extent to which royal ideology pervades the DM; it conveys the extent to which the text itself conveys this by virtue of its very structure. It demonstrates the agency of the text in serving as its own hermeneutic guide, prioritizing material through cues comprising its inherent structural organization. It therefore contributes not only to *what* we see in the text, but *how* we go about seeing it. It demonstrates a highly conscious organization of the fabric of the DM so as to mimic the qualities of the Goddess through three formal tropes: (1) the stream-of-consciousness-like nature of the opening frame and its interlacement with the first exploit depicting the Goddess as Mahāmāyā; (2) the expansive sequence of chapters resulting in episodes that contain thrice the number of chapters as the one before it; and (3) most significantly, the episodic balance accentuating the slaying of Mahiṣa as formally and thematically central to its fabric, and the interplay between the frame narrative and that textual mid-turn to constituting its narrative ring structure. Clearly, the story of Medhas, Suratha, and Samādhi does not function merely to latch the DM into the MkP; they serve to contribute to a rich, well-orchestrated ideological and structural whole.

In engaging the DM as intelligible literature, this research ramifies both western scholarship on South Asian narrative texts (especially the Purāṇas; discussed below), and literary theory more generally (discussed here). This work corroborates Eco's notion that texts are generally designed for the sake of interpretation; such is the case with the DM at any rate. This principle is not necessarily nullified when there are multiple authors at play, provided subsequent authors are attentive to the contours of the text they are adding to. In light of this process, narrative "accretions" *especially* constitute meaningful commentary on the thematic thrust of the text.

The synergy between Eco and Douglas is a potent one: in theorizing the model reader as integral to textual interpretation, Eco provides a "metanarrative" in which Douglas might ground her work; in exchange, Douglas' analysis of the nature and function of ring compositions concretizes the emphasis on the text as the locus of meaning which Eco proposes. Otherwise put, Eco articulates what Douglas assumes and Douglas exemplifies what Eco theorizes. Ring compositions are de facto guidelines for model readership, allowing the text to communicate by virtue of its very configuration much of what it expects of its model readership. Artistic motivations notwithstanding, model readership is arguably the very purpose for ring composition to occur. If, as Eco describes, texts are machines crafted for interpretation, ring compositions, then, are especially well-oiled interpretation machines. Given the utility of their theoretical union in broaching the DM, I can only begin to imagine what we may come to learn by mapping much more complexly enframed narratives as occurring in the epics and Purāṇas using the navigational prowess that Eco and Douglas collectively provide.

This is not the first work to examine a Sanskrit text through use of ring theory, though this enterprise is certainly yet in its infancy. Hans Hock, for example, builds upon Brereton's work (which demonstrates that Yājñavalkya's encounter at the court of Janaka in *Bṛhad Āraṇyaka Upaniṣad* (henceforth BAU)

3 is a ring composition framed by a simpler story occurring at *Œatapatha Brāhmaṇa* 11.6.3), demonstrating that this BAU passage "forms part of a much larger text (BAU 2.1–4.5), which is even more clearly a ring composition."[2] His process is worth mentioning here, given its resonance to the present research. In identifying the key elements of ring composition (recall Dorsey's proposed steps), namely the initial frame, the central point, and the terminal frame, he locates the core message of the text, with which he validates "an old argument about how this same *Upaniṣad* intended the '*neti neti*' statement of later classical *Vedāntic* thought."[3] He was able to speak *to the intention of the text*, based on its structural configuration, a configuration crafted for the specific purpose of encoding that intention. Moreover, and unsurprisingly, the structure of the text served to validate thematic intuitions already available to the reader, even in the absence of scrutiny of its structural mechanics. In the case of this present research, it has long since been clear to me that the central thrust of the DM was Durgā's function in restoring kingship, and thus guarding the globe, but it is only in analyzing the structure of the text that I come across persuasive, demonstrable evidence that the text overall agrees with me, while still leaving ample room for interpretation in the direction in which it points.

In reading the acts of Durgā alone, one may pick up on the centrality of sovereignty to those acts; however, whatever efforts are exerted in the composition of the work toward conveying this theme are amplified in the composition of its frame and ring structure at large. The narrative structure of the DM does not present as its centerpiece the amalgamation of liminal Goddess traditions, or any other such cultural issue. This is not to say they do not partake in the heritage of the text, but that they are not central to the problem the text addresses. The DM engages a dichotomy at the heart of Hinduism, as evidenced by Durgā's divergent boons, so as to privilege the themes of protection as necessary to life in this world, especially as incorporated into Indian conceptions of kingship. Suratha starts by asking why he is ensnared by illusion, but what truly prompts the telling of the greatness of the Goddess is his curiosity after the might of she who is sovereign of all lords. The problem of the loss of kingship inherent in the episodes as occurring on the heavenly level is only magnified by the frame narrative which grounds this problem in the human sphere.

The DM's frame narrative thus accentuates the text's ability to elicit interpretation in a manner cohesive to its core narrative. If this was not evident in unpacking the frame narrative alone, then it becomes abundantly clear when viewing that frame as a part of a chiasmic strategy, drawing on the work of Dorsey and Douglas, to highlight the central episode whereby Durgā manifests in the manner as does the Indian king, and her specific duty is to safeguard Indra's throne from the perils of tyranny. Indeed, it is only once she manifests and is anointed by the gods in preparation for royal battle that she is hailed Durgā, an identity which eclipses her function of Mahāmāyā. This attests to the general function of narrative to elicit interpretation, and the specific function of religious narrative to elicit ideological interpretation pertaining to religious themes encoded within.

This second, structurally oriented interpretational tool not only corroborates the textual locus whereby one ought to most rigorously apply the first, hermeneutic-oriented tool; it opens up an avenue whereby to gauge the richest thematic texture of the work. Ring structure not only highlights the interplay between center and circumference—that is, between mid-turn and frame—but also presents us with important parallelisms. These parallelisms firmly establish episodic corollaries, which avail avenues of thematic commentary imbedded within the work. That A should parallel A′, for example, necessarily calls us to compare the two in order to ascertain how the one might comment upon the other. This commentary might take the form of embellishment, mimicry, rejection, distortion, or mere simple parity. The task for the interpreter is to figure out *what* the parallelism says; by virtue of its very structure, the text has already communicated *that* it says something. Most important: this "figuring out" process need not be conclusive, or even ultimately restrictive. The interpretational guidelines provided by the text, if heeded, will in all probability curtail the range of angles you will be inspired to take; however, ironically, they point you in the direction of the greatest depths of the work. The chamber of the text might insist in guiding you to the wardrobe, and that process may feel stifling. The cramp might be unbearable. However, there is sometimes a world of possibilities laying within a wardrobe, one we miss by ignoring the structural pointers within the text.

Since ring composition spans too vast a history and geography to possibly stem from a common cultural source, some theorize that it is a function of how the human brain processes information. Yet, as demonstrated by both Biblical and Purāṇic scholarship, the sort of structural patterning appearing in the DM proves difficult to detect, much less interpret, for the modern reader. In speaking of the Hebrew Bible, Dorsey notes that

> these and related patterns are so foreign to modern readers that it is easy to miss—or misunderstand—them. To investigate structure in the Hebrew Bible, the reader must lay aside Western expectations and watch for these less familiar structuring conventions that were indigenous to Ancient Israel.[4]

Douglas, too, puzzles at length at why so pervasive a compositional phenomenon should remain undetectable to we moderns. Referring to the Book of Numbers, she maintains that despite its highly structured ring composition, it "is found to be quite impenetrable in modern times ... the book only seems disorderly because moderns are not used to reading in rings."[5] Eco might have an answer for Douglas' puzzlement, or at least another way of expressing the disjuncture between how ring structures expect to be read versus how we scholars proceed to read them, based on our own expectations of text. Eco notes that the model reader is one who can "observe the rules of the game,"[6] indeed even "someone eager to play such a game."[7] In the absence of this voluntary participation, one superimposes one's "own expectations as [an] empirical reader on the expectations that the author wanted from a model reader."[8] This appears to be why modern readers have had such difficulty detecting (much less deciphering) ring compositions.

The modern scholar's prowess pertains to reading *as an empirical reader*. The scholarly approach is a linear one, geared at uncovering answers, not necessarily recognizing artistry. We tend to approach texts more like newspapers than like symphonic compositions, even narrative texts, at least *while* we study them. For example, have you noticed the ring structure inherent in this book?[9] Regardless, does it add to the validity of my line of argumentation? Of course not; nor should it. During the act of dissertation, I make explicit throughout what it is I wish to convey, and so you need not look to my book's formal properties to corroborate my content: interpretation in this case need not be nearly so complex an enterprise as with works of literature configured as narrative rings.

The structure of this work is an *artistic*, not argumentative, aspect. It is not a requisite element in establishing my model reader, for my model audience is a *scholarly* one. The mode of scholarship itself requires that we say what we mean, and mean what we say, and that we convey what we think through logical, demonstrable, verifiable, explicit exposition. Conversely, the scholarly eye winces when meaning is obscured by symbolism, formal acrobatics, and contradictory stances. Hence, our very mode of inquiry readily serves as a potential handicap to accepting the criteria of model readership posited by ancient, mostly oral, works of art. If one can turn a blind scholarly eye, so to speak, and engage the work on its own terms, "playing the game," as Eco puts it, we might then, ideally, be able to infuse insights into our subsequent scholarly analysis. One might even be surprised at what light may be shed on the diachronic aspects of the work through intimate synchronic engagement, as with Hock's study noted above. Indeed, the very practices we toil to master in producing and interpreting sound scholarship counter the artistic grain of crafting and deciphering narrative rings. While the one is predicated upon direct lines of reasoning and presentation, the other is, quite literally, circular in its logic, and proudly so.

Frame III: history of scholarship

The first frame of this book looked to our colonial past, and traced the pejorative scholarly attitudes directed at Purāṇas, as disorganized, debased, "corrupted" texts. Received in the shadow of this scorn, the study of the DM exhibits the same dismembering for historical and cultural data as adopted toward the Purāṇas, and its frame narrative was frequently belittled as a conceit implemented by sectarian textual rogues intent on smuggling the Goddess into Mārkaṇḍeya's Trojan horse. If nothing else, it is my hope that this book demonstrates that the DM's frame is far from flimsy. As Safavi and Weightman observe, "whenever a work of some significance is universally criticized for being badly constructed, it is probably because it is not being read correctly and its genre is not understood."[10] Now that we are able to identify the DM's intricate frame structure, we are forced to view its frame as integral to a sophisticated whole. Speaking of narrative circles, Matthew Orsborn notes that

> rather than seeing a "chaotic" text reflecting the mind of a presumably "incoherent" author, quite to the contrary they show a highly ordered and even complex intelligence, wherein the relationships and positioning of parts within the whole are definitely intentional.[11]

The authorial choices behind creating these narrative structures themselves constitute religious authority, representing the voices of the traditions striving to secure cultural relevance, and ideological transmission.

The diachronic impulse behind the creation of critical editions tends toward treating the DM as a separate entity, branding it as a "late," "sectarian" (*Śākta*) interpolation of the non-sectarian "original" MkP, which necessarily views its frame narrative as a flimsy conceit. This same impulse caused 1500-year-old hymns to Durgā to be excised from the "critical edition" of the MBh. That hymns to Durgā occur immediately preceding the great war of the MBh is unsurprising when viewed from the interpretation of the text adopted in this research. Both this juncture and the plight of Suratha are united in a common theme: mythic moments wherein the rightful succession of sovereign power is to be decided through armed conflict. Who else would one want on one's side but she whose central purpose is the restoration of rightful kingship? However, cutting away these frames with diachronic shears obscures our view of portions of the texts we erroneously view as haphazard, sectarian framing. When we sufficiently suspend the disbelief espoused by our colonial scholarly forerunners in receiving the Purāṇic corpus, we may appreciate the crucial decisions consciously undertaken by the tradition's redactors in an effort to partake in a highly effective hermeneutic strategy: framing narratives with other narratives for the sake of ideological import.

Douglas emphasizes the significance of the ending in a ring composition given its ability to link everything, creating coherence for the text as a whole. Her spirited call to embrace such narrative structures *as literary wholes* is precisely resonant with the impulse behind this project, spawned by the fragmented manner in which they have been hitherto received. She writes:

> When the ending of a composition wraps up everything that is there, the whole is endowed with a special power. The same for a painting or a carving, or music—its dense coherence inspires feelings of respect, even of awe. It is something to be valued for itself, like poetry, regardless of what narrative or instrumental functions it may perform. You might use the picture for a blanket, the carving to stop a leak, the poem to advertise a brand drink. Its possible usefulness is irrelevant to its quality as a work of art. The thing is too impressive to be cherished for generations because of any incidental ability it may have to refer to something outside itself. It is not made for a practical purpose, like a map ... It is made to be itself, a complete thing in its own right.[12]

The methodological and theoretical approach adopted herein therefore counters the prejudice with which Sanskrit narrative enframement has been made to contend. The sentiments of J.A.B. van Buitenen and C. Dimmit are representative of this bias: they remark that the Purāṇas gathered accretions "as if they were libraries to which new volumes have been continuously added, not necessarily at the end of the shelf, but randomly."[13] The perceived randomness results from the mentality of we scholars searching for the linear "shelf," whereby we are rendered unable to register (much less appreciate) the sophisticated manner in which these tales within tales are orchestrated. Douglas' work on ring theory has proven a useful tool in "thinking in circles" along with the ancient authors of works such as the DM. We have become obsessed with "the" text and "the" historical horizon generating it, looking to the first to gain insights into the second, and vice versa. When both of these are murky, our process becomes akin to the partially blind leading the partially blind: progress can surely be made, but not without glaring blind spots. In the case of *purāṇic* materials, and their evident directive to preserve religious tradition, renovating along the way so as to prevent atrophy, older is not necessarily better. *Purāṇic* narrative by virtue of its very nature flows with the impetus of current concerns.

I willingly run the risk of overstating my synchronic emphasis qua *corrective*, not *replacement*, for historicist inquiry. Historical inquiry is a vital and indispensable branch of the humanities, to be sure; but so, too, is the study of literature, for it not only teaches us about the past, but about the present, and, ideally, about ourselves. As evidenced by this research, if you tilt your head in just the right manner, you will perceive why a conversation between a forest hermit and an exiled king makes for the perfect place to shelve the DM. Furthermore, we can readily understand why centuries of subsequent South Asian transmitters of this text neither contest nor amend its narrative shelving. This research aims to raise awareness of the centrality of Purāṇa to Hindu thought, and, more broadly, the centrality of mythic narrative toward religious understandings. It is my hope that this methodology will be harnessed for subsequent study of the mechanics of Sanskrit enframement, and the thematic import it encodes.

Framing the future

Now that the discursive frames of our thesis proper have been brought to a close, let us, like the DM's appointment of the future Manu at the end of *its* discussion proper, look to the potential future incarnations of the theory and method adopted herein. In addressing the question of why the DM should be framed by a conversation between an ascetic and a king, perhaps the next logical step would be to ask why it should occur within discourse on Manus, or indeed within the MkP at all. These questions well exceed the bounds of this current inquiry, but I will nevertheless share some tentative thoughts on the matter.

As the work of the making of the Manu equally entails the theme of preservation as with the work of our grand Goddess, it is perhaps not surprising that the sovereign of the universe would appoint the lord of an age in the form of the Manụ Sāvarṇi. As to why her glories relate to this specific Manu, among all others, I theorize firstly, drawing upon Douglas' work on chiasmus, that the positioning of the DM within the *manvantara* discourse of the MkP conforms with the symmetry innate to its intrinsic enframement. It occurs after the discussion on the previous seven Manus (the seventh of which reigns currently), and before discussion on the future seven Manus, indeed in the heart of the section. The DM is thereby casted as the mid-turn of a larger narrative ring, given seven (past) Manus are described before it, and seven (future) Manus are described after it, maintaining its narrative ring configuration, even within the *manvantara* section of the MkP. This suggestion is made by looking to the *form* of the narrative; much like the two-fold methodology adopted in this research, we need to find some corroboration by way of the *content* of the Manu narratives in order to make our case.

The Manu Sāvarṇi, along with the current Manu Vaivasvata, are offspring of the sun, which the DM reminds us of in its opening lines. The themes of sovereignty and preservation are not only equally implicated in the myths of the sun occurring in the MkP, but these myths are concentrated in a tripartite narrative whose structure parallels that of the DM, which I have tentatively dubbed the *Sūrya Māhātmya*. Harkening to textual architecture once again, its narrative "interrupts" the line of kings section of the MkP just as the DM's narrative "interrupts" the line of Manus section of the DM, and these *māhātmyas* furthermore occupy a quarter of their respective sections. Furthermore, that the DM occupies precisely one fourth of the chapters allotted to the MkP's discourse on the succession of Manus[14] makes for an intriguing parallel: the glorification of the sun occupying precisely one fourth of the chapters on the MkP's discourse on the succession of kings.[15] Moreover, let us not forget the ancient *Taittirīya Āraṇyaka* verse (third century BCE; duplicated verbatim in *Ṛg Vedic Khila, Rātrī Sūkta* 4.2.13), which hails Durgā as descended from Virocana (*vairocinīm*), a name of the sun. Such observations, powered by the methodological thrust of this book, give one pause as to whether the "placement" of the DM into the MkP was as haphazard as previously thought. I've in fact recently demonstrated both that the solar myths in the MkP framing the DM encode the astronomical alignment occasioning the proper timing of the Navarātrī festival at which the DM is ritually chanted throughout the Hindu world,[16] and that the symbolism of sun, Goddess, and king harkens to the inaugural frame of the MkP itself: inquiry into the function of preservation.[17] The approach I'm advocating might well uncover "method" within the purāṇic "madness."

What would happen if we viewed other works through the narrative ring composition? Take, for example, the *Vālmīki Rāmāyaṇa*: would we have an answer as to why its "prologue" (Book I) would necessarily incur an epilogue, particularly one whose name prohibits additional installments (*Uttara Kaṇḍa*, the "End Book")? Might we then make narrative sense of Rāma's otherwise senseless abandonment of Sītā in the final Book, impelled by the theme of separation established in Book I? Could this be why the central book of the series (IV) exhibits a complete absence of Sītā, who is kidnapped in the previous book, and discovered in the following book? Moreover, what about the myriad of textual junctures existing throughout the MBh and Purāṇas? How many of them may have partaken in narrative rings, waiting to be discovered? Yet these scholarly tales are a beast left for another day. While such queries are necessarily speculative, such is the manner in which one engages uncharted terrain. In reaching the final frame of this research, we arrive at a frontier of possibility wherein we might engage Sanskrit literary works in a manner acknowledging their agency.

Notes

1 Coburn, 172.
2 H.H. Hock, "The Yajnavalkya Cycle in the Brhad Aranyaka Upanisad," *American Oriental Society* 122 (2002): 278.
3 Orsborn and University of Hong Kong, *Chiasmus in the Early Prajñāpāramitā*, 28.
4 Dorsey, *The Literary Structure of the Old Testament*, 16.
5 Douglas, "Writing in Circles: Ring Composition as a Creative Stimulus," 43.
6 Eco, *Six Walks in the Fictional Woods*, 10.
7 Eco, 10.
8 Eco, 10.
9 Aside from closing off its discursive frames in this chapter in a reference to how they were opened in the opening chapter, its central argument associating Durgā with royal ideology is emphasized in its central chapter and therefore functions as the mid-turn of the thesis. This is further corroborated by the return to the research question during the culmination of that chapter, which appears in the first and last chapters. Secondly, the second chapter mirrors the fourth insofar as they both provide one of the two tools expected of the model reader in order to answer the research question: Chapter 2 provides an ideological tool (pertaining to content), and Chapter 4 provides the structural tool (pertaining to form), interlacing with the first tool to demonstrate the rich manner in which the text embellishes the essential conclusion we reach at the midpoint.
10 Safavi and Weightman, *Rūmī's Mystical Design*, 50.
11 Orsborn and University of Hong Kong, *Chiasmus in the Early Prajñāpāramitā*, 28.
12 Douglas, *Thinking in Circles: An Essay on Ring Composition*, 137–8.
13 Rohlman, "Textual Authority, Accretion, and Suspicion: The Legacy of Horace Hayman Wilson in Western Studies of the Purāṇas," 69; originally cited in Dimmitt and van Buitenen, *Classical Hindu Mythology*, 3.
14 See Pargiter, *Mārkaṇḍeya Purāṇa*. The Manu section occupies forty-eight chapters (53 through 100) of which twelve (chapters 81–92) are dedicated to relaying the glorious exploits of the Goddess, while Canto 93 tells us of the fate of Suratha.
15 See Pargiter. The genealogies section occupies thirty-six chapters (101 through 136) of which nine (chapters 102–110) are dedicated to glorifying the sun proper, while chapter 101 introduces the genealogies. See appendix 5.3 for the hymn-cantos in isolation.
16 Raj Balkaran, "The Splendor of the Sun: Brightening the Bridge between Mārkaṇḍeya Purāṇa and Devī Māhātmya in Light of Navarātri Ritual Timing," in *Nine Nights of the Goddess: The Navarātri Festival in South Asia*, ed. Caleb Simmons, Moumita Sen, and Hillary Rodrigues (New York: SUNY Press, 2018).
17 Raj Balkaran, "The Essence of Avatāra: Probing Preservation in the Mārkaṇḍeya Purāṇa," *Journal of Vaishnava Studies* 26, no. 1 (Fall 2017): 25–36.

Bibliography

Agrawala, Vasudeva Sharana. *Devī-Māhātmyam: The Glorification of the Great Goddess*. Varanasi: All-India Kashiraj Trust, 1963.

Bailey, Greg. *Materials for the Study of Ancient Indian Ideologies: Pravṛtti and Nivṛtti*. Torino: Ed. Jollygrafica, 1986.

Bailey, Greg. "The Pravṛtti/Nivṛtti Chapters in the Mārkaṇḍeyapurāṇa." In *Epics, Khilas and Purāṇas: Continuities and Ruptures*, edited by P. Koskikallio, 495–516. Zagreb: Croatian Academy of Arts and Sciences, 2005.

Bailey, Greg. "The Pravṛtti/Nivṛtti Project at La Trobe University. With Notes on the Meaning of Vṛt in the Bhagavadgītā," *Indologica Taurinensia* XIX (2006): 11–30.

Bailey, Greg. "The Purāṇas: A Study in the Development of Hinduism." In *The Study of Hinduism*, edited by Arvind Sharma (Studies in Comparative Religion). Columbia, SC: University of South Carolina Press, 2003.

Balkaran, Raj. "The Essence of Avatāra: Probing Preservation in the *Mārkaṇḍeya Purāṇa*," *Journal of Vaishnava Studies* 26, no. 1 (Fall 2017): 25–36.

Balkaran, Raj. "The Safeguard of Sovereignty: Focusing the Frame of the Devī Māhātmya." In *Proceedings of the 16th World Sanskrit Conference (Bangkok, 2015)*. Delhi: Motilal Banarsidass Publishers, 2018.

Balkaran, Raj. "The Sarus' Sorrow: Voicing Nonviolence in the Vālmīki Rāmāyaṇa," *Journal of Vaishnava Studies* 26, no. 3 (Spring 2018): 25–36.

Balkaran, Raj. "The Splendor of the Sun: Brightening the Bridge between Mārkaṇḍeya Purāṇa and Devī Māhātmya in Light of Navarātri Ritual Timing." In *Nine Nights of the Goddess: The Navarātri Festival in South Asia*, edited by Caleb Simmons, Moumita Sen, and Hillary Rodrigues. New York: SUNY Press, 2018.

Balkaran, Raj and A. Walter Dorn. "Violence in the 'Vālmīki Rāmāyaṇa': Just War Criteria in an Ancient Indian Epic," *Journal of the American Academy of Religion* 80, no. 3 (September 1, 2012): 659–90.

Basham, Arthur Llewellyn. *The Wonder That Was India: A Survey of the Culture of the Indian Sub-Continent Before the Coming of the Muslims*. New York: Taplinger Publ. Co., 1968.

Biardeau, Madeleine. "Brahmans and Meat-Eating Gods." In *Criminal Gods and Demon Devotees: Essays on the Guardians of Popular Hinduism*, edited by Alf Hiltebeitel, 19–33. Albany, NY: State University of New York Press, 1989.

Brereton, Joel. "Why Is a Sleeping Dog Like the Vedic Sacrifice?: The Structure of an Upaniṣadic Brahmodya." In *Inside the Texts, Beyond the Texts: New Approaches to the Study of the Vedas*, edited by Michael Witzel, 1–14. Cambridge, MA: Harvard University Press, 1997.

Brodbeck, Simon. *The Mahābhārata Patriline: Gender, Culture, and the Royal Hereditary*. Farnham, UK; Burlington, VT: Ashgate, 2009.

Bronkhorst, Johannes. *The Two Sources of Indian Asceticism*. Bern; New York: P. Lang, 1993.

Brown, Cheever Mackenzie. *God as Mother: A Feminine Theology in India: An Historical and Theological Study of the Brahmavaivarta Purāṇa*. Hartford, VT: Claude Stark & Co., 1974.

Brown, Cheever Mackenzie. "Kālī: The Mad Mother." In *The Book of the Goddess, Past and Present: An Introduction to Her Religion*, edited by Carl Olson, 110–23. Prospect Heights, IL: Waveland Press, 2002.

Brown, Cheever Mackenzie. "Purāṇa as Scripture: From Sound to Image of the Holy Word in the Hindu Tradition," *History of Religions* 26, no. 1 (August 1, 1986): 68–86.

Brown, Cheever Mackenzie. *The Devī Gītā: The Song of the Goddess: A Translation, Annotation, and Commentary*. Delhi: Sri Satguru Publications, 1999.

Brown, Cheever Mackenzie. "The Tantric and Vedantic Identity of the Great Goddess in the Devī Gītā of the Devī-Bhagavata Purāṇa." In *Seeking Mahādevī: Constructing the Identities of the Hindu Great Goddess*, edited by Tracy Pintchman, 19–36. Albany, NY: State University of New York Press, 2001.

Brubaker, Richard L. "Comments: The Goddess and the Polarity of the Sacred." In *The Divine Consort: Radha and the Goddesses of India*, edited by John Stratton Hawley, 204–9. Delhi: Motilal Banarsidass, 1984.

Burnouf, Eugene. "Analyse Et Extrait Du Devi Mahatmyam, Fragmens Du Markandeya Pourana," *Société Asiatique* 1, no. 4 (1824): 24–32.

Caldwell, Sarah. *Oh Terrifying Mother: Sexuality, Violence, and Worship of the Goddess Kāḷi*. New Delhi; New York: Oxford University Press, 1999.

Chakravarti, Prabhat Chandra. *Doctrine of Sakti in Indian Literature*. Patna: Eastern Book House, 1986.

Chapple, Christopher K. "Otherness and Nonviolence in the Mahābhārata." In *Nonviolence to Animals, Earth, and Self in Asian Traditions*, 75–83. Albany, NY: State University of New York Press, 1993.

Clark, Matthew. *The Daśanāmī-Saṃnyāsīs: The Integration of Ascetic Lineages into an Order*. Leiden; Boston, MA: Brill, 2006.

Coburn, Thomas B. "Consort of None, Śakti of All: The Vision of the Devī-Māhātmya." In *The Divine Consort: Radha and the Goddesses of India*, edited by John Stratton Hawley, 153–65. Delhi: Motilal Banarsidass, 1984.

Coburn, Thomas B. *Devī Māhātmya: The Crystallization of the Goddess Tradition*. Columbia, MO: South Asia Books, 1985.

Coburn, Thomas B. "Devi: The Great Goddess." In *Devī: Goddesses of India*, edited by John Stratton Hawley and Donna Marie Wulff, 31–48. Berkeley, CA: University of California Press, 1996.

Coburn, Thomas B. *Encountering the Goddess: A Translation of the Devī-Māhātmya and a Study of Its Interpretation*. Albany, NY: State University of New York Press, 1991.

Coburn, Thomas B. " 'Scripture' in India: Towards a Typology of the Word in Hindu Life," *Journal of the American Academy of Religion* 52, no. 3 (September 1, 1984): 435–59.

Coburn, Thomas B. *The Conceptualization of Religious Change: And the Worship of the Great Goddess*. Canton, NY: St. Lawrence University, 1980.

Coburn, Thomas B. "The Devī-Māhātmya as a Feminist Document," *Journal of Religious Studies* 8, no. 2 (1980): 1–11.

Coburn, Thomas B. "The Study of the Purāṇas and the Study of Religion," *Religious Studies* 16, no. 3 (September 1, 1980): 341–52.

Coburn, Thomas B. "The Threefold Vision of the Devī Māhātmya." In *The Great Goddess*, edited by Vidya Dehejia, 37–57. New York: Arthur M. Sackler Gallery, 1999.

Creel, Austin B., Vasudha Narayanan, and J. Patrick Olivelle. "Village Vs. Wilderness: Ascetic Ideals and the Hindu World." In *Monastic Life in the Christian and Hindu Traditions: A Comparative Study*, 125–60. Lewiston, NY: Edwin Mellen Press, 1990.

Dhand, Arti. "The Dharma of Ethics, the Ethics of Dharma: Quizzing the Ideals of Hinduism," *The Journal of Religious Ethics* 30, no. 3 (October 1, 2002): 347–72.

Dhand, Arti. *Woman as Fire, Woman as Sage Sexual Ideology in the Mahābhārata*. Albany, NY: State University of New York Press, 2008.

Dimmitt, Cornelia and J.A.B. van Buitenen. *Classical Hindu Mythology: A Reader in the Sanskrit Purāṇas*. Philadelphia, PA: Temple University Press, 1978.

Doniger, Wendy, ed. *Hindu Myths: A Sourcebook Translated from the Sanskrit*. London; New York: Penguin, 2004.

Doniger, Wendy, ed. *The Hindus: An Alternative History*. New York: Penguin Press, 2009.

Doniger, Wendy, ed. *Women, Androgynes, and Other Mythical Beasts*. Chicago, IL: University of Chicago Press, 1980.

Doniger, Wendy and J. Duncan M. Derrett. *The Concept of Duty in South Asia*. New Delhi: Vikas Publishing House, 1978.

Dorsey, David A. *The Literary Structure of the Old Testament: A Commentary on Genesis-Malachi*. Grand Rapids, MI: Baker Books, 1999.

Douglas, Mary. *Thinking in Circles: An Essay on Ring Composition*. New Haven, CT: Yale University Press, 2007.

Douglas, Mary. "Writing in Circles: Ring Composition as a Creative Stimulus." *Dwight H Terry Lectureship, Yale University*, 2005. http://terrylecture.yale.edu/previous-lectureships.

Eagleton, Terry. *Ideology: An Introduction*. London: Verso, 1991.

Eagleton, Terry. *Literary Theory*. Oxford: Blackwell, 1983.

Eco, Umberto. *Six Walks in the Fictional Woods*. Cambridge, MA: Harvard University Press, 1994.

Farquhar, J.N. *An Outline of the Religious Literature of India*. London; New York: H. Milford, Oxford University Press, 1920.

Framarin, Christopher G. "Environmental Ethics and the Mahābhārata: The Case of the Burning of the Khāṇḍava Forest," *Sophia* 52, no. 1 (2013): 185–204.

Fuller, Christopher John, ed. *The Camphor Flame: Popular Hinduism and Society in India*. Princeton, NJ: Princeton University Press, 2004.

Ghoshal, Upendra Nath. *A History of Indian Political Ideas: The Ancient Period and the Period of Transition to the Middle Ages*. London: Oxford University Press, 1966.

Ghoshal, Upendra Nath. "King's Executive Administration in the Dharmasutras," *The Indian Historical Quarterly* 21 (1945): 288–93.

Ghoshal, Upendra Nath. "Kingship and Kingly Administration in the Atharva Veda," *Indian Historical Quarterly* 20 (1944): 105–13.

Ghoshal, Upendra Nath. "Kingship in the Rgveda," *Indian Historical Quarterly* 20 (1944): 36–42.

Glucklich, Ariel. "The Royal Scepter ('Danda') as Legal Punishment and Sacred Symbol," *History of Religions* 28, no. 2 (1988): 97–122.

Gonda, Jan. *A History of Indian Literature. Volume II, Fasc. 1*. Wiesbaden: O. Harrassowitz, 1977.

Gonda, Jan. *Ancient Indian Kingship from the Religious Point of View*. Leiden: Brill, 1969.

Hazra, R.C. *Studies in the Purāṇic Records on Hindu Rites and Customs*. Delhi: Motilal Banarsidass, 1975.

Heesterman, J.C. *The Ancient Indian Royal Consecration: The Rājasūya Described According to the Yajus Texts and Annotated*. 's-Gravenhage: Mouton, 1957.

Heesterman, J.C. *The Broken World of Sacrifice: An Essay in Ancient Indian Ritual*. Chicago, IL: University of Chicago Press, 1993.

Heesterman, J.C. "The Conundrum of the King's Authority." In *Kingship and Authority in South Asia*, edited by John F Richards, 13–40. Delhi; New York: Oxford University Press, 1998.

Heesterman, J.C. *The Inner Conflict of Tradition: Essays in Indian Ritual, Kingship, and Society*. Chicago, IL: University of Chicago Press, 1985.

Herman, Phyllis Kaplan. "Ideal Kingship and the Feminine Power: A Study of the Depiction of Rāmarājya in the Vālmīki Ramāyana." Ph.D., University of California, Los Angeles, 1979.

Hiltebeitel, Alf. *Rethinking the Mahābhārata: A Reader's Guide to the Education of the Dharma King*. Chicago, IL: University of Chicago Press, 2001.

Hiltebeitel, Alf. *The Ritual of Battle: Kṛṣṇa in the Mahābhārata*. Ithaca, NY; London: Cornell University Press, 1976.

Hiltebeitel, Alf and Kathleen M. Erndl, eds. *Is the Goddess a Feminist? The Politics of South Asian Goddesses*. New York: New York University Press, 2000.

Hock, H.H. "The Yajnavalkya Cycle in the Brhad Aranyaka Upanisad," *American Oriental Society* 122 (2002): 278–86.

Humes, Cynthia Ann. "The Text and Temple of the Great Goddess: The Devī-Māhātmya and the Vindhyacal Temple of Mirzapur (Volumes I and II)." Ph.D., University of Iowa, 1990.

Inden, Ronald. *Imagining India*. Oxford; Cambridge, MA: Basil Blackwell, 1990.

Inden, Ronald. "Kings and Omens." In *Purity and Auspiciousness in Indian Society*, edited by John Braisted Carman and Frédérique Apffel-Marglin, 30–40. Leiden: E.J. Brill, 1985.

Inden, Ronald. "Ritual, Authority, and Cyclic Time in Hindu Kingship." In *Kingship and Authority in South Asia*, edited by John F. Richards. Delhi; New York: Oxford University Press, 1998.

International Congress of Human Sciences in Asia and North Africa, A. L. Basham, and Colegio de México, eds. *Kingship in Asia and Early America: XXX International Congress of Human Sciences in Asia and North Africa*. México, D.F.: Colegio de México, 1981.

Kinsley, David. "Durgā, Warrior Goddess and Cosmic Queen." In *The Goddesses' Mirror: Visions of the Divine from East and West*, 3–24. Albany, NY: State University of New York, 1989.

Kinsley, David. *Hindu Goddesses: Visions of the Divine Feminine in the Hindu Religious Tradition; with a New Preface*. Berkeley, CA: University of California Press, 1997.

Kinsley, David. "Kālī: Blood and Death Out of Place." In *Devī: Goddesses of India*, edited by John Stratton Hawley and Donna Marie Wulff, 31–48. Berkeley, CA: University of California Press, 1996.

Kinsley, David. *The Goddesses' Mirror: Visions of the Divine from East and West*. Albany, NY: State University of New York, 1989.

Kinsley, David. "The Portrait of the Goddess in the Devī-Māhātmya," *Journal of the American Academy of Religion* 46, no. 4 (December 1, 1978): 489–506.

Kripal, Jeffrey J. *Kālī's Child: The Mystical and the Erotic in the Life and Teachings of Ramakrishna*. Chicago, IL: University of Chicago Press, 1995.

Krosby, Kate. *Mahābhārata: Book 10, Dead of the Night. Book 11, The Women*. Vol. 1. New York: New York University Press: JJC Foundation, 2009.

Lyons, Tryna. "The Simla 'Devī Māhātmya' Illustrations: A Reappraisal of Content," *Archives of Asian Art* 45 (January 1, 1992): 29–41.

Malamoud, Charles. *Cooking the World: Ritual and Thought in Ancient India*. Delhi; New York: Oxford University Press, 1996.

Mani, Vettam. *Purāṇic Encyclopaedia: A Comprehensive Dictionary with Special Reference to the Epic and Purāṇic Literature*. Delhi: Motilal Banarsidass, 1975.

McDermott, Rachel Fell. *Revelry, Rivalry, and Longing for the Goddesses of Bengal: The Fortunes of Hindu Festivals*. New York: Columbia University Press, 2011.

McDermott, Rachel Fell, and Jeffrey J. Kripal. *Encountering Kālī in the Margins, at the Center, in the West*. Berkeley, CA: University of California Press, 2003.

McDonald, K.M. "The Sacred Aesthetics of Scriptural Illustration: An Analysis of the Devi Mahatmya." Ph.D., University of Wisconsin-Madison, 1997.

McLain, Karline. "Holy Superheroine: A Comic Book Interpretation of the Hindu Devī Māhātmya Scripture," *Bulletin of the School of Oriental and African Studies* 71, no. 2 (2008): 297–322.

Minkowski, C.Z. "Janamejaya's Sattra and Ritual Structure," *Journal of the American Oriental Society* 109, no. 3 (1989): 401–20.

Mirashi, V.V. "A Lower Limit for the Date of the Devī-Māhātmya," *Purāṇa* 10, no. 1 (January 1968): 179–86.

Monier-Williams, Ernst Leumann, Carl Cappeller, and Īśvaracandra. "Monier-Williams Sanskrit-English Dictionary (2008 Revision)," 2008.

Olivelle, Patrick. *The Āśrama System: The History and Hermeneutics of a Religious Institution*. New York: Oxford University Press, 1993.

Orsborn, Matthew Bryan and University of Hong Kong. *Chiasmus in the Early Prajñāpāramitā: Literary Parallelism Connecting Criticism & Hermeneutics in an Early Mahāyāna Sūtra*, 2012.

Pargiter, F. Eden. *Mārkaṇḍeya Purāṇa*. Calcutta, India: Asiatic Society of Bengal, 1904.

Poley, Ludwig. *Markandeyi Purani Sectio Edidit Latinam Interpretationem Annotationesque Adiecit Ludovicus Poley*. Berolini: Impensis F. Duemmleri, 1831.

Pollock, Sheldon. "The Divine King in the Indian Epic," *Journal of the American Oriental Society* 104, no. 3 (July 1, 1984): 505–28.

Ramanujan, A.K. "Two Realms of Kannada Folklore." In *Another Harmony: New Essays on the Folklore of India*, edited by Stuart H. Blackburn and A.K. Ramanujan. Berkeley, CA: University of California Press, 1986.

Ramanujan, A.K. "Where Mirrors Are Windows: Toward an Anthology of Reflections," *History of Religions* 28, no. 3 (February 1, 1989): 187–216.

Ramanujan, A.K., Vinay Dharwadker, and Stuart H. Blackburn. *The Collected Essays of A.K. Ramanujan*. New Delhi; New York: Oxford University Press, 1999.

Rao, Velcheru Narayana. "Purāṇa." In *The Hindu World*, edited by Sushil Mittal and Gene R. Thursby, 97–115. New York: Routledge, 2004.

Rao, Velcheru Narayana. "Purāṇa as Brahaminic Ideology." In *Purāna Perennis: Reciprocity and Transformation in Hindu and Jaina Texts*, edited by Wendy Doniger, 85–100. Albany, NY: State University of New York Press, 1993.

Richards, John F, ed. "Introduction." In *Kingship and Authority in South Asia*, 1–12. Delhi; New York: Oxford University Press, 1998.

Rocher, Ludo and Jan Gonda. *The Purāṇas*. Wiesbaden: Harrassowitz, 1986.

Rodrigues, Hillary. *Ritual Worship of the Great Goddess: The Liturgy of the Durgā Pūjā with Interpretations*. Albany, NY: State University of New York Press, 2003.

Rodrigues, Hillary. "Scrutinizing Devī: Does She Live Up to Her Portraits in Kinsley's Analysis?" *Studies in Religion/Sciences Religieuses* 30, no. 3–4 (September 1, 2001): 397–402.

Rohlman, Elizabeth Mary. "Textual Authority, Accretion, and Suspicion: The Legacy of Horace Hayman Wilson in Western Studies of the Purāṇas," *Journal of the Oriental Institute* 52, no. 1–2 (2002): 55–70.

Rushdie, Salman. *Midnight's Children*. New York: Knopf, 1981.

Safavi, Seyed Ghahreman and S.C.R. Weightman. *Rūmī's Mystical Design: Reading the Mathnawī, Book One*. Albany, NY: SUNY Press, 2009.

Sarkar, Bihani. *Heroic Shāktism: The Cult of Durgā in Ancient Indian Kingship*. Oxford: Oxford University Press, 2017.

Scharfe, Hartmut. *The State in Indian Tradition*. Leiden; New York: E.J. Brill, 1989.

Söhnen-Thieme, Renate. "Goddess, Gods, Demons in the Devī Māhātmya." In *Stages and Transitions: Temporal and Historical Frameworks in Epic and Purāṇic Literature: Proceedings of the Second Dubrovnik International Conference on the Sanskrit Epics and Purāṇas, August 1999*, edited by Brockington Dubrovnik International Conference on the Sanskrit Epics and Purāṇas; Radoslav Katičić and Hrvatska akademija znanosti i umjetnosti. Zagreb: Academia Scientiarum et Artium Croatica, 2002.

Taylor, McComas. "What Enables Canonical Literature to Function as 'True'? The Case of the Hindu Purāṇas," *International Journal of Hindu Studies* 12, no. 3 (December 1, 2008): 309–28.

Tiwari, J.N. "An Interesting Variant in the Devī-Māhātmya," *Purāṇa* 25, no. 2 (1983): 235–45.

Venkata Rāmaswami, Kavali. *The Supta-Sati or Chundi-Pat: Being a Portion of the Marcundeya Purana*. Calcutta, India: Columbian Press, 1823.

Werner, Karel. "The Long Haired Sage of Rg Veda, 10.136." In *The Yogi and the Mystic: Studies in Indian and Comparative Mysticism*, 33–53. Hoboken, NJ: Routledge, 1995.

Wilson, Horace Hayman, trans. *The Viṣṇu Purāṇa: A System of Hindu Mythology and Tradition*. Calcutta, India: Punthi Pustak, 1961.

Winternitz, Moriz. *A History of Indian Literature. 1, 1.* New Delhi: Oriental Books Repr. Corp., 1972.

Yokochi, Yuko. "The Rise of the Warrior Goddess in Ancient India: A Study of the Myth Cycle of Kauśikī-Vindhyavāsinī in the Skandapurāṇa." Ph.D., University of Groningen, 2005.

Yokochi, Yuko. "The Warrior Goddess in the Devīmāhātmya," *SENRI Ethnological Studies* 50 (1999): 71–113.

Index

Page numbers in **bold** denote tables, those in *italics* denote figures.

Agni 18, 70, 104, 109, 119n41, 119n42, 121n68, 146n62
Agrawala, Vasudeva Sharana 14, 96
ahiṃsā 2, 28, 38–40, 50, 53, 76, 129; *see also* nonviolence
Ambikā 5, 80, 131, 143, 146n68
araṇya 41, 49–50; *see also* wilderness
Arjuna 58n45, 72, **93**, 94, 114–15, 122n90, 122n98, 123n100, 135
Asuras 48, 58n45, 76, 79–80, 109, 131

Bailey, Greg 11, 35
band of mothers 55, 104, 132, 135
BhG 63, 91, 94, 114–15
Biardeau, Madeleine 108, 120n63, 145n43
Brahmā 1, 8, 47, 54, 79, 82, 85n54, 98–9, 105, 111, 143
brahmacarya 39, 45, 75
breast 124, 143; goddess of the 124–6; mothers 125–7, **125**; -tooth 124–5, **125**
Brereton, Joel 24, 149
Brodbeck, Simon 19
Brown, Cheever Mackenzie 14, 128
Brubaker, Richard L. 116
Buddhism 24, 35–6, 63, 69
buffalo demon *see* Mahiṣa
Burnouf, Eugene 9–10

Cāmuṇḍā 107, 132
Caṇḍa **90**, 107, 109, 110, 128, 134, 145n49
Caṇḍikā 5, 79–80, 109, 118n1, 132
Chakravarti, Prabhat Chandra 91
Chapple, Christopher K. 38
Coburn, Thomas B. 5, 7, 15–18, 59n58, 74, 82, 86n107, 87n114, 105–7, 115–16, 118n1, 118n12, 122n91, 123n100, 138, 146n62, 148
consort 48, **125**, 138; goddess 17–18, 125–7, **125**; male **125**; of none 138
Cosmic Man *see* Puruṣa
cosmic order 1, 66, 70, 82, 104, 106, 110, 128, 135

Daṇḍa 74
deposed king 1–2, 60, 83, **92**, 147
Dhand, Arti 25–6, 29, 33n103, 36–7, 45–7, 49, 77
Doniger, Wendy 7, 12, 40, 85n55, 89, 91, 124–6, 136, 138
Dorsey, David A. 23, 102, 150–1
double helix 28, 34, 41, 56, 62, 83, 91; *brāhmaṇic* 2, 41, **41**, 52, *52*, 83, 88, 100; *dharmic* 2, 4, 25, 28, 34–6, 40, 56, 63, 103
Douglas, Mary 4, 7, 21–4, 88, 99, 102, 110, 112, 114, 117, 149–51, 153–4
Durgā Pūjā 107, 115, 129, 148; *see also* Navarātrī
Durgama 5, 80, 136

Eagleton, Terry 19, 26–7
Eco, Umberto 3–4, 7, 19–20, 26, 88, 149, 151–2
exiled king 4, 21, 34, 41, 49–53, 56–7, 82–3, 154

forest dweller 34, 41–2, 44–5, 48–9, 51–3, 56, 95; *see also* hermit; ascetic 2, 21, 34, 43, 46, 51, 53, 83, 147; household 49; hunter 56; sage 34, 40, 56
Framarin, Christopher G. 135
frame narrative 1–2, 7, 22, 24–5, 29, 56, 68, 90, 98, 103–4, 111, 127, 133, 148–50, 152–3
Fuller, Christopher John 68–9, 106–8, 129

Ghoshal, Upendra Nath 70
Gītā 40, 91, 122n90; *Bhagavad* **93**, 122n98; *Devī* 128
Glucklich, Ariel 74
Gonda, Jan 69, 71–3, 75, 78, 81, 114
grāma 41, 49–50; *see also* village

Hazra, R.C. 11, 13–14
heaven **41**, 44, 48, 55, 75, 77, 104, 113, 129, 135, 142, 148, 150; king of 2, 60, 102; throne of 2, 104, 108
Hebrew Bible 23, 151
Heesterman, J.C. 4, 50, 60–6, 68, 73, 95, 140, 146n67
Herman, Phyllis Kaplan 70
hermit 43–6, 53; *see also vānaprastha*; forest 4, 34, 38, 41–7, 49, 51–3, 56–7, 154; household 41, 43–4
hermitage 42, 44, 47, 54, 90, 94, 96
Hiltebeitel, Alf 25
Hindu: classical 35–6; deities 75, 85n55; goddess 124–5; king 61, 64, 66–7, 107; myth 40; religious ideology 2, 35, 148; traditions 2, 66, 74, 130; world 3, 5, 21, 28, 36, 61, 75, 127, 148, 155
Hock, H.H. 149, 152
household 21, 28, 34–5, 39, 42, 45, 47–8, 52–3, 62, 148; *see also* forest dweller, hermit, Vedic; affirming 2, 28, 42; deities **125**; married 36, 40, 44; religion 62; sacrificial 42–3; village 41, 43–4
Humes, Cynthia Ann 141
hunter 44, 50, 56, 130
hunting 44, 50, 53, 56, 90, 122n91

Inden, Ronald 62, 64, 66–8, 73
Indra 60, 67, 70, 72–3, 75, 77, **90**, 102, **103**, 104–5, 108–10, **111**, 117, 119n41, 119n42, 121n68, 127, 129, 134, 141, 143, 148, 150
īśvarī 82, 86n107, 101, 111

Kaiṭabha **90**, 98–9, 141
Kālī 16, 74, **90**, 107, 109, 111, 124–5, 127–30, 132, 134–5, 143, 145n49
kingship *see* Hindu: ideals of 2–3, 70, 74; ideology of 2, 28; Indian 60–2, 64–6, 70–1, 81–2, 150; loss of 91, 94, 150; restoration of 114, 134, 150, 153; rituals of 17, 62, 107–8; themes of 108, 110, 148
Kinsley, David 16, 76, 106, 110, 126–8, 136, 138
Kṛṣṇa (Krishna) 3, 58n45, 72, 91, **93**, 94, 114–15, 122n90, 122n98, 135, 138, 146n62
kṣatriya 18, 35, 46, 49–53, 73–4, 95, 110
Kubera 70, 72–3, 104–5, 109, 119n42, 121n68

Lakṣmī 70, 82, **125**

McDermott, Rachel Fell 107
Madhu **90**, 98–9, 105, 141
Mahābhārata (MBh) 2–4, 12, 19, 21, 24–5, 28–9, 34–9, 41, 43, 45–9, 53, 56, 62–3, 70–2, 77, 96, 114–15, 148, 153, 155
Mahāmāyā 54, 91, **92**, 94, 96, 98–101, 111, 113, 118n5, 119n31, 137, 149–50
Mahārājā of Kāśī 12, 69
Mahiṣa 76, 82, 86n107, 89, **90**, 100–8, 120n55, 126–7, 129–30, 133–5, 141, 149
Malamoud, Charles 50
Mārkaṇḍeya 13–14, 17, 24, 89, **92**, 96, 102, 117, 118n5, 118n13, 152
Mārkaṇḍeya Purāṇa (MkP) 4, 6–7, 10, 13–16, 18–19, 24, 30n21, 57n11, 58n53, 70, 89, 100–1, 117, 118n13, 149, 153–5, 156n14
martial prowess 1–2, 76, 108, 131, 135, 139
Medhas 2, 13, 17, 24, 53–4, 59n58, 76, 81–2, 88–90, 95–7, 99, 101–4, 114–16, 118n1, 118n13, 133, 143, 149
Minkowski, C.Z. 24
Mirashi, V.V. 15
mokṣa 3, 38, 40, 43, 46–9, 56, 77, 85n68, 89, 95–8, 114, 142
Monier-Williams, M. 59n58
Muṇḍa **90**, 107, 109–10, 128, 134, 145n49
Mysore 107–8, 120n63

Navarātrī 1, 68, 107–8, 120n63, 155; *see also* Durgā Pūjā
Niśumbha 80–1, **90**, 109–10, 133–4, 136–7, 141, 145n49
nonviolence 2, 28, 36, 40, **41**, 50, 52–3, 56, 60, 63, 74–5, 83, 85n54, 88–9; *see also ahiṃsā*

Olivelle, Patrick 40, 42–5
Orsborn, Matthew Bryan 24, 152

Pargiter, F. Eden 6–7, 10–11, 13–15, 24, 30n21, 89, 91, 100, 107, 156n14, 156n15
Pārvatī 18, **125**, 143
Pollock, Sheldon 69–71, 114

power: cosmic 67, 113, 136–7, 139; delusive 113, 136; divine 65–6, 69, 104, 124; feminine 70, 138; field of 139–41; king's 60–1, 71, 73, 83, 90, 105, 140; loss of 103, 111, 147; martial 102, 113, 116, 130; mother of 1, 4, 16, 91, 136–7, 143; political 68, 74, 139–40; restoration of 101, 111, 134; ring of 102, 114, 117, 134–5; ritual 68, 139; royal 51, 56–7, 60–1, 63, 66, 69–70, 101, 103, 106, 108, 111, 114, 120n49, 130, 135, 139–40, 148; sovereign 88, 112, 117, 135, 139, 153; spiritual 68, 74, 139–40; universal 67, 113, 137, 139, 141
Prajāpati 75, 105
priest 47–8, 50, 63–5, 68, 71, 73, 75, **125**, 126
protector 18, 70–1, 79, 81, 83, 97, 100, 102, 130; divine 4, 60, 69; goddess 18; world 72–3, 104–5, 109, 119, 119n42, 120n48, 121n68
Purāṇas 6–14, 17, 19–20, 23, 29n2, 35, 45, 53, 73, 96, 148–9, 152, 154–5
Puruṣa 67

Queen Durgā 82–3, 89, 104

Raktabīja **90**, 127, 132–5, 145n42, 145n49
Rāma 40, 70, 75, 78, 108, 155
Ramanujan, A.K. 125–6, **125**, 144n7
Rao, Velcheru Narayana 8, 12
refuge 18, 51, 54, 78, 82–3, 87, 97, 104–5, 108, 130; of all 1, 39, 46, 77–8, 82
renouncer 2, 28, 34, 38, 40–2, 45–6, 49, 51, 62–3, 65, 70, 83n8, 95–6, 115, 122n91, 139–40, 142; ascetic 34, 140; celibate 40; ideology 21, 28, 148; tradition **41**
Richards, John F. 69
ring composition 3, 21–4, 27, 99, 102, 114, 134, 149–53; narrative 7, 21, 155
Rocher, Ludo 11–12, 14
Rodrigues, Hillary 16, 118n4, 138
Rohlman, Elizabeth Mary 9–10, 12
Rushdie, Salman 20

Safavi, Seyed Ghahreman 24, 152
Śakti 1, 54, 74, 103, 130, **133**, 134, 136–9
Samādhi 17, 88, 95–8, 114–17, 147, 149
Sanskrit 7–9, 29, 44, 97, 107, 154; great goddess 1, 107, 144n7; literature 24, 28, 53, 130, 156; narrative 1, 3–4, 22–3, 28, 53, 77, 153; text 1, 3, 23–4, 30n21, 149
Sāvarṇi 14, 77, **92**, 94, 116–17, 118n5, 147, 154–5; *see also* Suratha
Scharfe, Hartmut 72
seer 55, 96–7, 103, 118n12, 135
Śiva 1, 46, 69, 85n54, 104–5, 138, 142–3
Söhnen-Thieme, Renate 16, 99–100
suffering 37, 48, 54, 78–9, 89, 94–5, 101, 114–15, 117, 137, 141–2, 147; human 51, 91; king's **92**, 98, 101
Śuka 25, 47–8
Śumbha 5, 80–1, 87n113, **90**, 108–11, 121n68, 133–4, 136, 138, 141, 145n40, 145n49
Suratha (King) 1, 14, 17, 24–5, 53–4, 60, 82, 90–1, **92**, 95–9, 101, 103–4, 114–15, 117, 118n1, 127, 130, 134–5, 140–1, 147, 149–50, 153, 156n14; *see also* Sāvarṇi
Suratha 1, 14, 17, 24–5, 53–4, 60, 82, 90–1, **92**, 95–9, 101, 103–4, 114–15, 117, 118n1, 127, 130, 134–5, 140–1, 147, 149–50, 153; *see also* Sāvarṇi
Sūrya **92**, 104, 117, 118n5, 119n41, 119n42

tejas 72, 105, 120n49, 131, 139–40
Tiwari, J.N. 15
tooth 124–6, 131–2; *see also* breast; goddess of the 4, 124–6; mother 125, **125**, 127

vānaprastha 45, 48–9; *see also* hermit
vanaprasthya 44–9
Varuṇa 70, 72–3, 104–5, 109, 119n41, 119n42, 121n68
Vāyu 50, 70, 104, 109, 119n41, 119n42
Vedas 6, 8, 18, 48, 71
Vedic: culture 36, 42–3, 60; householder 48; initiation 45; lore 48; pantheon 1, 104; religion 18, 35–6, 39, 41–4, 50, 62; ritual 24, 41–3, 47, 49, 54, 61–2, 110; sacrifice 24, 35, 42, 46, 54, 60, 63, 89, 110; teacher 48; text 8, 61, 63; tradition **41**, 47; world 42, 62
village 41–4, 48, 50, 64, **125**; *see also* *grāma*, household; activity 50; culture 41–3, 126; life 42, 44
violence 2, 36, 38–9, **41**, 44, 50–3, 56, 73–5, 82–3, 88, 108, 110, 130–1, 135, 141, 148
Viṣṇu 1, 68, 85, **90**, **92**, 98–9, 101, **103**, 104–5, 111, **111**, 113, 135, 138, 142, 146n62; slumber of 54, 68, 98, 111
Viṣṇu Purāṇa 9, 13, 15, 29n2
Vyāsa 8, 25, 47–9

warrior 3, 39, 51, 56, 66–8, 74, 128, 130, 142; Goddess 17–18, 130
wilderness 41–4, **41**, 50, 94–5; *see also araṇya*
Wilson, Horace Hayman 6–7, 9–10, 13, 15, 24, 29n2
Winternitz, Moriz 9, 11, 13–14

Yama 70, 72–3, 104–5, 109, 119n41, 119n42, 121n68
Yoganidrā 98–9, 104
Yokochi, Yuko 16–19, 32n59, 120n55, 130

Printed in the United States
by Baker & Taylor Publisher Services